PENGUIN BC

# THE LOST PILOT

# THE LOST PILOT

A MEMOIR

JEFFREY PAPAROA HOLMAN

PENGUIN BOOKS

PENGUIN BOOKS
Published by the Penguin Group
Penguin Group (NZ), 67 Apollo Drive, Rosedale,
Auckland 0632, New Zealand (a division of Pearson New Zealand Ltd)
Penguin Group (USA) Inc., 375 Hudson Street,
New York, New York 10014, USA
Penguin Group (Canada), 90 Eglinton Avenue East, Suite 700, Toronto,
Ontario, M4P 2Y3, Canada (a division of Pearson Penguin Canada Inc.)
Penguin Books Ltd, 80 Strand, London, WC2R 0RL, England
Penguin Ireland, 25 St Stephen's Green,
Dublin 2, Ireland (a division of Penguin Books Ltd)
Penguin Group (Australia), 707 Collins Street, Melbourne,
Victoria 3008, Australia (a division of Pearson Australia Group Pty Ltd)
Penguin Books India Pvt Ltd, 11, Community Centre,
Panchsheel Park, New Delhi – 110 017, India
Penguin Books (South Africa) (Pty) Ltd, Block D, Rosebank Office Park,
181 Jan Smuts Avenue, Parktown North, Gauteng 2193, South Africa

Penguin Books Ltd, Registered Offices: 80 Strand, London, WC2R 0RL, England

First published by Penguin Group (NZ), 2013
1 3 5 7 9 10 8 6 4 2

Copyright © Jeffrey Paparoa Holman, 2013
Copyright © images author's collection, unless otherwise credited

The right of Jeffrey Paparoa Holman to be identified as the author of this work in terms of
section 96 of the Copyright Act 1994 is hereby asserted.

Designed and typeset by Anna Egan-Reid
Front cover image: see page 83
Back cover image: see page 120
Printed in China by South China Printing Company

All rights reserved. Without limiting the rights under copyright reserved above,
no part of this publication may be reproduced, stored in or introduced into a retrieval
system, or transmitted, in any form or by any means (electronic, mechanical,
photocopying, recording or otherwise), without the prior written permission of
both the copyright owner and the above publisher of this book.

ISBN 978-0-143-56876-6

A catalogue record for this book is available
from the National Library of New Zealand.

www.penguin.co.nz

The assistance of Creative New Zealand towards the production of this book
is gratefully acknowledged by the Publisher.

# Contents

|   |   |   |
|---|---|---|
|   | Japanese Foreword: Ritsu Hall | 7 |
|   | Explanatory Note | 11 |
|   | Introduction: Saving the Dead | 13 |
| 1 | St Valentine's Day | 18 |
| 2 | Dad's Story | 48 |
| 3 | Kokutai no Hongi: Japan as the Emperor's Body | 81 |
| 4 | Fubuki: Falling Blossom, or Human Sacrifices? | 112 |
| 5 | Japan Calling | 150 |
| 6 | On Kyūshū | 168 |
| 7 | Ishigaki Pilgrim | 215 |
| 8 | Ōsaka Soul Food: Okonomiyaki | 244 |
| 9 | The Old *Illustrians*: Writing from Memory | 281 |
|   | Epilogue: Te Taua Moana Marae | 296 |
|   | Acknowledgements/Mihimihi | 301 |
|   | Sources by Chapter | 305 |
|   | Index | 311 |

## Japanese Foreword

# RITSU HALL

　わずか六十数年前、日本は連合国相手に壮絶な戦いを繰り広げ、多くの生命を犠牲にした事実を忘れる程、現在は大変豊かな社会、国家へと成長を遂げた。このように平和に暮らせる時代に生まれて良かったと、この度の調査に同行し改めて痛感させられた。

　今回の調査の過程でいくつかの資料館を訪ね詳細な御説明を給わり、不知の事実が多々あり、戦争、特に神風特別攻撃隊の壮絶な戦いを知る事が出来た。空母を中心とした機動部隊は日本海軍が発案した戦法であり、神風特攻隊は日本人精神の誇りである。彼らは劣勢の戦況下、日本の勝利を信じ、また家族、皇国を死守すべく、自らの命を犠牲にし、爆弾と共に若くして散華した。しかし残念なことに、今日諸外国では特攻隊は自爆テロと同等に扱われ、英語圏での「KAMIKAZE」は皮肉にもクレイジーの意味で使用されているのが現状である。そこでこの本を通じ少なくとも読者の方々には、特攻と自爆テロの明確な違いや、特攻隊員等及び日本人が脈々と受け継いできた「大和魂」が少しでも理解されることを願ってやまない。

　最後にこの場をお借りしてご協力くださった皆様へ。
大刀洗平和記念館　北原様、鹿屋航空基地史料館
内門様、中俣様、和田様、熊本県遺族連合会事務局長
横手様。また、こちらから突然の対談申し入れに快諾くださった特攻隊員御遺族永田輝幸様、永田英治様、西田様。その他、皆様方の多大なるご協力のもと、今回の調査は完結いたしました。皆様方のご協力に私からも心より深謝し、お礼申し上げます。

２０１１年５月　　ホール　律

Japan has now grown into such an affluent society and state that one forgets the fact that just sixty or so years ago it was in an unfolding life-and-death fight against the Allies, and that many lives were sacrificed. Being part of the research for this book brought home to me once again how good it is to have been born in an era like this where we can live in peace.

In the process of this research I visited a number of museums, and was granted detailed explanations. There were many things I was ignorant of, and I was able to learn a lot about the war, particularly the life-and-death campaigns of the Kamikaze Special Attack Units. Having mobile forces focused on aircraft carriers was a Japanese Navy idea, and the Kamikaze Special Attack Units are a credit to the Japanese spirit. In a war situation where they were numerically weak they believed in a victory to Japan. Expected to protect their families and Empire to the death, they heroically sacrificed their own young lives. However, the unfortunate thing is that today outside Japan the Special Attack Units are viewed on the same level as suicide bomber terrorists, and in the English-speaking world as it stands at present, ironically 'kamikaze' is used to mean 'crazy'.

Accordingly, I will never stop hoping that through this book readers will at least understand, even if only a little, the clear difference between the Special Attack Units and suicide bomber terrorists, and the native 'Japanese spirit' that the Special Attack Units and Japanese people have inherited in an unbroken line.

Finally, I take the opportunity to address everyone who co-operated in this research: Mr Kitahara of the Tachiarai Peace Memorial Museum; Mr Uchikado, Mr Nakamata and Mr Wada of the Kanoya Air Base Museum; Mr Yokote, Head Official of the Kumamoto Prefectural Bereaved Families Federation; also Mr Nagata Teruyuki, Mr Nagata Hideharu and Mr Nishida, bereaved relatives of Special Attack Unit members who readily assented to my unexpected requests for interviews. The research here was accomplished with the co-operation of these and others. I too am deeply grateful for everyone's co-operation and I thank them from my heart.

Ritsu Hall
May 2011

To my father: William Thomas Holman, RN, RNZN
Chief Petty Officer (Yeoman of Signals) JX157199, 1939–45

My father (left), on the bridge of HMS *Illustrious*, somewhere in the Pacific, 1944–45.
The caption reads: 'Dad with Sid Hunt, both ex-*Furious*.'

# Explanatory Note

In the course of telling this story, I was well aware that this book was going to cross many genres: memoir, history, travel, a spiritual quest – and poetry. Not only does it do that, but in the process, various themes and styles and voices are interwoven, with leaps backward and forward in time. There are historical sequences where the personal interjects, and the register changes; my only guide was to make this history personal, to be fully engaged myself and to engage the reader. A word, then, about what to expect.

    The book opens with a scene where my father confronts his death, and the subject announces itself. The next chapter explores our relationship, the background to that scene, and the war between father and son. The following chapter returns to my father's life from birth until the time the war ended, building up to the attack on his carrier in 1945 – that moment captured so graphically in the image that sparked the storytelling.

    From there, the focus switches to the kamikaze pilots who died attacking HMS *Illustrious* that day, the wider kamikaze culture, and its emergence in modern Japanese history. It ends with a reflection on the possible meanings of ritual suicide in the culture of the war; of suicide itself, and what relevance this may have for us today. How like, and how unlike, are we and the Japanese – our fellow human beings?

From the historical to the personal, the next chapter looks at my early links with Japan and the way this book began as a question, an unlikely goal, on its way to becoming a real possibility with the award of the 2011 University of Waikato writing fellowship.

Moving continually in the present, the next three chapters chronicle a visit made to Japan in April and May of 2011, to meet the families of two of the men who died that day in April 1945. It was also to get some feeling for Japanese culture today, and to learn more of their history of the war while living amongst them. The writing here is more that of a travel diary than history or memoir, as it builds on all that has gone before.

A reflection on the act of writing itself and the place of memory in our lives follows. Here, I'm asking myself: Just how reliable is memory? What other choice do we have in recalling the past than to seek in its mists the ghosts that dwell there? The book ends in the recent past: a visit to the sailors' marae, Te Taua Moana, at Devonport Naval Base in Auckland, with a pōwhiri to lay those selfsame ghosts to rest. The journey, this kawe mate where the dead are brought into the meeting house to sleep with the ancestors, concludes with a poem for my father.

If this sounds like you, please read on, in full awareness that this is a very personal journey on many levels. There seemed to be no other way than to take and combine all the written forms I could possibly juggle, in an attempt to contain on the page what the last century and my father's clay feet have gifted to me. That gift has been a too intimate reminder of my own flawed humanity, of my deep kinship with him and with his former enemies.

I never heard my father speak against his German or Japanese foes: from 1939 until 1945, they were all in the same profession, trained in the arts of delivering death. Having once descended into that hell, there was no road back to innocence. We, their children, lived under those same roofs where nightmares pursued them from within, every waking day of their lives. This is a story of their shadows and their ghosts – English and Japanese.

Introduction

# SAVING THE DEAD

> So our memory is the only help that is left to them [the dead]. They pass away into it, and if every deceased person is like someone who was murdered by the living, so he is also like someone whose life they must save, without knowing whether the effort will succeed.
>
> *Theodor Adorno, 'Essay on Mahler'*

On a day in September 1972 in my mother's house at 11 Franklin Street, Greymouth, my father shuffled across the room in his dressing gown and broke down in my arms. He had just been delivered his death sentence by Dr Kibblewhite, who had then left quietly and driven away. The cancer treatment was not working: Dad was told he had perhaps a couple of weeks and then he would die. Cradling my sobbing father – when what I really wanted was for him to cradle me – has haunted me ever after. This became a poem in 1973 and, twenty years later, another writing of the same event when the seed lines of a poem I called 'As big as a father' ambushed me in the bathroom of a London council flat.

How do we react when told point-blank that the death we all know awaits us is about to arrive, is on the doorstep, knocking? My father sobbed on my neck, grieving for his losses, choking, 'My life's been such a bloody waste!' 'No, Dad,' I shot back at him, 'no it hasn't!' I still don't know how convincing I sounded – even to myself. Memory is tricky, but I did try to

Dad, on his final visit to my sister's farm at Barrytown in 1972, after he was diagnosed with both lung and bowel cancer.

console him, struggling with my own anger: What the hell was I doing being a parent to him? Again?

Ask any adult child of an alcoholic how this weird reversal comes about and they can explain – but I didn't know any of this back then. All I knew was that as his life collapsed around us, I couldn't stand to watch – but I had to. Was this really the man who had terrorised me and my family late at night: home slamming doors from the pub in Blackball, muttering to himself beyond the cracks of light glowering beneath my bedroom door as I pulled the sheets over my head, me listening to my brother swearing to kill him, my sisters waking in the next room, screaming?

Was this the man who had spent six years on active service in World War Two, a signalman and later a chief petty officer on huge aircraft carriers fighting the Germans and the Japanese, mythical figures who haunted the imagination of a boy born and raised in the shadow of the war? The same man who had seen a kamikaze flying straight at him in April 1945: diving for cover as its wing sliced through the radome on the bridge of HMS *Illustrious*, plane and bomb falling and exploding together in the waves beside the ship, just missing him and his shipmates? Lying with them flat on the signal deck, parts of the Suisei dive-bomber and its two-man crew showering down, scattering in smithereens onto the armour-plated flight deck as the great ship, shaken like a wounded beast, surged on through the seas off the Sakishima Islands?

He had a well-worn snapshot of the event taken from a nearby ship: the gout of water towering over the carrier, the bomb buckling the side plates but not piercing them, the nearest of near near-misses. Yes, this was my father – the man who had faced death as his paid employment, surviving to die twenty-seven years later in a hospital bed, with me just down the corridor. Dad was in the final stages of physical collapse and surrender; my malady was more mental and spiritual, the emotional burnout of watching my monster, my former hero, die.

The more I studied that picture over the years, the more I began to wonder who were those men that had attacked him that day, why they died and my father – and I in my father – lived; why they vanished, their sons

'Rage, rage against the dying of the light': the last photograph of my father, dated '16.9.72'.
He died on 2 October 1972, aged 50.

The moment of the 6 April 1945 attack on *Illustrious*, seen from the port side. SOURCE UNKNOWN.

and daughters never to be? How was their death sentence experienced and lived until that terrifying moment: from the hour they first knew they were chosen to die for Japan and the emperor, until black death swallowed them in fire and madness as the Allied ships rose up to meet them out of the shining sea in a storm of anti-aircraft fire?

Far from being the suicidal fanatics of Allied wartime portrayals and later comic book caricatures that I was weaned on, I would discover that these men were just like my father: the majority were young, aged eighteen to twenty-four, many of them university students, the educated flower of their country. They were the kind of men who could not stand to hear the clocks ticking the seconds away in their final nights and so smashed them; men who got drunk on sake, slashed light fittings in their barracks with samurai swords; some of whom were Christians, singing forbidden hymns, wrapping up bibles to carry with them on those flights to human oblivion. Men like him, yes, and men like me: complex and precious human beings.

This is the story of my search for my father and his enemies. I do not know at the point of writing this sentence where it will lead me. Like any journey worth taking, like any day we rise up and follow the path the sun takes until it passes over, the act of setting out is enough to begin with.

What can we possibly learn from men who saw themselves as 'sojō no koi' ('carp on the cutting board'), live fish awaiting the stroke of death in the midst of a ruthless, titanic struggle that threatened to obliterate any prospect of human choice and individuality? Yet even in this extreme situation, courage and its poetry survived the madness. So now I must go in the hope of meeting at least one of them and their relatives, of paying my respects to the living and the dead.

# St Valentine's Day

*He was born on St Valentine's Day 1922.*

Today is my father's birthday: he would have been 89 years old. I have two books of naval history beside me now, precious souvenirs that remain from breaches in the family walls whereby our enemies got in and laid waste: post-traumatic stress disorder (blame the war); alcoholism and gambling addiction (blame the Fall, blame the genes, take your pick); divorce (see first choices); and long, deeply nursed resentments all around (blame yourself).

I *did* have the one letter he wrote me, after a visit in early 1972, when he came to see me in Christchurch and stayed in my upstairs flat on Carlton Mill Road. We were both in transit: I was back at university, trying to hold myself together, and my relationship with the mother of our son who was thinking things over far away. Dad had been kicked out of the home he and his second wife had set up in Nelson, and was living alone in a forestry camp at Golden Downs. We were both – strangely for everything that had happened – men alone together. I had agreed to see him even though we were officially estranged. It was not the easiest of meetings.

'Ball at Naval Base, Auckland', Devonport, c. 1953–54. Mum and Dad in happier times; he in his post-war demob three-piece.

Dad kept 'popping out' (I suspect to the Carlton Hotel just down the road, and the RSA), probably putting a bet on, and maybe later buying the Bonus Bonds he gave me as a present. Picking up my English literature studies after a five-year-long sabbatical from high school, a fish out of water from the world of hard men I'd dropped out into, I even tried to persuade him, at something of a loose end in his life, to enrol as an adult student and do something with his always formidable intellect. He was a ferocious reader, devouring half a dozen novels in a day or two — sometimes almost overnight, if sleep deserted him.

He marred the moment with an attempt to balance the books over his relationship with my mother — ended when my brother and I had moved her out of the family home — telling me there were always two sides to a story. One day, I might understand (he'd been out drinking, so he was well oiled). I do understand them both much better now than I did then; but it was not a good move on the day. I closed the subject down. The letter, which came after he'd left and gone back to his forestry hut, thanked me for lending him Thomas Hardy's *The Mayor of Casterbridge* and William Faulkner's *Light in August* (two of my course texts). He confessed he hadn't been able to get into Faulkner, but had read the Hardy novel, and found in the dark and stubborn character of Henchard (a man who sells his wife when drunk) a sobering measure of identification.

I see this now as my father's first attempt at confessing his part in his downfall. He had never been quick to admit a fault – not that I could recall. Did I grasp the poignancy of his admission: that he'd seen something of himself in a fictional character, a man destroyed by pride? Perhaps. There was so much murky water swirling beneath too many broken bridges. He did try and explain himself further, quoting the saying attributed to Robert Louis Stevenson (among others), that 'There is so much good in the worst of us / and so much bad in the best of us, / that it ill behooves any of us / to talk about the rest of us'. I wasn't about to swallow that, either. I just wanted him to say he was sorry, outright – which I think he came close to on that day in September 1972 when Dr Kibblewhite gave him the bad news.

I kept the letter as well as a leather pencil case he had sewn in prison, both of them together. Their importance grew over the years, two rare mementoes that linked us post-mortem. For some reason I had them both in the pocket of a backpack in the study of the house where I now live; around ten years ago, a young escapee from Kingslea Children's Home in Christchurch broke in and burgled us. Shoulder packs are just fine for filling up with loot, so he'd emptied my books onto the floor and shoved in the VCR, and whatever other electronics he could easily transport for the hop, step and jump to the second-hand shop. That was the last time I can remember seeing the letter and the pencil case – my guess is they got dumped in a skip with the pack when he'd done his deal.

The fact that he was caught some time later and confessed to raiding our place for drug money and sundry needs, along with a string of other break-ins, was not a lot of comfort. The irony of where the pencil case was made – behind bars, where this wayward kid was now spending some more time himself – was not lost on me. But the loss of the letter still hurts. I have hunted everywhere, yet that one piece of evidence of Dad's world meeting mine remains stubbornly disappeared. What I do have – and what the kid could not steal – are memories and the power to commit them to a record even he might get to read one day. Stranger things have happened.

And there is something else: two history books, links to my father as I call out to the dead, to see who will answer for them from among the living. *Illustrious* (the ship's story) was written by Kenneth Poolman and published in 1955 – the year after she was decommissioned, a year before she was broken up for scrap at Faslane Naval Base on the Clyde. The other is *Wings of the Morning: The Story of the Fleet Air Arm in the Second World War*, by Ian Cameron, published in 1962. Between the giving and receiving of these two veteran hardbacks, still in my possession, runs the difficult and painful current that sparked and flared in the relationship with my father as I entered puberty the son of a sailor, a miner – and a thief.

Am I being too frank in exposing the family laundry and judging my father harshly? Nothing of this on the page compares to what it was like in the cold light of day in a West Coast coal-mining town when your world comes crashing down one Sunday morning: family friends arrive to haul your father out from his miner's sleep-in, carrying the books for the school committee funds, pointing out the discrepancies, calling the police, the squad car arriving, him being taken away, all in the space of a few hours. Everybody knows. Everybody is forming an opinion. And suddenly, you are the family not of a sailor, not of a miner, but of a criminal.

It wasn't the first time: Dad's gambling addiction and his recourse to making withdrawals from other people's social funds had already got him kicked out of his beloved navy. Back in Christchurch in 1955, he'd got into debt with the bookies and raided the mess funds at HMNZS *Pegasus* in Montreal Street. I still can't drive past that building, mast and flags, and not have this incident reach out and touch me. Dad's disgrace, broken from the naval career that was really all he'd known since 1937 – 'Discharged: Services No Longer Required' – saw him handed over to the police and the civilian courts.

Mere children, we didn't really grasp what was happening then. My mother, in shock, still somehow believing in all his rationalisations, led us to believe Dad had gone into hospital and not Paparua Prison. For her, his Blackball dip into the school committee funds was the final indignity – and this time, I was thirteen, not a gullible eight-year-old. It went through us all like an invisible knife, a blade that hollowed me out, snapping whatever faith

I held in adult authority and setting me up for years in the needy role as a caretaker of female pain. I became my mother's helper and confidant, the boy who knew too much. I was building up a set of defences and dependencies that would cause me – and others – a whole heap of trouble up ahead.

This is where those two books come in: sooner or later, the prisoner comes home – to what? In my case, it was a cold fury, a sullen silence that did not want our betrayer and shamer back in the house where I had taken over much of his role. And for a good while he was on the outer, living in a little bach up the road. He wasn't supposed to be coming home: Mum had taken out a separation order – a brave act in 1961 – and it seemed that he was history. Thanks to the intervention of a well-meaning prison chaplain who came to see her, armed with Dad's promises of reformation, and his own conviction that 'your husband has changed, Mrs Holman', she began to reconsider. Henry Ivor Hopkins: what might have been had you never arrived on our doorstep with your family, locum Anglican priest in Westport over that summer while your counterpart enjoyed the charms of Paparua, ministering to your flock of inmates amongst whom in his white cook's uniform sat my father?

In some ways, the prison was familiar: military rules and uniforms, a sense of order almost naval, and Dad as a cook was back in tropical whites. I was later to go and stay with the Hopkins family at Paparua, having made a firm friendship – based on mutual aero-modelling and a general attraction to zaniness (The Goons, *Mad* magazine) – with his eldest son, Jim. Under lock and key, I went to church with them there one Sunday. As Padre Hopkins stood before us and the prisoners filed in, my father sat down behind me and patted me on the shoulder. I have no idea what I felt at that moment: it's down there somewhere in a file marked 'Leave well alone'.

Of course part of me wanted my father: for as long as I could remember, I had worshipped and feared him. This man had been my hero, the runaway sailor who had left us in England to sail to New Zealand, then deserted us there as well when he sailed for Korea. In Blackball we were left again, this time to fend for ourselves in a small town suspicious of my mother's imagined part in his embezzling of the school committee monies ('she must have been in on it, she'd have known'). In the prison chapel, I was just confused. It was a comfort of sorts to see him – and a burning shame.

Dad says goodbye to me in Galloway Road W8, just before sailing off to New Zealand in 1949: 'Go away, Daddy!' I was heard to rebuke him.

They filed out at the end, sins confessed, sins forgiven; and I went back to admiring Jim's latest acquisitions at the manse: an Airfix Wellington bomber kit and his trendy Vance Vivian stovepipe trousers.

There were other issues – my sisters confronted at the primary school by spiteful children whose parents had shared the bad news about the Holmans over the mince and spuds: 'Your Dad's in prison. He's a thief!' Fifty years on, they have not forgotten. My mother, fearing I would get the same treatment in my first year at high school in Greymouth, rode there on the New Zealand Railways Road Services Bedford bus and spoke to the principal, that ferocious-looking martinet Percy Muirhead. Running a school populated by the sons and daughters of bolshie West Coast miners, sawmillers and the like was no sinecure, but Percy was well and truly up to it. In the days when the cane still ruled, he was feared – and respected. Hearing her concerns about my brother and me being taunted, Mr Muirhead was blunt: 'Mrs Holman, if I hear of anything like this, I will deal with it with utmost ruthlessness!' Bless him.

Nothing of that came my way that I recall, but there were ripples in the family following Dad's departure. My brother – in the absence of a father in the house – made friends with a neighbour who took him deerstalking, let him learn to drive in his flash green Vauxhall Wyvern (we never had a car), and early into that fourth-form year, persuaded Eric to leave school and go working down at Haast on the Ministry of Works roading project connecting Westland with Otago. When a parent leaves, things change for the children – and nowhere is this truer than with a prisoner's kids. Into that vacuum nature abhors stepped my maternal grandmother; she had come out from England in the early 1950s and lived with us until her death in 1967. She had never quite taken to Dad it seems, and here was further proof of his fecklessness; she was with us in Christchurch at the first manifestation of his gambling addiction so this was the final straw. How could he bring such shame and odium on the family – again?

Eunice Winifred Airey – henceforth 'Nanny' – was a remarkable woman. Born in 1878, to a peripatetic sea engineer, Peter Daniel Bywater, and his wife Mary, she was no stranger to slings and arrows. Her first love, Carl Hasenburg, a somewhat devious German suitor, had got her pregnant, at a time when the shame of such a thing for middle-class Victorians would – I assume – have been intense. So much so that Nanny was shipped off to relatives in Pennsylvania to give birth to a baby boy and have him adopted. Bereft of the only son she would ever have, she carried back with her on the ship to Liverpool a lifelong wound; a wound deepened and made bitter by the discovery on her return that this same Carl had begun a romance with her elder sister Lily – and that they would later marry. Her feelings are not hard to imagine.

She would go on to marry three times, survive the death of two husbands,

Nanny: Eunice Winifred Airey (1878–1967), my mother's mother and my storyteller. This is the only image ever taken of her while she lived with us in her last ten years, snapped with my first camera, a Box Brownie.

the infidelity of a third (kicked out), the death also of her first daughter Lillian, my aunt, aged twenty-eight, two world wars (including the 1941 Liverpool blitz and German V-weapon raids on London from 1943 onwards), and finally travel as a one-way immigrant to New Zealand in her seventies. At the end of a long life, she was now privy to her daughter coping with her son-in-law's indiscretions on the public stage. She was tough and resilient, having crossed the Atlantic several times; she could recall with clarity the *Titanic* sinking, and became in the domestic sphere my teacher of living history. She was not backward in declaring that my father – in absentia – was 'a wicked man, he must never come back and hurt your mother again'. This kind of emotional cocktail was poisonous but I would sit faithfully at her bedside, smelling the eau de Cologne she so loved to use, almost masking – but not quite – the old woman smells in the bright sunporch where she slept and her busy Singer sewing machine sat. It must have been bloody freezing there in a Blackball winter. Not as cold as her welcome for him, should he ever darken the doorstep – as indeed he did.

Dad came back to Blackball at the end of his sentence in 1962 and faced the music – I give him a good deal of credit for that. That first day back at work: what was that like? He was living in that tiny bach up the road to begin with, so we were not likely to hear. I was fourteen, going on fifteen, when he walked back into my world. For eighteen months there had been no man in the house – except for the occasional visit from the local cop. My brother and I had developed some anti-social tendencies (such as shooting out street lamps with his Diana slug gun, raiding old people's orchards – normal boy's stuff in the country). Life had been good without a father: there was no tension, no late-night returns from the pub and, best of all, I was the man of the house. Mum even started giving me her fags (I was smoking anyway) and we would sit down to talk while her coffee percolator bubbled and bloop-bloop-blooped on the stovetop and we puffed away on Pall Mall plain. Jim would come from Christchurch and stay with us, reciprocal visits when we would stay up half the night copying graphic art from *Mad* paperbacks and eating sandwiches in bed, while he regaled me with his latest fifth-form literary discovery (*Catch-22*, in one memorable example). I already knew about anti-heroes.

It was a time that would never come again – a moment of post-pubescent discovery when the world was both way too big and far too small. The possibilities seemed endless – and the boredom too, in lazy waves. Over this emergence of an imagined autonomous self, my crazy mixed-up enthusiastic insecure and arrogant dose of narcissism, fell the shadow of my father. My mother was still holding out, but granted him the odd invitation to come and have a meal with his children; we would visit him half a mile up the

Main Road, as he slowly began to work his magic. My sisters — especially the elder of the two, Jill — were more vulnerable; and she, being his favourite, was pretty well disposed. He had certainly changed: he was going to church on Sundays and he wasn't going to the pub (or putting bets on — was he?). He even helped the vicar paint the tiny old Anglican church. This was a man I can hardly ever recall — a veteran of a London council house tenancy culture — exhibiting the remotest trace of that pioneering Kiwi DIY spirit. His post-prison behaviour began to alter my former image of him and, like it or not, however wary, at fourteen a boy needs a father.

Whatever my mother was thinking, it came to a head one day when she took my brother and me aside and said that she and Dad had been talking about the possibility of him moving back in: what did we think? We would have to agree to it and she wouldn't do anything over our heads. There are some days in your life when everything changes, when so much hangs on whatever you do and say next. As we cannot read the future, such days never seem as momentous at the time as they prove later to be. It was all too much: we should never have been put in that position. It was the wrong amount of power and responsibility to give to teenagers — but what else could she have done? There was nobody else to ask. I know what my grandmother would have said, and my sisters were just too young to be faced with that kind of decision.

I have no idea how long it took for us to come up with an answer: what actually passed through my mind, or what my brother thought. It was impossible to make a perfect decision — there is no such thing at a time like that. Part of me, I'm sure, wanted the status quo: I had power over him and, presently, outranked him. If he came back, I think I knew that would have to change. That other part of me, the son, the child, wanted a father who would be stable and secure, to make the hard calls and take away from me the burden of being my mother's emotional rescue service. I was a trainee co-dependent who just wanted to be fourteen again. We said yes.

Or, we said something that amounted to yes — let's give it another try — and so my father moved back into the house, into the marriage bed, and back into my life. What was she thinking and feeling on that day? The woman who had turned her back on him that shameful Sunday when the cops came, saying, 'How can you do this to us again, to your family?' She had her needs as well, her own feelings: this was the man she had married in haste in 1943, at a time when perhaps that night, or the next day, you would die. It was a time when life was short and expectations shorter, when men and women had intense opportunistic sex, got married and had more sex with no great thought of tomorrow, a time when tomorrows were hard to come by and marriage was not quite what it had been in the days of peace. Years later, long after he was gone, I asked her, 'Mum, did you ever love Dad?' – and she answered yes, of course she did. But there was a footnote: if you try hard enough, you can work at killing love, and eventually it will die. Her confession is a comfort to me now: back then in 1962 my jury on him was well and truly out.

All ex-prisoners face the same communal retrial: will they do it again? My role now was to fall in behind and give my father another chance. Fat chance! Once he was back in the house, I began to freeze him out. I can't recall when I made the decision to send him to Coventry, but I soon put into play what a perceptive friend would later describe as one of my 'Wagnerian sulks'. I refused to speak to him, refused to acknowledge him at all; whatever I had thought I was doing when I agreed with my mother that Dad should come back into the fold, when it actually happened, emotionally I could not cope. I felt I had lost my powerful position in my mother's needs and affections and now I was expected to just be the son again, not the 'husband', to allow him back in and have charge over me.

Perhaps I experienced his return as a form of rejection on her part: oh Oedipus! I can only speculate on the unconscious anger of a teenage boy who seems now like a stranger, but those books tell a story that has some tangible evidence. The copy of *Wings of the Morning* that sits beside me now has an inscription on the inside facing page: 'Jeff Holman, Christmas '62. From Mum and Dad. Main Road. Blackball.' Had he moved back in then? My memory is not up to that kind of detail; certainly, the book (which I had asked for) was a gift from them both. At forty-two shillings and sixpence, it wasn't cheap: apprentice mechanics at that time were only on about five pounds a week, so it was easily two days' wages for some of my old schoolmates.

My asking for and being given a book about the Fleet Air Arm suggests some kind of rapprochement going on. Something about the date inscribed

Precious books: peace offerings between father and son.

in my old copy of *Illustrious*, however, makes me think he was still not quite back in the house by that Christmas. I know that I bought this book for him – as it plainly says 'To Dad from Jeff. 20th July, 1963' – and when and why I gave it. It was my peace offering and a white flag of submission. My behaviour towards him was destructive, but I'd got into such a tailspin, I couldn't get out under my own power. The two of them finally called me in one day and sat me down; it was my mother who opened the confrontation. She told me quietly but firmly that my attitude was not helping, that she and my father were trying to make a go of things and that I had agreed to support them. This surly behaviour would have to stop.

I can't recall feeling betrayed by her taking 'his side' – or even if my father had to chip in much – but there was some measure of relief because the adults had taken a stand. Teenagers – no matter what they say – don't want to run families. I backed down – maybe I even apologised – and the book about HMS *Illustrious* became my peace offering. I didn't have it with me – it would have been ordered soon after – but I know that I gave him *Illustrious* as a sign he was back in command of the family, that I was willing to co-operate. *Aye, aye, Captain.* Many years later I inscribed on the opposite inside cover page the full text of his favourite hymn: the Sailors' Hymn, 'Eternal Father, strong to save / Whose arm hath bound the restless wave ... O hear us when we cry to Thee / For those in peril on the sea'. It was sung on 5 April 1939 at the Vickers-Armstrongs shipbuilding works, Barrow-in-Furness, at the carrier's launch. According to Jim Hopkins, it was also the hymn my father used to request in the prison chapel Sunday services.

So life with my father as household head began again; and as I scrutinised all sides of the new leaf he professed to have turned over, there were some encouraging signs. I was in the fifth form by now, and 1963 was a big year for me. School Certificate pressure was mounting, and I was adding intellectual and hormonal growth rings. By the end of November, as I turned sixteen, the president of the United States was assassinated – my world was turning around and expanding. Dad was back at work down the mine, digging the garden at home – never had I seen him do that before – and tarring the iron roof with a mop dipped in hot pitch. Horticulture, house maintenance, even church attendance – and what's more, he was walking past the pubs every night and coming straight home. I have one golden memory of him working in the garden, freshly laid out by the coal heap. He was all sweaty in the summer heat, clad in his white singlet and baggy white ex-navy shorts (tropical issue), his pale and gnarly miner's body bent over whatever humble crop was struggling to survive in the thin soil that topped the stony glacial moraine on which the town rested.

As he dug, cricket blared from the transistor – England were playing New Zealand in February and March of 1963 – and as the radio crackled away, I ferried him cordial made up by my mother and we chatted. The English (his team, I suppose, though he never seemed to care) had David Sheppard in their ranks, a man of the cloth known as the Playing Parson (he would go on to become the Anglican Bishop of Liverpool, opposing the worst of Margaret Thatcher's excesses). My father noted this as an oddity, the one thing he said that I recall from that halcyon afternoon. Like the mythical bird that nests in the sea – from which the latter expression comes – we were floating in our newly refurbished nest, the winds and the former waves all seemingly charmed away.

I began to conceive of a spiritual hunger: in church one Sunday, I heard the call to confirmation classes and signed up to attend. Blackball lay in the Nelson Diocese – the strange connection of a well-to-do middle-class bishopric to a radical coal-mining town that during its bolshie heyday in place of Sunday school had run classes in communism for its children. Our vicar, Barry Loveridge, seemed a fish out of water, nice as he was – he was not of the Coast at all. He did though have a flash Mark III Ford Zephyr, which to me at the time was akin to a very luxurious spaceship. Trips to confirmation classes over at the vicarage in Ahaura and bible class camps in the Moonlight Hall had their advantages. The sadness of damp bibles and prayer books, the musty perfume of old tongue-and-groove rooms inside weatherboard halls under corrugated-iron roofs upon which the endless rains thundered, has stayed with me longer than anything they taught me – a somewhat bewildered but willing disciple.

I learned that good followers of Christ should be witnesses, and so practised on Ken, my best friend: did he want to come to church with me next Sunday? No. No, he did not. And while we had been drifting apart (he had been in Woodwork at high school for three years by this time, and I was now in the academic stream), I think the long boyhood friendship of two overweight lads (Beefy and Biff) took a fatal hit that day. My confidence was shaken and I did not repeat my evangelism. Then the Reverend Loveridge failed an important test. He flunked the question that starts to bother many teenagers: Why is the world so marred by evil and suffering? We were driving back from a class at Ahaura in the flash Zephyr and as we approached the Blackball Bridge in our chariot, I casually asked him, why – why were human beings so nasty, cruel and sadistic?

I'd been reading some heavyweight tomes: *The Scourge of the Swastika* (evil Germans) and *The Knights of Bushido* (sadistic Japanese). I was genuinely disturbed by – yet compelled to view and review – the gruesome images of the Holocaust and the death marches. What sort of world was this? I'd also had some personal experience of human frailty by this time, and while I wasn't exactly asking him, 'Vicar, why did my Dad steal money from the school?', perhaps that lurking question was in the mix. Barry Loveridge replied that he felt human evil could be sheeted home to the work of the devil in our midst. I may be misrepresenting him: he may have finessed this opening gambit in all sorts of ways – but that was what I heard and what stuck. It rang hollow then, as it does now: I couldn't see any devils herding Jewish children into gas chambers in the photographs in Lord Russell's books, nor demons decapitating and bayoneting pregnant Chinese women – but I could see men.

That failure to address what I knew – that I too could be cruel and nasty, could hate, and despise, could steal and cheat, even from my friends – gave Old Nick the chance he was looking for. I began to doubt the vicar's credibility. When the Bishop laid his hands on my bowed head some weeks later in the tiny Anglican church near the old Domain where rugby league was king, nothing happened. I silently ceased to nourish my shoots of faith. Where was this promised Holy Spirit? I waited: his hands felt warm and heavy and I wished he'd take them off me. Goodness knows what it was I needed from these men, but I couldn't get any of it. I probably wasn't ready. I have no problem accepting the existence of a Devil today – I have a living God in my life – but I take responsibility for my own behaviour as an adult. Even in 1963, I knew there was no free pass, no shuffling the blame off onto invisible entities.

And anyway, in my father's life I had the evidence: he had been very bad, and now he was trying very hard to be good. Slowly, however, the first cracks began to appear in his reformation. Certainly by the following year, 1964, University Entrance exams, Bob Dylan and the Beatles as my soundtrack, we were heading back into troubled waters. I suppose it started again on a long-forgotten night when he neglected to pass by one of his old watering holes, the Club Hotel, the Dominion or the Workingmen's Club – and popped in for a quiet beer with his mates.

You can imagine the pressure from within and without: the joshing remarks of his miner mates, the buried horrors of old internalised battle fatigue. To complete his rehabilitation in a tough community, he had been trotting off home obediently after his shift came down from the mountains: the road from Roa on the miners' bus, dropped off outside the mine office, walking back to his family down the long Main Road – while those he had sweated with all shift strolled through the doors of the pub, or gathered

A drinker's view from the bar of the Dominion Hotel, Blackball (now, Formerly the Blackball Hilton).

round the horseshoe bar of the Club. You could almost feel the slaking power of that first eight-ounce beer as it coursed over their dry tongues, working its smooth alcoholic magic in their systems. 'Ahhhhhhhh, didn't even touch the sides!' Today I don't drink: but I confess to feeling just a little thirsty after that sentence, trying to imagine his thirst, his physical longings for relief and release and the emotional need to belong – to be accepted again and respected by his peers.

So, one day, he simply rejoined them: just for a five ounce, just for five minutes, just for a round of darts, a game at which he had a deadly aim, going on to win the West Coast Singles Champs more than once, even making the National Championships one year. Practice in darts came – mostly – from time spent in bars, the smoky haze and the male hubbub, intoxicating. Nineteen sixty-four: still six o'clock closing, smoke as much as you like, few women seen or welcome in the public bars, a male domain serenaded by race commentaries on the radio, buffering the man's world of work from the domestic pressures at home. From the moment that beer slipped on down my dad's throat, from the instant he put the first bet back on some hopeful nag, he was disappearing from the garden and the church – and from us – all over again. He was travelling within to where the demons of addiction with their dice-shaped genes and their insatiable wounds were happy to be bathed once more in alcohol and adrenaline.

At home waiting, my mother and my grandmother were also victims of the post-traumatic stress disorder my father was trying to medicate. They'd both been bombed and blasted in 1940 and 1941 by Goering's Luftwaffe in Liverpool, during that port city's vicious blitz; and then again in 1943, when they moved to London and ran the gauntlet of the V-weapons that rained down on them there. They survived the unpredictable and deadly V-1 flying bombs, then the terrifying V-2 missiles that came with no warning, blasting whole streets before people knew what had hit them. They were, all three of them – like so many returned services personnel and civilian survivors of World War Two – deeply damaged, struggling inwardly to adjust and make new lives in the post-war peace. This was especially true when New

Inspecting the remains of a V-2 rocket, Chinatown, Limehouse, East London, March 1945. Blast damage has destroyed the street. IMPERIAL WAR MUSEUM: HU 44973.

Zealanders – antipathetic as they were to Poms – did not always have the ears to listen to their own veterans' stories, let alone those of English immigrants; and civilians at that. Somehow these women bottled it up, while men like my Dad turned to the bottle instead.

Much more is known about these conditions now; back then, few knew about post-traumatic stress disorder and cared even less. Stoicism ruled. Bite the bullet and get on with it: the men could go to the RSA and share their experiences in a silence where even the unsaid was a kind of saying. For the rest, it was Anzac Day for the public acknowledgement of such wounds; and for boys like me, it was war comics and war films. None of which was of much help to my mother on this particular evening, as she waited for her reformed husband to come home early in his new and welcome practice. What was she feeling as the time ticked by and echoes of the old patterns began to ring alarms – as six o'clock came and went and still he wasn't home? The plate of meat and veggies was slid into the oven under a lid, drying out slowly as the gravy congealed and darkened.

I'm inventing detail, of course, but this kind of thing did happen; there were triggers for her, as there were for the rest of us. When he did come home, late and lit up, was he perhaps all bonhomie from the refuelling stop, or just a little bit aggressive in defence of his broken promises? The exact moment is lost, but there was a beginning to this backward slide, down a slope that took us all with him into the distorting mirror world of the alcoholic and the addict. You sense in your gut this is not going to turn out well, that something you can't name is happening all over again. Your eyes begin to turn away, avoiding the painful reality of seeing an adult become a child once more – while you, the real child, are forced to grow up ahead of time.

This doesn't happen overnight: days, weeks and months slide by while the erosion of faith goes deeper. Children, after all, having pretty acute antennae for their parents' behaviour, are also uniquely self-absorbed. My brother had left home for the Ministry of Works in Haast; I was head down in University Entrance homework every night, feeding on my teachers' approval, respect which was not forthcoming from my father. He had gone with my mother to a parents' evening the year before and came home telling me my fifth-form history teacher, Bernie Conradson, had called me his 'star pupil'. I tried to get him to help me with algebra homework (not my strong suit), but his 1930s methods and mine were incompatible. Friends have reminded me of him taking the St John First Aid classes and the Boy Scouts for lessons in tying knots and making signals; as the booze and the betting took over, we were the ones that became entangled. His domestic communications with his own flesh and blood spoke of an increasing self-absorption, which did not bode well.

I retreated into my own world: obsessive schoolwork and model-making, trips alone down the bush or sitting up in a beech tree in our paddock, smoking, thinking, watching the world go by. I was in flux: being sixteen, going on seventeen. I would have made some form of private world even in a happy and stable environment – but watching my parents' descent into alienation simply increased my loneliness, my cynicism and my anger. Dad would bring home mates from the pub, dropping them unannounced on my mother, who then had to find an extra place at the table. The two men would talk to each other, fuelled with a skinful while we all watched – and waited. I took to going away for weekends to stay at the homes of sixth-form friends: this proved a revelation, as the host family sat down to meals together. They all seemed to have cars, and most went to church. They were not all saints, nor problem-free, but it seemed to me they were living as families – while we were not. Dad was back living in a kind of ersatz navy culture: you did your job, went ashore, had some fun, staggered back to the ship, crashed in your hammock – and somebody else did the worrying about what came next.

Some nights he would come home late from the pub, well after we had all gone to bed and the radio was switched off (there was no television or internet to keep us up). The front door would bang shut, hard on the creaking of his shoes on the verandah; lights would go on in the lounge and the kitchen, then the radiogram would start to tune up: Nat King Cole, 'Rambling Rose'. I still can't listen to it. Dad would talk to himself, argue with himself, cook up a feed of bacon, make cheese and onion sandwiches, then sing along with Nat. The smell of the food would fill the house, the light under my bedroom door flicker as he walked up and down, and finally into the marital bedroom. Voices would rise: if it got bad enough, I would pull the pillow over my head, my sisters would start crying – and then screaming.

Angry young man: my sister Jill with me, outside our house in Blackball. Judging by the finery, I'm dressed up ready to catch the old NZR Bedford bus to Greymouth for the pictures on a Friday night (fashion courtesy of the Mersey Sound).

Nightmares can be both waking and sleeping: over that year we had both. I came into the kitchen one morning to find my mother staring fixedly out of the window with a faraway look. With a stab of anxiety, I asked her what was wrong. She started talking about a blue tree, out there on the back lawn – couldn't I see it? I don't know how we got her back from that place. The parents of a high-school friend brought me home from a weekend stay one Sunday: they owned a Mark I Ford Consul and had taken me on a family drive around the Grey Valley, before the home delivery. Invited to stay for tea, they were treated to my father's declaration at the meal's end that he had no need to do the dishes, when he had 'a sixteen-year-old slave to do them for me'. That was me. I can almost feel the burn of shame and rage that rose from my soul to my cheeks – how *not* to deal with a teenage boy.

One night around this time when I'd had my fill, it came to an inevitable head. I excused myself from the table after having had enough of him, more so than the food. My mother asked me if I wanted dessert: I just said, 'No thanks' – and got up. 'Don't you talk to your mother like that!' he growled. That was it: *he should talk!* 'Fuck off!' I shot back, bolting for the front door. Dad leapt from his chair breathing fire and draught beer vapours, and threw a punch, just missing my head. Mum pushed herself between us yelling, 'Leave him alone! Leave him alone!' My sisters I can still hear screaming as the family went into meltdown. God knows where my grandmother was – offstage most likely in her sunporch room, trying to make sense of the ruckus.

That peak Oedipal moment finished us off for good – right up until the day in 1972 when he was dying, and crying on my shoulder. I knew he wanted to kill me and the feeling was mutual. The homicidal jealousy a dominant male can conceive against his young male offspring – especially if he suspects, probably rightly, that his female mate has transferred her affections to the son – face to face is very frightening. To somehow sense that your father wants to take your life is the absolute reversal of everything you instinctively feel should happen. To feel within you that same hatred is even worse.

If this sounds a bit like the gorilla cage at the zoo – male, female, mate, offspring – it is because these primal moments, the dark depths of human nature, are not hard to access. It is our reserve of civilised behaviour that needs nurturing and cultivation; the bedrock survival stuff seems to kick in without any training at all. I put my head down and fled the house – somewhere, anywhere, the hell out of there. Father and son: we were finished – he knew it and I knew it. Unless he was able to reassert the adult part of himself and turn his life around, I would never ever trust him again. Looking back, the whole scene seems to have leapt fully formed from a Tennessee Williams script. Dad and Mum would stagger on for two more years after I left home in 1965, dropping out of university in the following year and running away on a shearing gang with my brother. Dad's attack on me, and my course over the next few years, seem deeply rooted in that one act.

We came home for the Christmas of 1966, and while we were all up in the old Dominion getting well and truly sloshed with Dad and his mates – smoke, bonhomie, darts and bullshit – my mother changed the game. Abandoned by all the males in her life for the charms of the public bar, she took an overdose in the middle of the day. Rather than a well-planned suicide attempt, it was really a desperate cry for help from a woman at the end of her tether. As we swayed home from the pub mid-afternoon, we met my elder sister running up the road screaming. A flying trip down the Grey Valley in the back of my brother's very quick Fiat 1500 got her to the hospital and the stomach pump. My father showed us the note she had left: from the male arena of the noisy bar, suddenly sober, it felt like my family was falling to pieces.

Eric and I talked it through, leaving Dad out of it. We couldn't go back up north and leave her after this and we didn't want to stay either. We visited our pale and chastened mother in the hospital, after her appointment with Dr Couston, the psychiatrist from Seaview Hospital in Hokitika. 'Mrs Holman,' he advised her, 'I don't seriously think you have a mental illness. From what you have told me, the problem lies with your husband.' He'd obviously dealt with his share of alcoholics and their families. We talked things over with her: 'Mum, we can't go and leave you like this. What do you want to do?'

She was sorry for what she had put us through, but she could see what had to happen. 'I should have left him when he went to prison – I should never have let him come back.' She wanted to get out this time and that was enough for us. We said we would help her do it and be there for her until she found a place. We went straight out and found a cheap old ruin in Murray Street, Greymouth; within a week, we had moved the family out of Blackball and into town. We told Dad what we were doing, but he didn't seem to grasp that we were serious. On the day we had the moving truck ordered, he went to work as if nothing was happening; not for nothing is alcoholism called the disease of denial.

The truck arrived and we went to work loading up enough of the household effects to get Mum started, leaving the basics for him to get by on. My poor sisters were not consulted: we simply uprooted them and they had to come with us, as did Nanny Airey (no doubt quietly cheering). The neighbours would have got a good nosey: the Holmans packing up and getting out of town. Some close friends were deeply saddened, while other smaller-minded pundits were satisfied to be proved right. In January 1967, walking out on your husband was a brave thing for a woman to do, in those years prior to the arrival of the Domestic Purposes Benefit. Making sense of those Blackball wives of the town who would cross the road in Greymouth when they saw my mother coming must have been cruel for her: did some of them wish they could abandon their abusers too? Then there were those of his old drinking mates who would ring her at night, asking, was she lonely?

Many things were left behind: my sisters' best friends, the familiar landscapes of our growing years, precious pictures, childhood photos that would later go into a new household, his next relationship, failing too in its time – our treasures fired off into the Nelson dump when she kicked Dad out. It returns to me now – details blurred – as a kind of Raymond Carver short story, a tale of blue-collar misery and courage that never deserved to end that way, yet it did. Many times I have wondered about the scene unfolding as my father came through the door of his deserted house that night, looked around and counted his losses. How did that feel? What did he do next? More Oedipal guilt: what a mess.

Once Mum was established, we headed back up to the Wairarapa, leaving her to survive on her own with an ailing mother soon to die and two very unhappy uprooted daughters. Dad, home alone from the pub, would make phone calls to her, sarcastic and threatening: he was going to go for custody of my sisters. 'Over my dead body!' said Mum. 'Your body was never much use to me dead or alive!' he fired right back. He always did have an acid tongue; now, she could just hang up and he couldn't touch her. She took out a non-molestation order against him and began her painful journey to independence.

Eric was turning twenty-one in February of 1967 and his host family at Waituna near Pahiatua were putting on a party. Mum and the girls came up – a long trip from the West Coast back then, by railcar, inter-island ferry and train – but our father wasn't there. I was not to see him again until late in 1969 when I came back home after eighteen months away shearing in Western Australia. Roma Towton, my wise country landlady, after many long nights with a sherry or two by the fire had worked me out. 'Go home, Jeffrey,' she said, 'and sort it out with your Dad, before it's too late.' She wasn't far wrong.

I booked a flight and went home for a break. Staying with my mother, visiting my Nanny's grave, falling in love with the girl next door – in between all this, Roma's voice in my head kept nagging at me: 'Go and see your father.' So I rang him, made a day, hired a car and drove up to Blackball. Seeing the old house again and him ensconced there with his new partner and her kids was very unsettling, but we did our best to make it work. It was a start: the place had been renovated from our time there and the lawns and garden were very shipshape. Corinne was not of the same stripe as my mother and he seemed to be back on his best behaviour again. I can't recall a thing that passed between us. I can't even see him there. I do remember driving the rental Ford Anglia into the yard, past my old bedroom, parking beside the coal heap opposite the moss-covered water tank on its supports, down which the overflow of water in winter would freeze into thick icicles. It was a kind of thaw: Dad had started over and I'd made a first attempt at reconciliation.

His next act in my life would be to die. I'd gone back to Western Australia – mission accomplished – but I didn't stay long. The girl next door was calling me home; and shearing merinos was not looking like a long-term career move. Australia was just too damn hot, my back was giving me hell and I was starting to write poetry again – tiny steps, but they were there. I came home to the Coast in 1970, moved back in with my mother and got a job with the Forestry Service on a tree-planting gang: relief work for the small but growing band of unemployed. Working on greasy slopes, spading *Pinus radiata* saplings into burned-off second growth, release-cutting the older trees from the sea of gorse that surrounded them, getting a handful of prickles, and when it rained really hard, playing cards in the back of the smoke-filled yellow Bedford truck – the winter passed. Writing poems on the back of tobacco packets, my relationship with the girl next door on the rocks, I discovered my father had moved up to Nelson. I was marking time.

Then Theresa, the woman I would fall for, a teenage ghost from high-school days, walked into my life. She was at university in Christchurch and it wasn't long before she'd persuaded me to re-enrol and try varsity again. Love is strange. My application to return to study in 1971 was accepted: I sold my car, moved over the hill and we were together. By the year's end she was pregnant, and by the beginning of 1971 we were separated. Our on-again, off-again roller-coaster relationship presented us come mid-winter with a son – still apart and thinking things over. Dad's visit to my flat came in this limbo time; after he had returned to his lonely forestry camp, Theresa and I got back together. By Easter of 1972, my mother was visiting Flat 3/3 Carlton Mill Road with a bunch of chocolate eggs that our boy happily smeared all over his angelic dial.

The world soon took another turn: news began to filter through that Dad was in hospital, in the cancer ward at Christchurch Public. I have a copy of his letter to my younger sister, written in May 1972, where he speaks of the treatment he's having, the hopeful tests – and of 'Terry and Jeff' paying him a visit. It's the same half-formed hand I remember from my missing letter, this one signed off 'Your Loving Father'. He was planning to make a visit to her when he was able; in the event, he would move back to the Coast for his last weeks on earth. All this came hard upon the time when my mother's beloved new partner Dick had killed himself; yet even in the midst of her own fresh grief, she took my father in so that he would not die alone. Time away from him had transformed her from passive sufferer to active agent.

Dad, with my sister Beth and his grandson Craig, Barrytown, 1972.

In this selfless act of forgiveness and reconciliation, she enacted a healing process that would help to release us all.

It was payback time: whatever we might have done for her, she now did for us and for him. He moved into 11 Franklin Street, Greymouth with his painful suitcase of regrets, hoping against hope that the treatment Dr Kibblewhite was experimenting with on him might just work. He wanted to marry her again, so that she would get the Widow's Pension: Mum refused. This was strictly a nursing care arrangement – although there must have been moments when the finality of his circumstances provoked some honesty and healing by the winter fire. He asked if he could take her dancing (my mother loved to dance); so one night he struggled up the road with her to the nearby Recreation Hotel. They managed a couple of turns around the floor before he had to give in (I have visions of a scene in a Robert Altman movie). At home in her house, he would lie on the couch in his dressing gown with a glass of port, the *Greymouth Evening Star* and a fag: 'Home is the sailor home from the sea, / And the hunter home from the hill'. He never quit smoking.

One by one, he made what peace he could with his children: I would travel over from Christchurch for the weekend, sometimes on my own, and for his last days, with my wife and son. He once asked me to be taken down to the Greymouth Workingmen's Club for a beer and a game of darts, so I borrowed my brother-in-law's Vauxhall and drove him into town. Darts were my father's talisman: whatever else he missed, he could hit the bull's-eye, double tops and triple tops, with monotonous regularity. This day, he stood at the line and fired: the dart travelled halfway to the board and sank into the floor. His playing career was over. He had a drink at the bar, made some small talk I suppose – and then I drove him home.

He visited my sisters and admired the newborns: like a wasting patriarch from an antique land, he was burning from the inside out before our eyes. There was still my brother in Australia to come home; letters and phone calls were fired off to Perth, advising him of the old man's tenuous hold on life. He would arrive just in time to fashion a difficult farewell with a father whose grip on reality was slipping away, laying bare his subconscious. The day I have recounted earlier, the doctor's death sentence, was shortly followed by Dad's admission to Grey Hospital and the onset of the last days and hours.

Terminal cancers rise up inside the living as well: from mine shafts long since sunk deep down, charged with the power at work in the dying. My father's slow death – and the rocky road I had travelled in my personal life in the previous eighteen months – was about to tip me over. My brother Eric says they had no idea what to say to each other: 'We hugged as best we could but the gap between us emotionally was just too wide to bridge in those few short minutes I spent with him. He was so sick and I'm sure just hanging on to say goodbye to me before he said goodbye to this world. He died that night.' He remembers – after the funeral – punching the old Prestcold fridge at our mother's place, the same one Dad had bought her as a present in 1957 and she ended up paying off.

The atmosphere was a hothouse of unresolved childhood feelings: how dare he die and leave us all stranded with so much unspoken raw material that would never be addressed? Dad, you old bastard – there you were, leaving us again, so often not there and now, never more. Some families have constructive goodbyes, but this one was driving me crazy. When my wife said she would go back to Christchurch with our son to take some pressure off me, I cracked. Another desertion. Dad lay a mile away: virtually silenced, a wraith with the yellowish thrush on his lips, tended by the nurses and prayed over by the local Anglican priest Peter Swears – another naval veteran. In his delirium, my mother had heard Dad mumble, 'Our father in heaven, Thy will be done . . . is that what you want?' – as if dismissing an annoying shade.

At the news Theresa was going, I opened a door inside myself, entered and shut it – shut down and closed off. I walked out into the night, up the road towards the hospital, muttering and raving to myself with snatches of *King Lear* bubbling up incoherently (we'd been studying it in English at varsity and there'd been a powerful production at the Court Theatre; I was full of its lines). 'Poor bare forked animal . . . poor bare forked animal' – words that might have been written to describe my father's condition as his life left him. I really did want to go mad – but like Lear, I was still sane. I babbled deliberately and repeated myself as I rushed up the road, leaving confusion and distress in my wake. I found myself in the bus shelter outside the hospital, muttering away; my brother-in-law Gavin who lived right across the road, dispatched to find me, sat there beside me while the ambulance was called. They thought I had flipped completely, but I was never mad: beside myself would be nearer to the truth – and soon, beside my father.

I was admitted and assessed: I continued to quote a garbled Shakespeare as a mode of communication, refusing to speak about what I was really feeling. I shut my family out: cruelly multiplying whatever distress they were already going through. The doctors were about to admit me to the local psychiatric hospital at Hokitika, discussing the prospect with Theresa, who had wisely stayed put. Two of the Grey Hospital staff snapped me out of it just in time: a young doctor who knew his Shakespeare and quoted him back to me and an older nursing sister, who knew what buttons to push, gave me the room to be angry – but knew I was never mad. I decided to come back: there was nowhere left to go in the place I had driven myself. While I was coming out of my corner overnight, just down the corridor, my father died.

Restored to my family – bless them – now we had to bury the sailor. The helpers appeared: the man from the RSA; Ron Neilson, Dad's mate on the coal at Roa from his mining days; the Reverend Swears; and the funeral director. A trip to the undertaker's premises to see him laid out in a coffin, his last little boat for that voyage to the underworld, set me off again. They'd dressed him up in what looked to me like a choirboy's outfit: frilly white silks, which in view of the life he'd led, looked completely bizarre. I appealed to the family: we couldn't let them bury Dad like that; he needed to be in his everyday clothes so we could shut the lid on somebody we knew – not whatever fancy dress funerary fashion was dictating. They agreed (whether to humour unstable me, I'm not quite sure): so out came his Bob Charles T-shirt, the baggy grey slacks, slippers, and his darts blazer with the ribbon that held his triumphs. That looked better.

Two years later I would write a poem, 'Choir Boy', that went like this:

*The burial of*
*the London*
*dead requires*
*the dress*
*they lived*
*in: take from*

## The Lost Pilot

*my Cockney father*
*long-time sailor gypsy*
*those choirboy capitalist*
*William the Conqueror rags*
*of death, bastard silk he*
*never wore and put*
*him down*
*positively,*
*perhaps*
*playing darts*
*in his*
*pyjamas*
*at the burial*
*of London's Dead.*

He took some putting down. At the graveside, I was not given the same amount of rope as my brother. As we lowered him into the ground, I was forced to sink to my knees and finally, lean down into the pit as far as my arms would stretch before the coffin hit rock bottom. Dad, you damn near took me in there with you! All my life, one way and another, I'd been trying to get close to you; you always kept moving away. Now you were dead, it would be a different kind of distance. I would have to cross it by writing you. Yes, old man, you became my subject. Help me bring you back this one last time. You always seemed to be a sailor to me, and an old man; but once you were a boy like me. That's where I have to go: searching for your childhood and manhood, following your footsteps out to sea towards the Sakishima Islands.

# St Valentine's Day

Dad, prior to leaving the navy for Civvy Street; Mum, recovering from her near-death experience in February 1946, in delivering my brother Eric into the post-war world (London W8).

# 2

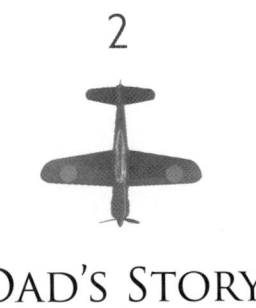

# Dad's Story

> Peril and abyss has God to the sea given
> And yet made it the mirror of heaven.
>
> *Fernando Pessoa*, Portuguese Ocean

> One of the pale-faced clairvoyants lifts himself on his elbow, reckons and numbers the fighters present and to come – thirty millions of soldiers. Another stammers, his eyes full of slaughter, 'Two armies at death-grips – that is, *one great army committing suicide.*'
>
> *Henri Barbusse*, Under Fire: The Story of a Squad

My father was born in Hammersmith Hospital, Du Cane Road, London W12 on St Valentine's Day 1922, in the cooling breath of the world's most recent act of mass slaughter, the Great War. He was delivered in time to reach the green age of seventeen by the arrival of the next act of mechanised homicide, World War Two. In between, he experienced the hunger and poverty years of the Great Depression, shadowing his childhood and adolescence with a vulture-like presence that goes a long way to explaining the man he would become. It was boyhood-to-manhood with not much between and then total war, as the Royal Navy took him and shaped him for life. By some miracle, some sublime calculation infused, we are free to believe, by the leaven of divine providence, he survived all of this and came back alive. Alive, yes, but someone other than who he might have become had he known the benison of the post-war boom years I was to enjoy growing up in New Zealand.

Three years ago, I went to the funeral of an old Blackball identity: Ivy McGuire, the wife of the late licensee of the Dominion Hotel, Bebe McGuire (the pub now known as Formerly the Blackball Hilton). There I met and talked to a number of ageing Blackball hands: one of them, George Reynolds, told me this story about my father from back in 1959, on the day of his mother's funeral in the town. As the procession rolled slowly down the

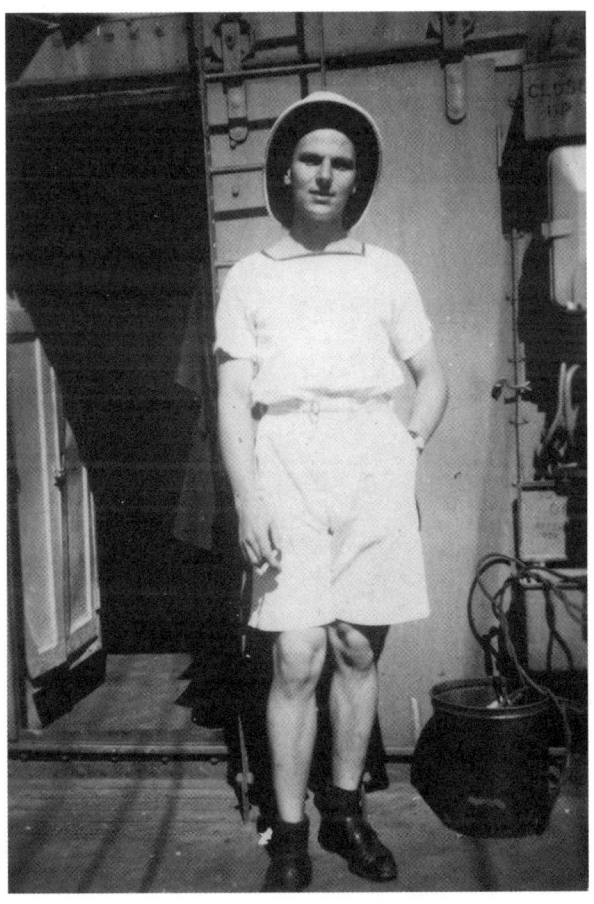

Dad gone troppo. The caption reads: 'Mombasa July '42' in my mother's hand.

I play Dad: fancy-dress ball in the Blackball Miners' Hall, 1961–62.

Main Road past our place, on its way to the local cemetery at the top of the Big Hill, George observed my dad on the side of the road, out mowing the lawns. Seeing her pass by, my father hauled himself up to his full five foot eight and a half inches and saluted the passing parade with naval precision. What amazed George was Dad's attire: 'He was standing there, saluting us at attention in his long white shorts and singlet.'

That I suppose is my abiding image of him: a former navy man, a person from another time and place, a past country we could never enter. The war, the armed forces and the bitterness of his exclusion from that privileged male world of the petty officers' mess seemed to define him. His old naval uniform still hung in the wardrobe in the parental bedroom; I borrowed it once to wear to the Kids' Christmas Fancy Dress Party in the cavernous Miners' Hall. I still have the picture of me parading with the other kids, marching around in my father's robes. My head is down and I seem preternaturally absorbed for a boy on the cusp of puberty. What did I want from that mask of his, that suit of adult armour?

Somehow it's a reminder that just as I was a child then, he too had been a boy like me. He barely spoke of his childhood, except to remind us with dinnertime cracks over the knuckles for insubordination that we had better clean up everything on our plates, and we'd sit there till we did, or have it for breakfast. Didn't we know that he and his family had lived on bread and dripping three times a day in the Depression when his dad was out of work for eighteen months and his mother, from a long line of laundresses, kept them from starving with her meagre income in the family trade? No, we did not – and the smell of the mushy Brussels sprouts still made me want to vomit, no matter how hard it had been for him as a child.

Weirdly, he still loved that bread and dripping treat, spreading the melted and congealed fat from Sunday's roast onto dry white bread, lashing it with salt and pepper. True, with the best dripping, it doesn't taste too bad; between the flour and the fat, and a bit of meat jelly – yes, I suppose you could survive on it. Survive they did, stunted by a poor diet, those pale little Shepherds Bush babies. West London was the manor into which he was born, just north of the Westway and Wormwood Scrubs Park; carried home as the firstborn of Florence Annie Sands and William George Holman of 81 Davisville Road W12 – my paternal grandparents. He would grow up around that area, roaming the streets between Uxbridge and Goldhawk Road, off to the football at his beloved Queens Park Rangers on Loftus Road. Sometimes he would cross London to the Borough, his father's old manor, to stay with his cousin Joe Line and family in Tabard Street SE1, close to the eponymous inn where Chaucer's pilgrims had once set off on their storied walk to Canterbury Cathedral in Kent.

Not that he was aware of the illustrious literary ground on which they played, near the site of the house in which they all crammed together like a nest of sparrows on his dad's old stamping ground. William George Holman was a Borough boy: he'd fought with the West Kent Buffs in the Great War, serving at Gallipoli, in Mesopotamia, India, and Iraq. After the war, he had moved across the town, somewhat akin to changing countries and religion; he'd fallen in love with our Nanny, Florence Sands, who wasn't about to leave

Heinkel He-III bomber, over Wapping and the Isle of Dogs, 6.48 p.m. on 7 September 1940, at the start of the Luftwaffe's evening raids. IMPERIAL WAR MUSEUM: C 5422.

her West London haunts for anybody. In view of the terrible pasting his part of London would take during the next war's Blitz, when the Luftwaffe sent waves of bombers over the central city night after night, it was in hindsight a very good move. There is a famous image of a Heinkel He-111 bomber over the Isle of Dogs in September 1940, unloading its deadly freight onto the working-class poor in their dingy rooms by the snaking Thames. A mere quarter of a mile to the west of the plane's port wingtip lies Tabard Street.

Nor would they escape in the West, not least in the last two years of the war when V-1 and later the V-2 terror weapons rained down on London and the Home Counties as Hitler threw his last destructive dice at England

and my father's family. In a war estimated to have cost upwards of 60 million lives – almost 400,000 of them United Kingdom service personnel, as well as 67,000 civilians – every one of my father's and my mother's immediate families came through with almost no visible scars. To a boy born in the early 1920s, before the stock markets fell in the Great Crash of 1929, this was all still very far away. The little I know of these growing years comes from his younger sister, my Auntie Pat: stories emerging long after his death, tales of an older brother much revered who had a reputation for standing up for the underdog against street bullies. Ten years older than her, he would vanish into the arms of the navy when she was seven or eight, reappearing infrequently on leave, before and during the war. Came the peace and in 1949 off he sailed to New Zealand – she would never see him again.

Pictures of his family left with my mother after Dad died show a robust and cheeky-looking boy, sitting on pebble beaches with his family on the annual excursions to the seaside; then one of him much later, captured in a family group by a street photographer. In most of these grainy snaps, he looks confident and extroverted: grasping handfuls of pebbles, climbing on harbourside frames, holding a spade to his cheek on the sands, his pale skin bared to an unfamiliar sunlight, the usual shock of spiky black hair hidden under a beret. In the family street portrait, he is almost as tall as his cloth-capped father (fag-on-lip, looking for all the world like Andy Capp save for his owlish spectacles). There they all are: Flo, mother-survivor with her tiny suitcase, Doreen the elder of his two sisters, a shy Pat, the next girl in line, and baby Geoff, a toddler in a pushchair that had seen better days. Geoffrey, born in 1932 and looking here about two or three, dates the picture at around 1934–35; little more than three years later, on 21 February 1938, Dad would enlist in the Royal Navy at the training establishment HMS *Ganges*, Shotley, Ipswich as Boy 2nd Class Holman.

From all accounts he was a clever kid at North Hammersmith School, above average; by the time secondary school was in prospect at the age of eleven, he had sat and gained his scholarship. He'd earned the right to enter the next level of education, but right there, my father's life took an all-too-common turn. He was now eligible to go to a grammar school, to place another foot on the ladder of education that might have helped him climb out of his origins into a different world. Like so many bright children of

The Holman clan, c. 1934–35; Dad is on the far right, rear.

his generation, it was not to be. He was the eldest child and marked down for work as soon as he could legally leave school. The family badly needed the money he could earn, so he stayed where he was until the leaving age of fourteen – then went to work for a bookie at the White City dog tracks. Class was against him as well as the times – but for England then, this was a given.

Entering White City must have been quite a thrill, euphoric even, as the great cloth-capped crowds gathered in the early 1930s to put their money on anorexic greyhounds flashing around the huge stadium's track. Built for the 1908 Olympic Games, the stadium was a vast field of dreams where urban hounds could chase an artificial hare. Roars of approval, hope and despair filled the atmosphere, swallowing up for a moment the drudgery and the frustrations of working-class London life. Perhaps it was here that seeds of my father's gambling addiction were sown; certainly his tendency to light-fingeredness soon manifested. He stole money from his employer, ending up in front of the local magistrate and facing borstal in a blatant example of 'theft as a servant'.

His good fortune was not to have been born a hundred years earlier, when transportation to the colonies would have been his reward. As it was, he would get to travel overseas, but at His Majesty's expense in the Senior Service. The magistrate gave his parents a choice: either send this boy to the navy, where good armed forces' discipline would straighten the bent vine – or he would be sentenced to a spell in a reformatory for wayward youth. 'The navy, sir,' said his mother, giving him cause for a deep resentment (so my own mother later told me). And so my father's long and successful naval career began – as it would end – in debt to the bookies.

It fascinates me how willing we are to spend bottomless sums of money locking people up – or, as in this case, sentencing them to no effective purpose – in order to cure something that is only now being recognised as the cause of so much social disorder and criminal behaviour. Gambling addiction changed his life, as it would later change mine and those of all the other members of his family. The Royal Navy – and the wars for which it prepared its men – continued to nurture in my father and countless others the adrenaline addictions that active service and years in harm's way would create for him and for the veterans of today. Post-Vietnam, the Gulf War and Desert Storm, Iraq and Afghanistan, men are living daily with the condition clinically recognised as post-traumatic stress disorder – shell shock as it was called after the Great War; then latterly, combat fatigue. Today, many working in the field, assisting all manner of chronic sufferers of such stresses, are dropping the medical appellation altogether, as it smacks of some incurable deficiency: thus 'PTS', not PTSD.

My theory goes like this: fill human beings up with daily doses of the fight-or-flight chemical that helps us avoid danger and eventually our systems, habituated to alertness and danger, will come to crave it. Until they crash. Once discharged from active service, such a person can never be the same again, in the sense of enjoying a normal civilian life. They are changed, chemically rearranged, and in many cases will have to find ways of obtaining and repeating that 'hit'. Gambling is one of them: not the winning, but the betting, the waiting, watching, praying, as the horse comes flying around the track, as the levels of excitement rise, and rise some more, as the beast flies at the line. Yes! No! It doesn't matter! Win or lose, what matters is the high – and then the low – that sends you back to the tote again, or the next glazed pull on the pokie's handle. The insanity of putting all you have on the line, win or lose – it's not about the money; it's all about the adrenaline, the things going on inside your poor demented bodily functions: glands, brain, heart, lungs, the whole damn shooting box. A sane-looking individual will risk their reputation on a throw of the dice, the body of a horse, the turn of a card. They don't need jail – they need help.

I look now at his picture, taken in 1944: the face of a man after five years on active service. He looks burned out, inwardly darkened by months on duty, years compounded, days when you never knew if you would live through the next watch, trained to suppress your reasonable fears. I once spoke to a former Royal New Zealand Navy seaman who as a mere boy of sixteen had managed to get on board the famous cruiser *Achilles* in 1945 and sailed to join Task Force 57 off those same islands where the attack on *Illustrious* took place. Pita Tauwhare was a seaman boy ammunition loader on an Oerlikon machine gun when the ship was attacked by kamikaze during the later attack on Truk. A skinny Māori kid strapped into an anti-aircraft gun, 'adrenaline pumping through my veins', he blazed away at the incoming plane with the spent shell cases rattling and bouncing all around his feet. It was over in seconds – an instant it seemed to him – and once the attack had ended, his 'stomach was going one to the dozen. After the adrenaline had left me, I felt as weak as a kitten.' It is this same concentrated after-effect I can read in my father's eyes – the inner war of fight against flight.

All this was still to come, when in February 1938, as a raw Boy 2nd Class, also a mere sixteen, he was marched through the gate of HMS *Ganges* for a year's training, to ready him for his first ship. He would be posted to the venerable and veteran fleet carrier, the converted Great War cruiser HMS

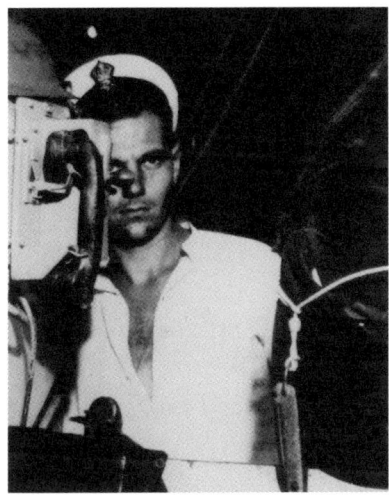

On duty, British Pacific Fleet, 1944–45.

*Furious* (lucky man: had he been assigned to its sister ship, the *Glorious*, he would have been among the 1207 men who died – or possibly, the forty-three who survived – when she was sunk by the German battleships *Scharnhorst* and *Gneisenau* on 8 June 1940, returning home to Britain after leaving Norway). A stroke of a pen could decide your fate: my father's postings would show a magnanimity working for him that was not granted to others who passed through the gates that day from the streets of Shotley, Ipswich. Shotley had been opened to train boys for naval service in 1905, and was renowned for its harsh treatment of raw recruits.

There were reasons for this harsh introduction to naval life: the instructors were usually veterans, counting among their ranks survivors of British naval engagements in the Great War – Jutland and Gallipoli men. Within twelve months, these boys would be turned from skinny pale city kids into fighting men who could perform their duties under fire. At Shotley, on *Ganges*, you learned to shinny up the 143-foot rigged mast, especially for the mast-manning ceremonies when a brass hat came to visit and inspect you. Uniforms, making beds, mopping up, marching, rifle drills, sport – football, rowing, swimming, and water polo, at which my father did well – all designed to make the recruit part of a team, a sailing machine that would obey orders instinctively. As the basic drills and patterns were laid, it was back to school to learn the myriad trades and professions a fighting navy required – in Dad's case, the vital art of the signalman.

A month before his first posting to the *Furious*, he has risen from Boy 2nd and Boy 1st class to Signal Boy, and in a matter of weeks, he will be on the signal deck of a huge carrier, sending and receiving the messages that were often a matter of life and death. I once saw his HMS *Ganges* magazines with photos of life in training and crudely drawn cartoons, along with jokes about navy provisions: 'Charlies', aka 'fly cemeteries', or raisin slices, were very popular targets. At the same time – during our rapprochement in 1963 – he showed me his exam papers from the final tests he sat, to become that graduate signal boy. I can still recall being amazed – as a schoolboy myself, in the fifth form at the time – at his pass marks. The lowest was 98 per cent, the next highest 99 per cent, and others were the full one hundred. 'Dad,' I wanted to know, 'how did you get such high marks? You must have been really smart!'

He laughed at my naivety: 'Any less and they failed you. They only allowed you two mistakes.' I was incredulous: it seemed so unfair, and I said so. 'Nothing to do with being fair,' he corrected. 'If the Officer Commanding sends you an order from the bridge, "Signal Fleet prepare to alter course 25 degrees to starboard", and you send the message 25 degrees to port, and they obey that message, you'll collide.' It had to be exact: there was no margin for error. Even then, he could still read Morse code; called in to teach the Blackball Scout troop, he could still instruct in semaphore with flags. Lost arts today, but in 1939 with war looming, expert communications were vital. His role as a cog in the great Royal Navy wheel was just as important as the man in command of the fleet who made the decisions and gave the orders. The navy is an image of the greater human organism: flotillas on the waters, arraigned in this case to defend – and attack. There was no room for compromise and none for error on the signal deck.

New recruits were knocked into shape with practised ease by the petty officers who roared them up with their 'Wakey, wakey!' in the early dawn: marched them, inspected them, divided them into their roles as seamen, signalmen, cooks and stokers, kitted them up with kit bag and uniform and ordered the dispatch of civilian clothes home. No reminders of the boy that was: from now on you were to be 'proper pusser' (turned out always in a service-like manner), bell-bottomed trousers and suits of navy blue. They marched and drilled, learned how to salute, and how to turn the world into a ship with a new vocabulary: floors were decks (and swabbed!), walls were bulkheads, the Main Gate was the gangway, and the humble toilet the heads. Weeks of intensive training left them fitter than ever, and the relentless discipline and lack of privacy instilled an ability to live between decks under wartime conditions, in the Arctic and the tropics, freezing and overcrowded, or suffocating in unbearable heat with metal scorching to the touch.

Graduating from this induction on 12 April 1939, my father joined the shore establishment HMS *Drake* at Devonport the following day, and from there, a month later, complete with his official service number JX157199, joined HMS *Furious* on 16 May as a signal boy. By 15 August, just weeks away from war, he was promoted to Ordinary Signalman aboard the world's first aircraft carrier. *Furious* was a very odd-looking warship, betraying her origins as a modified *Courageous*-class cruiser, converted to operate Sopwith Camels in 1918. Among the battle honours in her long career was the first successful naval air raid in July of that year when her planes attacked the Zeppelin sheds at the German naval base in Tondern, destroying two of the

HMS Furious, 1939: 'The eyes and ears of the fleet' – Dad, far right.

airships that were bombing British towns and cities. With my father aboard, she would serve in the abortive Norwegian campaign and later, ferrying planes to the beleaguered Mediterranean island of Malta in 1941. Included in the more unusual feats of her career was the shipping of £18,000,000 sterling value in gold bullion to Halifax, Canada, returning with more aircraft for Britain and all her available spaces crammed with sugar for a Britain on rations.

She was sent back to the US in September 1941 for an extensive refit after two busy years of constant movement and combat, in which time my father had been blooded as a naval signalman and promoted twice, up to the role of Acting Leading Signalman. It was here in America that he changed ships, joining the heavily damaged carrier HMS *Illustrious* on 19 October of that year. From the oldest carrier in the fleet, he was moving to one of the most modern: *Illustrious*, launched in April 1939, was the first of a new class of fleet carriers, noted for their speed and highly effective armoured flight decks. In her case, this aspect of her makeup had been tested almost to the point of destruction when the ship had been mortally wounded and nearly sunk by German dive-bombers in the Mediterranean, early in 1941. Stung by the carrier's successful strike against the Italian fleet in Taranto in November of 1940, the Germans had stationed expert Stuka dive-bomber pilots of Fliegerkorps X in Sicily. On 6 January, the Ju-87s attacked, behind a diversion by Italian bombers that had drawn off the carrier's fighters; with her 6500-square-metre deck, she presented an unmissable target to hardened Luftwaffe veterans.

From the resulting seven direct hits and five near-misses, the ship sustained 217 casualties and was crippled, limping into Valetta Harbour at Malta where the Germans launched further attacks to finish her off – and failed. Herculean efforts by British and Maltese engineers and dock workers culminated in the miraculous escape of the battered ship to Alexandria, where she remained under repair until March, slipping through the Suez Canal to Durban for more repairs and assessment before crossing the Atlantic in early May for the massive refit she would undergo in the US Navy yards at Norfolk, Virginia – where my father joined her. She would remain there until 28 November before leaving – virtually rebuilt, with a longer landing area, a more effective catapult for launching aircraft, updated radar and armament – on 12 December, five days after Pearl Harbor. This event changed everything for the ship's prospects and for Britain's. America was now in the war: Germany's fate – and eventually, too, Japan's – had been sealed.

From this point onwards – his joining the new ship, and the attack of the kamikaze aircraft in 1945 – there are few personal details, except for a shadowy relationship in America and his marriage to my mother in 1943. There is an abundance of information about the carrier's movements and the theatres in which she served which does need mention, but in the tradition of the silent generation post-war, almost nothing of his life aboard ship. Nothing of his messmates, the places they visited and went ashore (Durban, Mozambique, Trincomalee, Sydney) – nothing. Nothing except the handful of photographs that show he was there. There is a telegram to my mother, to mention later; but just as his wartime family (and later, his new wife) heard almost nothing from him, he would become a blank-page war veteran to his children. He did, however, let slip to me one personal item.

This came during that visit to my Christchurch flat in 1972: a brief wartime assignation he spoke of, while on shore leave after joining the ship in the States. Memory is tricky. I think I asked him if he'd had any other relationships before he met my mother, and he spoke of a girl he met in America – that they went out somewhere during the day. Coney Island? Who knows now. There are two things about that conversation that I won't swear to, but I can't get out of my mind either. One: that she had dark hair; and two: that she was Jewish. There's a sneaking suspicion that something happened between them, that he saw her more than once, that they might have had sex – but that too is vague; that is the shadow. There was a girl, he told me that much. Who, how, when, where and what, that's all gone now.

There was certainly a collision at sea: *Illustrious* and her sister carrier HMS *Formidable* collided in heavy seas on the way back to England. But by March 1942 his ship was working up for her new life and on her way to Madagascar to attack the Vichy French warships in Diego Suarez, docking at the main Eastern Fleet base at Mombasa in May. Here my father appears in photographs for the first time in his tropical whites, cockily sporting a pith helmet in one and posing in another with a telescope. He's human again: joking, ironic, far more angular and gaunt in his aspect than the chubby-faced teenager seen in the early shots on the deck of the *Furious* in 1939, with his signal-boy mates. He's been at sea now for three years, two and a half of those on active service: by June he'll be a Leading Signalman and six months later, in January 1943, he's Acting Yeoman of Signals. They didn't give these promotions out for long service: you had to be good to get them, and I believe he was (in the Royal New Zealand Navy post-war, he was encouraged to take officer training, but resisted, not wanting to leave his petty officers' mess: class again).

The ship operated in the Indian Ocean in the latter half of 1942, but the British fleet there was considered too weak to risk a head-on encounter with a Japanese carrier force, and she was withdrawn, to return with the beefed-up British Pacific Fleet in 1944. After a refit in Durban and a return

Dad: 'Mombasa July '42' in my mother's hand.

to action off Mombasa, she left for Birkenhead on 13 January 1943 – for another major refit; and for my father, a crucial meeting. She remained there under refit until 7 June – by which time my father had blind-dated, courted and married my mother. As the great carrier sailed up the Mersey on 23 February, he was on watch on the signal deck on the bridge, and in telephone contact with the Women's Royal Naval Service operators onshore at Western Approaches HQ in Liverpool's Liver Building. The woman on the other end of the line – whom he promptly chatted up once the official exchanges were completed – was Mary Elisabeth Woollam, WRNS Writer, my future mother.

I wish I could say that romance was in the air – or the Mersey fog – but the blind date Dad proposed to my mother was both pragmatic and a bit

Diary page: from my mother to my father, 1943, after their marriage.

sly. Would she meet him and his mate for a drink? Maybe. Did she have a friend? Perhaps. Well, then, why not: under the clock at Lime Street Station? She'd see what she could do. What the hell, it was war – why not? They agreed a time, and she went off air and found a friend to come along: what a lark. Cheeky thing: but at twenty-one and in love with dancing, she was game. Now the story does get interesting, and not only because the great clock high on the wall of Lime Street Station was a famous assignation spot where prostitutes met their clients (I have no idea which of them suggested this venue). The fallback position of my father and his mate was later revealed to her; the boys would sneak up on the waiting girls and spy them out from cover. If they were tasty, well and good, full speed ahead; but if not, then a hasty retreat to a nearby pub and who knows – fairer prey?

Happily for the waiting princesses, the navy frogmen did like the look of my mother and her friend, enough to kiss them – more if more was forthcoming – and to head for that nearby pub. A whirlwind and familiar wartime courtship ensued: Dad, who could be very charming and was something of a wit, proposed to her soon after on the top deck of a Liverpool bus. My mother had been waiting for Fred Street, a much more level-headed and suitable suitor, to get his act together. Fred was too slow and in the heat of battle my father prevailed. She accepted and the die of my life was cast: once they were engaged (what did my Nanny think of this London sailor boy?), the next move was geographical. Mum was to live in London, near his extended family in the streets of the West. On 25 March 1943 – just over a month since they'd met – my parents were married in St Luke's Parish Church, Hammersmith, witnessed amongst members of the extensive Holman clan by my great-uncle Ulysses J. Bywater and his sister, my bewildered grandmother, Eunice.

I have known for some time that the courtship was brief – looking at these times and places afresh is a reminder of that pressure to live in the moment the war had produced in people's lives. To meet and marry so quickly, to move hearth and familiar home, well aware that soon after they had married, my father would be called back to sea and she would be alone with virtual strangers – what does this say about the forces of social change unleashed by such a global conflict? Not just the front lines, the daily deaths and the wounding, but the manner – and speed – in which local mores and wider ways of life were overturned and in many cases vanished. They went for their honeymoon in Great Missenden, Bucks, on a series of country rambles my mother would later describe as 'a pub crawl'. They would rise in the morning and after a leisurely breakfast at the country hotel, my father would suggest a walk: 'There always seemed to be a pub along the way, about lunchtime,' she recalled, where Dad would happily smoke and down country pints.

Alcohol and abandonment were lurking from the beginning; by 26 July, he was back at sea off Norway, as the ship worked up on her third commission before she left for the Mediterranean to join Force 'H', reinforcing Malta's aircraft fleet and supporting the Salerno invasion in early September. At home, his new bride waited for the letter that never came. As the weeks became months and she fretted, it is interesting to speculate just what her mother was saying to her about the missing husband. By this time, Nanny had also relocated from her familiar Liverpool and was living in London with my mother. Mum became so distressed after weeks of no news (presumably, his parents around the corner at The Curve had no contact either) that she went to someone in Queen Anne's Mansions near the Admiralty where she

Semaphore signal for the letter 'J', given to me by Derek Taylor, an old *Illustrian* and shipmate of Dad's, in memory of my father, 1993.

was now based, and reported her concern for him. Was he dead? Missing? Had something happened to the ship? Why hadn't she heard?

The wheels began to turn: this was not acceptable behaviour. The navy contacted the ship's captain, who on hauling my father in, asked why he had not been in touch with his new wife these months past? Finding there was no good reason, he ordered my father to do something about it. I can feel his rage: he never really forgave her for showing him up like that, no matter how well deserved it was. It wasn't the first time he'd gone AWOL emotionally, and it wouldn't be the last; who was he, really, and who was my mother, to choose such a risky prospect? Dad was good-looking, and charming; yes, she had fallen in love and under his spell. True, there was that spirit of *carpe diem* abroad, but none of this explains why she was such an easy target for his charms and why – once those early flushes of infatuation and headiness had worn off – she stayed so long and put up with so much from someone who had not the slightest desire to change.

The woman my father met and fell for under the Lime Street Station clock was a five-foot two-inch beauty with Greta Garbo hair and sad eyes: Mary Elisabeth Woollam, Wren Writer 15416. She had joined the WRNS on 29 April 1941 and was appointed for training and service to the shore-based sloop HMS *Eaglet*, the flagship of the Commander-in-Chief of the Western Approaches Command at Liverpool. She had been a kennel maid at the outbreak of war; she and a friend had opened their own business, Abbey Kennels of 17 Hunters Lane: 'All pets boarded. Good exercising.' The war killed that off: pets, especially dogs, fretted under the stress of blackouts, sirens and the terror of the air raids. Pets were sometimes put down, sent to the country, or even abandoned; the business folded. Their own terrier worked out his angst as the sirens howled by chewing a block of wood under the table.

Without an income, she was manpowered into the local tax office, and from there, bored after a time, she joined the navy. From August 1940 to January 1942, the Luftwaffe bombed the city in a series of assaults, which would cost over 4000 civilian lives, second only to London in bombing casualties (30,000 there by the war's end). At the time she joined up, the city was experiencing a prolonged seven-night aerial assault from 1 to 7 May: the so-called 'May blitz', when over 600 German bombers pounded the city

Nanny Airey and Mum with dogs, Liverpool, 1941.

and the docks with bombs, mines and incendiaries that caused almost 3000 casualties and rendered large parts of Liverpool uninhabitable. My mother and my grandmother were still telling me hair-raising stories of survival over twenty years later: not that long, in a human life, to recover from nights of terror. Parachute mines landing in the garden next door; high-explosive bomb blasts blowing down the nearby church's doors, scattering pews, ricocheting off the back wall, and flipping the pews back the other way as the blast bounced back into the streets. Incendiaries would smash through the roof and damp nights were spent in Anderson shelters dug into the back garden; the searchlights probing, the sirens, the ack-ack fire – and then in the cold daylight, dust, death and tumbled ruins.

Nanny was an Air Raid Warden, prowling the streets to check on the blackout curtains; everything was rationed except the death waiting at your elbow. 'Civilian casualties' was an antiseptic way of avoiding the literal truth: 'headless corpses, scattered body parts'. In this new form of total war, the front line was not some faraway designation in a newspaper headline, but your own address. What my mother, her mother and the entire Liverpool community went through was a trial by fire every bit as deadly as that faced by my father and his shipmates at sea. It would be returned – with savage interest – on German civilians; for now, she had become part of the war machine that would introduce her to Acting Yeoman of Signals William Thomas Holman, two years on.

New Zealand's wartime Prime Minister, Peter Fraser, meets Mum and other Kiwi sailors rounded up to greet him, Liverpool, 1941.

Shortly after she joined up, Peter Fraser, the New Zealand Prime Minister, came to Liverpool while on a visit to England and five New Zealanders serving in the Royal Navy were rounded up to meet him, including my mother – who happened to have been born in Wanganui to English immigrant parents in 1921. In a photograph she has left behind, it's 1941: there she is, just twenty years old, beaming past Fraser who stands beside her, looking towards the grinning matelots. She could barely remember the land of her birth: there had been so many changes since then, and many losses. Her mother was a widow who in 1910 had married a second time; with her new husband, my maternal grandfather, Samuel Thomas Woollam, a dairy farmer and milkman from Cheltenham, they left for New Zealand after the end of the Great War with her daughter Lillian Mitchell, the child of her first marriage.

She was an aunt I was never to meet: born around 1906 to 1907, a book of poetry she owned is inscribed 'Invercargill Girls' High School 1919', while she was in the third form. She was thirteen at that time; fifteen when my mother was born. Grandad Woollam has proved a shadowy figure to pin down: cherished in my mother's memories as the funny Papa, the 'great rhinoceros' to her 'hippopotamus' at bedtime. Certainly he cuts a beatific, cuddly figure in the surviving photograph of him leaning on the posts of a tennis court net somewhere in New Zealand, a twinkling smile, watch chain swinging over the paunch swelling his waistcoat. He was born in 1878 at Caergwle near Wrexham, North Wales, the son we are told of the local squire's dalliance on the wrong side of the sheets with a serving girl, my great-grandmother. She would later move to Leicester and marry a Mr Woollam, leaving little trace of her son's paternal line.

Grandad was a Salvationist who had marched with Bramwell Booth; he never forgave the Army, so it was said, for deposing the great general. At some point during his earlier time in the colony with his first wife, he had farmed at Parewanui near Bulls. When my mother was born, they were living at Castlecliff in Wanganui, with his occupation given as a 'toymaker'. The chronology is a little garbled now: there was a store in Winton, which burned down uninsured; he had heart troubles, and they moved to Christchurch, where my grandmother ran a boarding house for single men in the grounds of the former St Margaret's College. It seems he was not fit enough to work, but by dint of her hard labour, Nanny created a sound business, later sold as a going concern to pay the family's passage back to Liverpool. They were part of that boomerang pattern of immigration: he had lived before in New Zealand, returning to England with his ailing wife who later died. When my mother was six, he sailed home again with his second family, in a world about to slide from Great War into Great Depression.

Nanny was certainly tough: they set up shop in Birkenhead, and started again. Her own father, the redoubtable Welsh adventurer P. D. Bywater who rode with Buffalo Bill Cody on the Pony Express, died in 1930, followed closely by my mother's father. Grandad Woollam had persistent heart trouble after his return to England; he lay down one day for his afternoon nap while my grandmother closed the shop to get more supplies, telling my mother to stay and play, and look after her father. Her nine-year-old memories were clear enough years later: Daddy was breathing heavily, asleep upstairs, when the noisy breathing stopped. When my grandmother returned, she told her, 'Mummy, Daddy must be better now, he's gone to sleep!' The old man had suffered a massive stroke: at sixty, he was dead, a great rhinoceros gone to the Lord. This, as they say in the novels, was when my mother's trials began.

Losing her beloved Papa was one thing; next, it was her mother and sister. My Nanny found herself running a shop and trying to care for a grieving child. When my mother came home from school and my grandmother was out buying supplies, little Mary began to roam the streets – so goes the received version. No doubt there were some issues of care and control, but the solution Nanny came up with seems extreme by today's standards: my mother was sent to the Bluecoat School in Wavertree, an orphanage and boarding establishment founded in 1708. In retelling the story of her banishment from the family hearth, my mother was always quick to explain that her wandering ways, unsupervised, had left her mother with little choice – but she was not so reasonable at the time. She cried virtually non-stop for a week, quite inconsolable; and on the seventh day – she rested.

Bad move: later it was revealed that Matron, in despair and frustration, had told her staff, 'If that girl cries for one more day, I am sending her back to her mother!' Poor mother: 'If only I'd known,' she told me, 'I'd have cried for another week.' Those familiar with the research done by Professor John Bowlby in the 1950s on maternal deprivation and later, attachment theory, will have some idea of what my mother was going through: losing two caregivers in a short period of time and left with affectionless strangers, she was bellowing her protests until finally – when no help came – subsiding into the blank resignation of deep grief. She once confessed to me that her responsibility in the marital difficulties that later ensued was down to one simple fact: 'I was too selfish to let anyone get close to me again.' In the

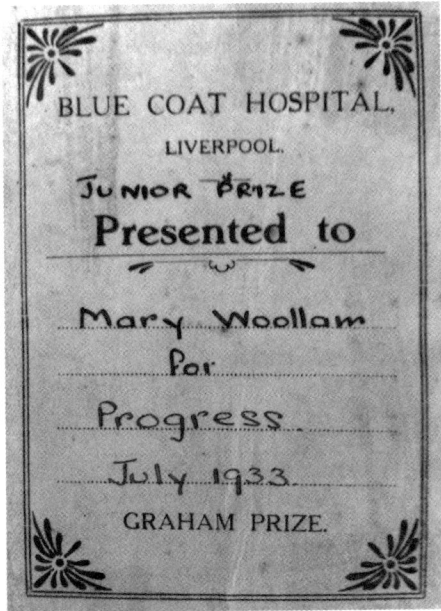

'For Progress': *The Poetical Works of Wordsworth*.

light of her cruel introduction to the Bluecoat experience – and the next six years she spent incarcerated there – that sounds like a sensible precaution against any future rejection that might bring with it wounding and pain on the scale of that already endured.

Hearing these stories, I always imagined the school was far away. But it was literally around the corner from 17 Hunters Lane, Wavertree where my grandmother set up house – a ten-minute walk. Parents of boarders were allowed to visit at Easter and Christmas, but would sit in the school hall while their children filed past and took their seats: you could look at each other, but not touch. Food was adequate, with no frills; material care ensured you were clothed and kept clean – but it was a loveless childhood and adolescence. One day someone will do an in-depth analysis of how boarding schools fucked up the English – instructed by my mother's heartbreaking anecdotes, I'll support their findings in advance. If they went home for Christmas at all, I have no idea – but even if they did, in her case the damage was done.

She did, however, get to go home at least once that I am aware of: in 1934, her older sister Lillian died of Hodgkin's lymphoma – a cancer originating in the white blood cells. Considered now to be one of the more curable forms of lymph tissue cancer, in those early days of radiation and chemotherapy treatment it was a virtual death sentence – renowned for striking most often in young adulthood (Lillian was around 28 years old). My grandmother was stricken with grief: little Polly (as she called my mother) was allowed home from school, but prevented from going to her sister's funeral. She was packed off to Uncle Phil's in Leicester while the adults mourned and then sent straight back to the Bluecoats.

Mary Elisabeth Woollam, thirteen years old, on her way back to the Bluecoat School after her sister Lillian's funeral in 1934.

## Dad's Story

A picture of her as a thirteen-year-old near this time – in buckled tweed coat and matching cloche hat, shiny buttoned shoes and white socks, gloves and a purse – gives nothing away, save for a wariness I think I can detect through my knowledge of what she was passing through. By now, she had survived five years of abandonment, and absorbed some very hard lessons: life was unpredictable, sometimes it left you to your own devices and those you loved were always taken away. She still had some more time to serve at the Bluecoats; eventually, she would escape the institution and stand on the threshold of the adult world – a world where Adolf Hitler in her cousin Pip's Germany was exhorting his bitter and resentful people to awake from the torpor of the Great Depression, throw out the wreck of the Weimar Republic experiment, rearm and prepare to avenge the betrayals of 1918. Before 1934 was out, however, her mother had been courted and wed by the interesting Mr Airey, a man whose name Nanny would carry to the grave.

If my mother was to prove vulnerable to a man in her need, her mother at this time was showing the way. Fred Airey began making moves shortly after Lillian had died, and over the next few months, sensing his opportunity, made her an offer. Nanny – still grieving the loss of her daughter, and the death of her mother Mary shortly after – wrote in the diary Lillian had left behind: 'Mr Airey asked me to marry him.' She soon agreed, but it was not a union fated to endure. Fred is another shadowy figure in the family story, something of a bit-part player with nobody much to take his side. His role, sadly, is that of the philanderer: travelling home on a bus not too many years into the marriage, Nanny witnessed the disturbing sight of her husband leaving a lady friend's house before crossing the road to board the same vehicle. Lying low until their mutual stop, she disembarked behind the unsuspecting love rat, took him by the collar and guided him home: 'Mr Airey, you can pack your bags!'

At this point he disappears: by all accounts, he raised little protest. Nanny, in order to supplement her meagre income, began again to take in boarders – and at sixteen, my mother fled the Bluecoat School forever and returned home. Her mother's capacity for assessing the character of men was still suspect; she had allowed under her roof a predator – anonymous now – who groomed my mother and sexually abused her. His threat, of course, was the same reptilian machination employed by all such inadequates: 'If you tell your mother, she won't believe you.' Young Mary Woollam was to carry another private hell of abandonment into the coming storm and her whirlwind marriage to my father. My heart aches for these two women: one long gone, the other a more recent loss; and yet, in my experience of them raising me to manhood, there remains a memory that is deeper and more pervasive than the wounds and disappointments in their lives and loves that would come to entangle me. It is indefinable: mana, integrity, a dignity conferred through survival that taught me it was possible to endure the worst, to face down bullies and tyrants, to keep living life to the full.

In October and November of 1943, *Illustrious* was back in the UK; there would have been leave available and, no doubt, conversations between my parents about Mum calling the captain in to tear a strip off my father. She was working in London and based at Queen Anne's Mansions; on Sunday 18 June she was not on duty when her fellow Wrens narrowly missed being killed. A V-1 flying bomb crashed into the nearby Guards' Chapel; it caused

London WRNS larks. Caption in my mother's hand: '24.6.43. All my love darling, Paddy', written just after their marriage.

only light damage and minor casualties where the women were working, but others were not so fortunate. The massive explosion of this direct hit on the adjacent church killed 121 worshippers and injured 141 others – it took two days to dig all the dead and injured out from the collapsed roof rubble. These attacks were part of Londoners' daily lives for nearly a year, until the Allies overran the launch sites in Holland and Germany. 'Like motorbikes in the sky, they sounded,' my Nanny later told me.

My father meanwhile has sailed away once more, leaving the civilians in his family to face this wave of Hitler's revenge weapons – and the terrifying V-2 missile, which nothing could stop – to confront the Japanese in the Pacific. In January 1944 the carrier was at Trincomalee naval base in Ceylon, working up to a March meeting with the American carrier the USS *Saratoga* for combined operations against Japanese-held oil refineries in Indonesia, the former Dutch East Indies. Denying the Japanese fuel oil was part of the grand Allied strategy to run her war machine dry and starve the population as well, by sinking huge amounts of merchant shipping carrying food supplies just as Doenitz's U-boat fleets had attempted to strangle Britain in the Battle of the Atlantic. While some of the American commanders – notably the Anglophobe Admiral Ernest J. King – had no wish to see the British join forces with their own battle fleets and be in at the kill, the American sailors were pleased to see them, in spite of the fruity jibes that were signalled between the ships when they met: 'Hey, Limeys, what took you so long?' Some equally tart responses were shot right back: 'We blew a trumpet in 1939 – it took you bastards till 1942 to hear it!'

That story my father did tell me; he never mentioned that in order to work with the Americans, ships of the British Pacific Fleet had to learn the US Navy signal system from the deck up – something that would have required a major and rapid re-education on his part, and those under him. A Yeoman of Signals by now, it was down to him – again, men could die if you made a mistake. In April, *Illustrious* returned to Trincomalee and exchanged the underpowered and poorly performing Fairey Barracudas for two squadrons of the latest American carrier-based bombers, the rugged and dependable Grumman TBM Avengers. Despite the Barracuda's battle honours in the north, the British warhorses had not functioned well in the Pacific heat: their poor high-altitude performance and speed-sapping

Dad with the Signals' Mess: Ceylon, 1944, British Pacific Fleet.

external bomb load meant they were unsuitable for the attacks on the oil refineries.

The heat made it tough on the crew, too: that picture of my father on watch on the bridge in 1944 (see dedication page) shows him with white shirt half open down his chest, and a shine of sweat on his features. Everything on deck was too hot to touch, and below decks, in the engine rooms, in the hangars and in the hammocks at night, conditions in the tropics were close to unbearable. Despite all this, they had to function – and fight. Pilots strapped into their machines on deck, engines powered up and ready to go, experienced energy-sapping sauna baths on a daily basis. Battle fatigue was a real enough problem in any event, but these conditions only multiplied the stresses of front-line service at sea. This, however, was what these men were trained for. In the company of the Royal Navy's most modern carriers – *Indomitable* and *Victorious* – the crew of *Illustrious* began to form what would prove, in terms of sheer firepower, to be the 'strongest strike force the Royal Navy had assembled up to that time', Task Force 57. It was certainly the largest and the most powerful squadron of British and Commonwealth warships to operate as a single unit in the war. They were about to show their teeth on Sumatra.

Before she could join this fleet, *Illustrious* was dispatched in September to Simons Town naval dockyard in South Africa for a final refit prior to the long campaign ahead. From a two-week shore leave in Durban dates the one surviving wartime communication from my father to my mother – a telegram. Sent from Twines Hotel in the city, it's no billet-doux, but rather a brief request for money: 'Cable L15 c/o Mrs Rudolph Twines Hotel Durban – Bill Holman.' A translation, based on earlier – and later – form might read: 'Paddy – in Durban and have run out of money. Please cable fifteen quid – Bill.' Imagination must fill in the blanks: did he lose on a game of Crown and Anchor, or on the horses? What did she think when this arrived on 11 September at 71 Talgarth Road, West Kensington? That was quite a decent sum of money, and her income would not have been great. One month later, on 30 October 1944, Wrens Writer Woollam 15416 was discharged to shore on compassionate grounds, and her naval career was over – why is unknown, the record does not say. She may have been finished with the navy – but the navy was not finished with her.

On 20 December 1944, *Illustrious* was part of a strike force which attacked the Japanese-held oil refinery at Pangkalan Brandan on Sumatra, but bad weather frustrated the Avengers' bombing mission. Joined now by HMS *Indefatigable*, on 24 January 1945, all four fleet carriers took part in successful raids on the Pladjoe oil refineries at Palembang (Operation Meridian), losing seven aircraft, and shooting down fourteen Japanese planes with sixty more damaged or destroyed on the ground. The Pacific

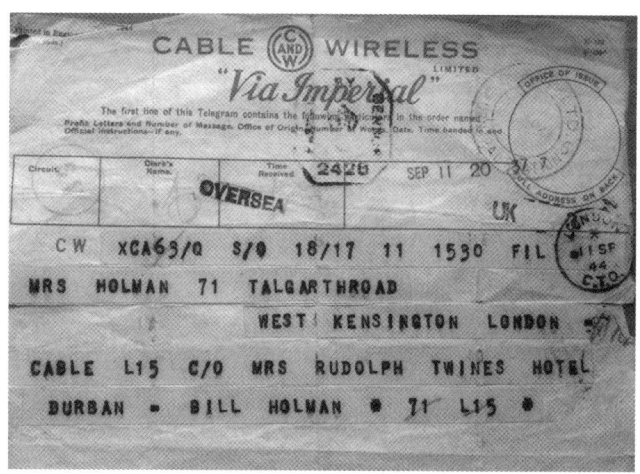

'Cable L15': the 'billet-doux' from Durban.

# The Lost Pilot

Dad (far right) on the deck of HMS *Illustrious* in Sydney, 1945, listening to Earl Mountbatten exhort the crew. STILL FROM PATHÉ PICTURES NEWSREEL, OCTOBER 1945. USED WITH PERMISSION: 45-74.

was hotting up now for the British, as well as the New Zealanders of Task Force 57 – by this time, at least ten per cent of Kiwi volunteers for aircrew had been diverted to the Fleet Air Arm. New Zealand pilots were amongst the action and the casualties – two of the airmen lost on this strike were Kiwis: Sub-Lieutenant Haberfield of HMS *Indomitable* and Sub-Lieutenant Baxter of HMS *Illustrious*. Captured, they later died in a notorious war crime at Singapore's Changi Prison in July 1945, where they were executed with seven other Fleet Air Arm officers.

The second strike on 29 January against the Soengai Gerong refinery across the river was also successful, helping to cripple Japanese oil supplies; a strategy which would eventually starve the kamikaze squadrons of high-quality aviation fuel. A reprisal attack by Japanese planes on the carriers was seen off with no damage, but 'friendly fire' from other ships damaged the *Illustrious*'s island (command centre), causing thirty-three casualties. It was now time to retreat to the fleet's Pacific base at Sydney, prior to joining the American fleet for the assault on Okinawa. *Illustrious* in particular was in need of attention in dry dock, with defects in her centre propeller shaft damaged

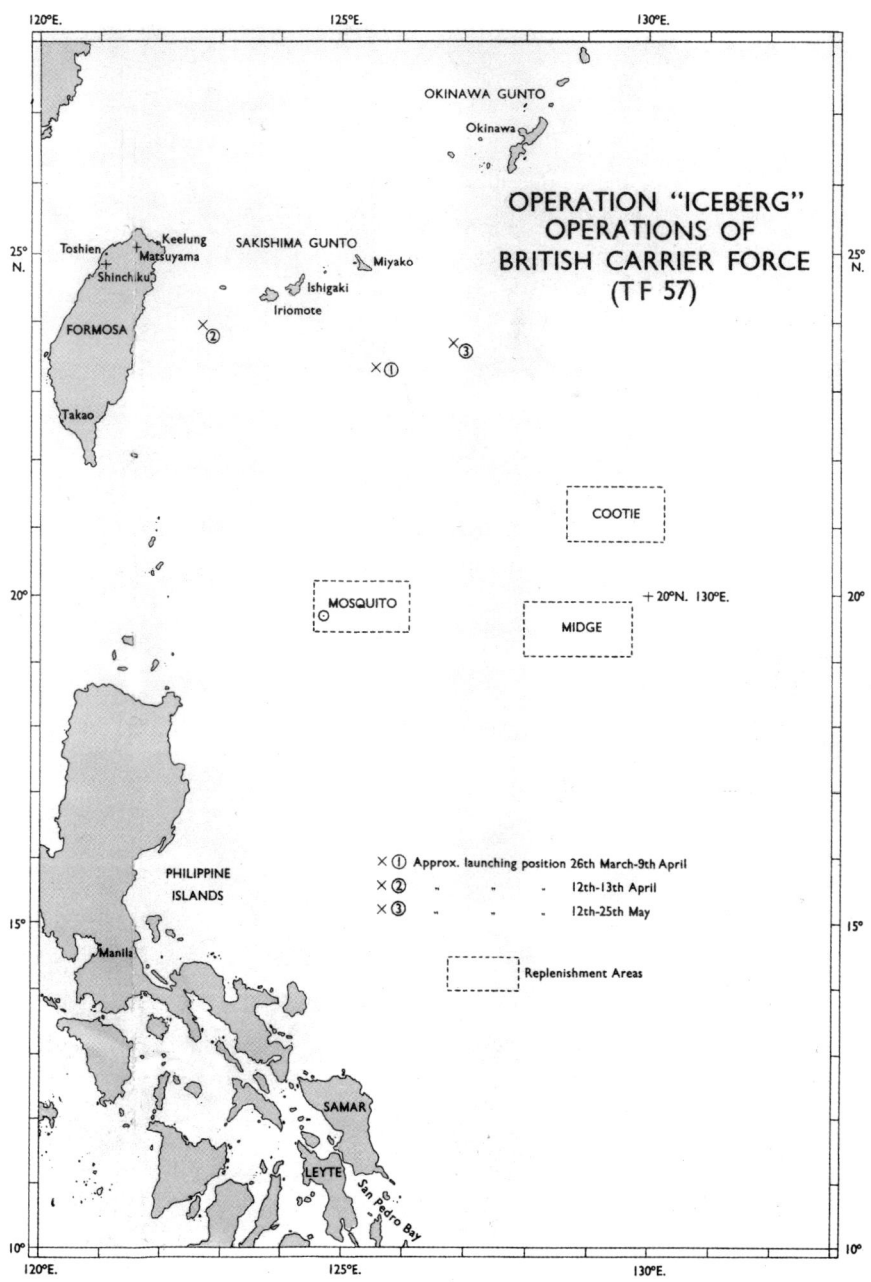

Map showing the area of operations of Task Force 57 in early 1945. The 6 April strike on HMS *Illustrious* took place at the site marked 'I'. NATIONAL ARCHIVES UK.

in the Palembang attacks; she was still carrying frame damage from the 1941 dive-bombing by Stukas in the Mediterranean. The carrier was starting to show serious wear and tear from her battle scars – and there was more to come. Over the course of the next month – my father and his messmates had plenty of shore leave in which to create mayhem – the centre propeller was removed, reducing the ship's speed from thirty to twenty-four knots.

On 7 March, the veteran carrier sailed north to its forward base at Manus in the Admiralty Islands north of New Guinea to prepare for the start of Operation Iceberg – and my father's close encounter with the men of Niitaka Squadron, kamikaze pilots based at Tainan on the island of Formosa (today's Taiwan). In late March, a photograph was taken of members of this unit of the Imperial Japanese Navy – the 102nd Special Attack Group of the 701st Air Corps – immediately after their naming ceremony. With their fast and deadly Yokosuka Suisei dive-bombers, ten of them would go on to form the Chusei Tokkōtai based at Hinschu, ready to meet the oncoming Allied naval forces with Japan's final weapon: a generation self-destructing. Four short weeks later, they would all be dead – six of them on the fatal day in April when they came within inches of killing my father and many of his shipmates, and sinking the old warhorse that had miraculously survived against remarkable odds. Who were these men – the kamikaze – and how did they arrive at such a fate?

# 3

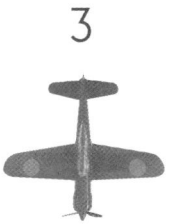

# Kokutai no Hongi: Japan as the Emperor's Body

*... the harmonious unity of the ruler and the people, the whole nation as one family under the rule of the emperor, his line unbroken for ages eternal.*

Itō Tasaburō, *Kokutai kannen no shiteki kenkyū*

Approaching 1500 hrs on 6 April 1945, three of the remaining five Suisei dive-bombers were warming up at Hinschu base as their crews received the orders to attack and drank their final cups of sake, exchanging them with each other. Ranging in age from nineteen to twenty-five, three pilots and three navigator/gunners prepared to die – along with hundreds of other young Japanese men who at that very moment were hurling themselves onto the decks of American ships and into the sea off Okinawa. These six had a different target: the carriers of the British Pacific Fleet, strafing and bombing Japanese airfields on islands of the Sakishima Gunto south of the main invasion. The Royal Navy's mission was to support the US landings by preventing Japanese aerial reinforcements from flying north. Jaguchi Maasaki (pilot) and Kiyoshi Iida (navigator) were one crew; Yoshio Minami (pilot) and Chiharu Nagata (navigator) another; Hajime Kitagara (pilot) and Hisashi Nishida (navigator) were the last. Clambering into their Suisei dive-bombers and strapping themselves in, they had just over 120 minutes to live.

HMS *Illustrious*, February 1945: what the kamikaze pilot would have seen as he began his seven-second final dive. The carrier was swerving violently and pouring anti-aircraft fire up at him. IMPERIAL WAR MUSEUM: A 27998.

After a two-hour flight northeast, they came within sight of Task Force 57 one hundred nautical miles west-southwest of Ishigaki Island, resuming its strikes on the Ryukyu Islands after a refuelling session to the south. At dusk on 1700 hrs, the tokkōtai spotted the *Illustrious*, and prepared to attack. They were picked up by the ship's radar: fighters of the Combat Air Patrol bounced them ten miles out. One of the Suisei was shot down; the other two got into the clouds, emerging to a barrage of anti-aircraft fire from the destroyer screen. A second plane was hit and destroyed, but the third eluded the Corsairs and Hellcats. Lookouts on the carrier spotted the kamikaze bursting out of cloud cover at 3000 ft and into its final dive. The ship took violent evasive action as the AA guns blazed away for dear life.

At the Suisei's controls, one of those three pilots, Maasaki, Minami or Kitagara – with his crewman – lined up the carrier and plunged down at speeds approaching 400 mph. Concentrating all his training, nerve and skill, he aimed the plane right at the island and the bridge as my father, his mate and everyone else dived for cover. The tokkōtai training manual told pilots never to close their eyes as the enemy ship loomed up prior to impact – they might veer off course. The manual spoke of the moment of impact: 'You are now 30 m from the target. You will sense that your speed has suddenly and abruptly increased. You feel that the speed has increased by a few thousand-fold. It is like a long shot in a movie suddenly turning into a close-up, and the scene expands in your face.' The writer's imagination was running hot: 'The moment of the crash. You are two or three metres from the target. You can see clearly the muzzles of the enemy's guns. You feel that you are suddenly floating in the air. At that moment, you see your mother's face. She is not smiling or crying. It is her usual face.'

Four gunners on a Bofors unit did have their eyes wide open: they fired a series of bursts, blowing the aircraft's tail off, and the pilot lost control. At 500 ft, seconds from oblivion, the accurate fire sheared off a wing and the plane began to fall apart. The starboard wing skidded past the radome on the bridge ten feet from Captain Lambe, slicing the installation open. Plane and bomb together smashed into the sea a mere thirty yards from *Illustrious*, exploding in a giant waterspout towering over the ship, buckling

The picture that started it all: the Suisei explodes in the sea alongside *Illustrious*, 5 p.m., 6 April 1945.

# THE LOST PILOT

'HMS *Illustrious*, forward part of the island, showing damage caused by kamikaze "Judy" which crashed alongside, on 6th April 1945.'
COURTESY FLEET AIR ARM MUSEUM.

its thick steel side plates, lifting her massive bulk several feet in the water. Fragments of the plane smashed onto the deck, skidding across its armour-plated runway: body parts, aircraft parts, a cylinder head from the great radial motor, a skull with an eyeball attached, a red and yellow inflatable life raft – all scattered at random in an instant. Its crew was dead: my father and his shipmates were all still breathing. This time.

A witness to and survivor of the attack, Corsair Pilot Lt Cdr Norman Hanson, has written graphically of its impact: his cabin was shaken by the 4.5-inch battery above him opening up. Hearing the Bofors guns start to fire, he rushed up towards the flight deck as 'the whole ship jumped three feet in the water. Torpedoed!' He thought a submarine had got them. Milliseconds of courage and carnage exploded together as the gunners' accurate fire rendered the dive-bomber uncontrollable and sent it off course. Pilots leapt for their lives from Corsairs ranged on the deck for takeoff, one without shutting down his idling engine.

The pilotless plane taxied off, rescued from a watery grave by the quick response of a very brave electrician who scrambled aboard the moving fighter and hit the foot brakes, inches from disaster. Thirty-five years later, Hanson reflected, 'it should be recorded that *only seven seconds had elapsed* between the Kamikaze's first appearance through the overcast and his explosion in the water. It was without doubt, one of those occasions when seconds can stretch into eternity.' Seven seconds: in little more than the time it will take you to read this sentence, the action began and ended.

A Seafire from the carrier, on the tail of one of the other kamikaze, had been shot down by that same Royal Navy anti-aircraft barrage. For the ship, it was one more narrow escape. The next day, the attacks on Ishigaki continued as the war ground on: six anonymous Japanese scattered in the East China Sea and another New Zealand pilot, Lieutenant Churchill, lost strafing and bombing the Ishigaki and Miyako airfields. Dead men with names, shipmates one day, empty bunks and hammocks the next; anonymous enemies, their remains dispatched off the flight deck with high-pressure hoses. The next mission was flown, the next enemy strike defended. Task Force 57 kept up its relentless attacks on the airfields, striking south at Taiwan from where the early April attacks had come. This pattern was repeated until the Japanese gave up using the Sakishima Islands as a staging post, once the Okinawa airfields were overrun. By the end of May, the last

Remains of D4Y-3 tail section, USS *Kitkun Bay* (CVE 71). GILBERT J. RAYNOR AND THE USS *KITKUN BAY* ASSOCIATION.

mission was flown and the British Pacific Fleet withdrew to Sydney to refit. The bloody and costly assault on Okinawa continued, ending with the surrender of its few remaining Japanese defenders on 21 June 1945.

*Illustrious*, however, had beaten the rest of the fleet to Australian waters, dispatched to Leyte in the Philippines a month earlier on 14 April for inspection of the bomb damage to her outer plating and internal frames, then sailing south. The ship had flown 643 sorties in nine days off the Sakishima Gunto, losing five aircraft to enemy action and seven others to accidents – now, her war, and my father's, was over. On the first of May, she sailed to Sydney at a restricted speed of nineteen knots, undergoing emergency repairs in Australia and landing her remaining aircraft and some aircrew. An aircraft carrier with no aircraft, a ship without a war: by 24 May it was time to go home. As she sailed through the Bismarck Straits, the end of the war in Europe was announced over the Tannoy, and celebrations broke out. Guns were fired off in wild abandon, blazing away at an invisible enemy cheated for now: death. The ship spliced the main brace and drank Nelson's blood; a piano was hauled from the pilot's wardroom into the hangar and wheeled onto the lift, whence it emerged from the bowels of the ship with a pianist hammering the keys 'to the accompaniment of massed cheers and whistles'.

In the Mediterranean, the captain hove to and piped 'Hands to bathe', whereupon a mass ocean dip took place, before the ship moved on to Gibraltar to lay in supplies of liquor for the homecoming. On 27 June, with her paying-off pennant trailing, the great ship sailed up the Firth of Forth to Rosyth, the same body of water where my father had stood on the deck of the ancient *Furious* in 1939, a fresh-faced signal boy, returned now to Mother Britain, the veteran survivor of a six-year world-changing war. Most of those who left the ship that day would never see her again; life was certainly never the same for Yeoman of Signals Holman. He was going home to his wife and the post-war world. Nine months later my brother was born; a new Labour government in Britain was about to create the modern welfare state in which Eric would begin his life – and I would follow.

Apart from a brief stint on HMS *Gambia* – a cruiser seconded to the RNZN in 1943, and accorded the honour of firing probably the last naval shots of WW2, on the day the Japanese surrender was announced – my father

# Kokutai no Hongi: Japan as the Emperor's Body

From cover of *Life* magazine (vol. II, no. 11), 15 September 1941. The ship in its pomp, before the Mediterranean Fliegerkorps X attack. COURTESY DEREK TAYLOR.

was shore-based on HMS *Drake* and HMS *Mercury*. He was discharged ashore by purchase – unhappily and unwillingly – on 13 June 1947, as my mother, in poor health after suffering a near-death experience with pregnancy toxaemia while carrying and giving birth to my older brother, was four months pregnant with me. Dad's commission had not expired, but because Mum was a near invalid in the year after her first delivery, she needed to be cared for. My grandmother had obliged to begin with, but now it was his turn. He resented having to leave his life in the Senior Service: forced to enlist by his mother, now forced to resign because of his wife's infirmity (or so he felt) – with the added insult of having to buy his way out of the final months of his service.

The irony was that my mother had been ordered by her specialist Dr Spitzer never to have another child: therefore, no me. The eclampsia that had nearly killed her, causing a brain haemorrhage and temporary blindness, had left her in the condition of a stroke victim. In another pregnancy, it might very likely reoccur and finish the job. My father, however, had other ideas: he was not at all happy with having an only child, so he persuaded my mother they should try again. His naval discharge, then – a result of my

4 The Curve W8: the Holman, Airey and Woollam families gather for a post-war family snap – probably taken early in 1947. My elder brother Eric is the new addition.

journey into the world – was much of his own making. While his family was returning to some kind of normality – and the Holman clan, complete with a brand-new post-war baby, gathered at 4 The Curve, Westway W8 for a family snap – on the other side of the world, a battered and numbed Japan was counting the cost of the imperial madness that had swept her into an unwinnable war. Instead of delivering power and prosperity, her military dictators had brought down an epic disaster on most of Asia and the Pacific, and then the final cataclysm of atomic warfare on their own people.

In a desperate and bloody bequest, the kamikaze phenomenon had scythed a harvest of death through her best and brightest young men. Japan was in shock, denial and mourning: in the family homes of those six men who had died on 6 April and in countless others, the military portraits of flyers, some in their teens and others just out of them, were hung with great sadness on the walls, beside their dead forebears. Many, of course, had no one to remember them and many families had no homes or walls on which to hang anything: the firebombing of the great cities had devastated Japanese life, causing far more deaths and casualties than the two atomic bombs of

## KOKUTAI NO HONGI: JAPAN AS THE EMPEROR'S BODY

6 and 9 August 1945. Major-General Curtis LeMay, the pyromaniacal commander in charge of B-29 bombing operations against Japan in the final months of the war, was running out of cities to raze – but he was not allowed to touch Hiroshima and Nagasaki, for reasons which soon became obvious. If the last days of Hitler's Third Reich were a vision of Götterdämmerung, Japan's were a hell of flame beyond the capacity of myth-makers to imagine.

Modern Japan grew out of the pre-modern era that came to a dramatic end with the arrival of Commodore Perry's ships and the American imperium in 1853–54. The Japanese imperial line that became so important politically and symbolically in the nineteenth and twentieth centuries stretched back in time to the sixth century AD, with the Yamato dynasty that would later claim descent from twenty-eight legendary ancestors back to the seventh century BC. These emperors gradually lost power in a feudal society, divided geographically and politically into small local fiefdoms. By the ninth and tenth centuries, the imperial line was producing emperors who lived sheltered lives in Kyōto, akin to Shinto priests; this connection between hereditary rule and religion would become a feature of the mythos of modern Japan.

By the tenth century, a samurai (or bushi) warrior class was emerging, eventually gaining some equivalency with the hereditary aristocracy. By the thirteenth century, the first shoguns, or generalissimos legitimised by imperial recognition, emerged to form bafuku or military governments, having little wider control beyond their local and regional boundaries. Communications were difficult in Japan due to its mountainous geography and the long stretch of the main islands (Hokkaido, the northernmost, was not pacified and included until the nineteenth century). In the fifteenth and sixteenth centuries, daimyō, or local military lords, with their samurai warriors presided over hundreds of jealous fiefdoms, until the more powerful were able to establish some measure of hegemony. The arrival of Western missionaries in the sixteenth century bringing God and, more decisively, guns, increased the power of those rulers in establishing greater centralised control.

In terms of religion and culture, Japan, while geographically divorced from the Asian mainland, was open to Chinese and Korean influences: Buddhism and Confucianism entered via the close connection to nearby Korea and were well established by the seventh and eighth centuries. They sat beside and in some respects merged with the local animistic religion of Shinto ('the way of the spirits'), which was mainly rural, dedicated to local deities (kami) and forces worshipped in physical shrines that remain in use to this day. Buddhism emphasised the essence of life as suffering and the illusory nature of reality; Confucianism, a set of moral and ethical teachings, stressed filial piety and respect for ruling elites. The good kingdom was a stable kingdom and the unquestioning obedience of its subjects was mandatory. These foreign teachings percolated downwards from the imperial court and the aristocracy to the wider society – in written Japanese forms of the Chinese script. A twin emphasis on the transitory nature of human existence and the demand to respect authority – along with a reinvention of imperial power and Shinto divinity on a national scale in the nineteenth century – would create an intoxicating and seductive environment, nurturing and ennobling the spirit of military sacrifice in the years ahead.

It is important to note that none of these beliefs were religions in the Judaeo–Christian sense of having a supreme being, or a sacred set of texts that involved a fall, sin, redemption and the final judgment of the individual beyond death. Kami, the Shinto spirit beings, were mortal and they could die; they were more in the realm of demi-gods, spirit beings or powerful natural forces. The imperial line was said to descend from the sun goddess Amaterasu; the reinvention of the emperor's divinity after the Meiji Restoration in the mid-nineteenth century was not a written dogma, but had become a general assumption in Japan by the onset of the Second World War. This was more an expression of the new nationalism and patriotism of the Japanese than the theological expression of a belief system (Shinto is plainly lacking in sacred scriptures, but clearly bound up in localised ritual in its origins).

The post-feudal shogunate continued into the nineteenth century under the Tokugawa dynasty which had pacified large areas of the country from the seventeenth century onwards. Their bafuku military government, however, was unable to resist what came from without, in the form of the American warships of Commodore Matthew Perry, sailing into Edo Bay in 1853. The Americans had been ranging across the Pacific, north and south, for many

Commodore Perry (1853), through Japanese eyes. COURTESY LIBRARY OF CONGRESS.

years, whaling and trading. Perry was a veteran of the US war with Mexico in 1845, and the campaign to overthrow Spanish control of Cuba in 1847. The Americans wanted coaling and trading facilities for their imperial adventures in the Western Pacific and Asia; it was even mooted that Japan should be colonised. Britain was making the running in China, exploiting military weaknesses and divisions there, by forcing on the Chinese a hated series of unequal treaties.

This was now to be Japan's fate: a form of colonial client status. While the Americans did not invade her, they did something equally as damaging – they humiliated the Japanese through the 1854 Convention of Kanagawa, and in 1858, the Harris Treaty of 'Amity and Commerce'. There was to be little amity but much commerce. The 1854 treaty had opened up two Japanese ports to the US, under the threat of war; the 1858 accord opened three more, and allowed American citizens to live and trade in Japan under legal extraterritoriality. They were not subject to Japanese laws; they were entitled to low import duties; and missionary activity was legitimised. In one stroke, the apostles of free trade and the evangelists of an unknown god gained access to the bodies and souls of the Japanese people – in the process storing up huge resentment and, later, revenge. This was humiliation on a grand scale: accelerating the demise of the old shogunate and ushering in the Meiji Restoration, which would quick-march Japan into modernity and globalisation.

This new stage of Japanese development coincided with a growing sense of nationhood that had not existed prior to Perry's incursion. By the time of the attack on Pearl Harbor in 1941, it was America that had virtually given birth by Caesarean to modern Japan, by first cutting her out of the womb of seclusion, then forcing her to enter the modern world on their terms. They were sowing the wind: the more the American traders violated Japanese sovereignty and ran their own affairs, unaccountable for the blows inflicted on local pride, the more they helped to create a united Japan hitherto non-existent in its feudal, divided past. By 1867, a disaffected self-educated samurai, Sakamoto Ryoma, from Nagasaki had studied Western political institutions in sufficient depth to devise a blueprint for the state beyond the shogunate model. The emperor was to preside over two legislative bodies, upper and lower houses, in a form of constitutional monarchy; a constitution would be drawn up and a new meritocracy would administer the imperial rule.

In 1868 the Meiji era ('enlightened rule') began when many of his ideas were adopted in the Charter Oath of the restoration. The old order, the bakufu forces of the shogun, was not about to go quietly and see its power disappear; bloody civil war ensued until 1869, when the imperial forces defeated them at Aizu. Western weaponry and superior numbers ensured the forces of modernity won the day and the era: in a chilling prelude to the kamikaze phenomenon seventy-five years later, many young samurai in utter despair committed sepukku – ritual disembowelment. Many others had flung their bodies willingly into the withering fire of Maxims and artillery barrages: a doomed era of archers and horsemen hurling themselves onto a future of rifles, machine guns and field weapons. The emperor was now moved to Edo (Tōkyō), ending a millennium of separation from the seat of government. The modern imperial era began as it would end – in bloodshed.

There was more political instability to come, but in spite of teething troubles, the new Japan went full speed ahead into a frantic period of modernisation, industrialisation and militarisation. The best way to resist the barbarians was to adopt their tricks. Envoys were dispatched to the West to learn everything that could help Japan modernise – and compete. German advisors came to reform the military and conscription was begun; what had started in a defensive nationalism soon progressed to an aggressive colonialism. In 1882 the Rescript for Soldiers and Sailors – an imperial edict – set out the duties for the armed forces: absolute loyalty and unquestioning obedience. In a dark analogue of the Apostle Paul's vision of the church as the loving servant body of Christ on earth, the troops were to be the arms and legs of Japan's imperial body with the emperor as its head (along with his political and military advisors). Young, uneducated conscripts from rural areas learned to read and write in the military, force-fed and brainwashed by state propaganda.

Emperor worship – a very unhistoric invention – became a touchstone of the new Japan's national identity (and superiority); right-wing and fascist tendencies were ever-present to deal by assassination with any liberal forces and democratic aberrations that might threaten the rise of their militancy and colonial ambitions. In the first Sino–Japanese war of 1894–95, a weakened Qing dynasty was forced to cede Formosa to Japan. The Chinese were also forced to recognise Korean independence, which an emboldened Japan would soon nullify by annexing her neighbour between 1905 and 1910. Before long, she was to announce her new status amongst the world's powers by soundly thrashing the Imperial Russian Navy in 1905.

This was an event closely watched by a relative of mine: the naval expert Hector C. Bywater, Nanny Airey's brother and my great-uncle. He enters this story of Japan's rise as one of the foremost naval commentators of the early twentieth century – whose work and writings will shortly appear here. He was not alone in watching the increasing friction between Japan and her Russian neighbours, who were steadily encroaching in Manchuria and Korea and gaining railway concessions. Japan saw this as her colonial backyard: a raid on the Russian outpost at Port Arthur in southern Manchuria was prophetic of the Pearl Harbor tactics, struck without a declaration of war. What followed – when the Russians replied by sailing their fleet all the way around the world and into the Sea of Japan – was a decisive and humiliating Japanese naval victory at the battle of the Tsushima Strait in May 1905. It was

# The Lost Pilot

Hector C. Bywater's prophetic book *The Great Pacific War 1931–1933*, published in 1925.

a harbinger of what was to come: the downfall of the old order in the West and the rise of the Pacific and the East – America, Japan and, latterly, China.

Racial theories in Europe and America may not have been much revised by these events, but naval strategists the world over with any powers of observation and analysis had seen a radical shift in the balance of world sea power. With the outbreak of the Great War (in which Japan was aligned with the Allies) came more opportunities to test her strength and status as a major military player. In the event, she never engaged in the endless war of attrition that bled the West dry, but as a manufacturer of armaments was given a golden opportunity to prosper without losing her manpower. By 1920, Japan was far stronger and better equipped to wage a war than the exhausted colonial powers of Europe. Due to her late engagement in the war in 1917, America, too, had emerged with her industrial might greatly strengthened, with a relatively small loss of men.

Two confident and well-equipped powers now faced each other across the broad expanse of the Pacific. While America had taken the Philippines from the Spanish in the 1890s, and gained Eastern Samoa as a coaling station in 1900, Japan too was becoming a regional coloniser in the Pacific. After the German defeat in 1918, as well as acquiring their former Chinese colony in Shandong, Japan also took German colonial outposts in Micronesia (Saipan, Truk and Kwajalein). This was part of a League of Nations mandate and Truk became a principal base for the Imperial Japanese Navy in the lead-up to World War Two. As the great powers wrangled over naval strengths, the numbers and sizes of guns on cruisers and battleships, a few far-sighted individuals such as Brigadier General Billy Mitchell of the US Army Air Service were demonstrating to the unbelieving battleship men of the US Navy that a bomber could sink a battleship (in 1921, he bombed and sank the captured German battleship *Ostfriedland*). The next major sea battles would not be fought as were the great battleship engagements of the Tsushima Strait conflict of 1905 – but at huge distances, foe invisible to foe, as fleets of aircraft carriers launched their shipborne planes to establish mastery of the sea through control of the air.

All the elements were lining up for the run to Pearl Harbor: Japan's strategic outlook had moved from alliance with the West to independent operation in the East. This stance was bound to bring her into direct confrontation with Britain, the European powers and America, the original colonisers of Asia. In bringing Japan into their orbit of trade, they had helped to transform an isolated rural culture that was internally self-sufficient and largely agricultural into an outwardly confident nation with an injured sense of pride, now heavily industrialised and resource-hungry. With few natural deposits of the vital elements needed in the industrial revolution (coal, steel and oil), she had begun to look elsewhere. She could bargain for her needs by trade – or take them by force.

Commodore Perry's arrival did not in itself turn the Japanese into Asian colonialists in competition with the West: this was their choice. A combination of hubris – and a raw inferiority complex – saw her dispatch obedient armies to defeat Korea and China, demonstrating Japanese superiority to her neighbours and the watching world. Meiji and early Taisho Japan aped many European ways in order to show them she was not at all as backward as those older Asian cultures to whom she owed so much of her own inheritance. The post-war, post-atomic Japanese victimhood and memory loss regarding atrocities committed in the course of her stated desire to liberate colonial Asia from the British, the Dutch and the French remain in the court of history as familiar examples of a bully's self-piteous reaction when his nose is bloodied in defeat.

Emperor Hirohito, in whose name this war had been fought, was to escape punishment for his responsibilities in both approving its being waged and then not intervening later when it was clearly lost and he might have called for its ending. Even General Hideki Tojo, the wartime prime minister hanged with seven others for war crimes in December 1948, said in his trial that nothing could have been done without the emperor's approval: 'no Japanese would dare act against his will'. He later changed his testimony under pressure from the Americans and the Allies; they wanted to use the once-divine emperor as a demoted 'symbol for unity' – a leading figure who was now to be shielded from the consequences of his actions. To the Japanese, it was plainly wrong that the servants who carried out orders under imperial mandate should hang while the top man escaped any censure. Even today, the memory of war criminals such as Tojo can find shelter under the same umbrella of self-pity, as obedient servants wronged by an injustice.

The all-pervading doctrine of kokutai no hongi ('the sacred national body') allowed this to happen. After the Meiji Restoration – and by the onset of World War Two – the emperor had been refigured as the embodiment of Japanese-ness, the Yamato spirit. Divine in descent, he was (metaphorically, at least) Japan itself to the Japanese. He was their head, they were his body:

Emperor Hirohito riding Shirayuki during an army inspection in August 1938.
WIKIPEDIA COMMONS.

the Japanese individual subject was dissolved into the imperial object. Yet while he was said to be in control of the country, in effect he was not: while responsible as head, he was not decisive in day-to-day matters. Democracy in the 1920s Taisho era of renewed Westernisation was stifled by a reactionary right-wing backlash. By 1940, the country was effectively ruled by the military, enacting this sovereignty (including colonialism and war) on the emperor's behalf.

East Asia was seen as Japan's rightful sphere of influence: its inhabitants would be grateful to be rid of the hated Western colonisers; liberated by the Japanese, they would be happily included (as second-class citizens) in the imperial polity. They would become slave labourers in a militaristic theocracy suffering from a pathological sense of inferiority when it compared itself with the Western powers. The only way to expiate this historical debt of shame was to defeat the Americans, the British, the Dutch and the French colonisers in East Asia and the Pacific; in much the same way as Japan had the Russians, in 1905. With the emperor as the head of the national body and his war ministers carrying out his perceived will – to make the world Japanese – all members of his armed forces were therefore executing their orders in a divinely ordained mission. The immediate superior who gave them an order was, in effect, the mouthpiece of the emperor.

During the mid to late 1930s, the generation which would carry out this mission swelled Japan's armed forces, along with those who from 1944 onwards would provide the bulk of the kamikaze pilots. With an average age of nineteen, these young men were born like my father between the years 1920 and 1925. Schooled from the outset in obedience, by the time they reached high-school age (from 1937 onwards) the pernicious kokutai doctrine was being institutionalised. Japan's leading scholars had been engaged by the Ministry of Education to create a document that gave the official teaching on every aspect of domestic policy, international affairs, culture and civilisation. Pupils were indoctrinated with the idea that they must put the nation (that is, the emperor) before themselves; that they were part of the body of the state (the imperial body) and must be prepared to die without question as the price of that belonging. They were also taught the doctrine of hakkō ichiu (literally, 'eight cords, one roof'), which meant that Japan's imperial rule had been divinely ordained to expand until it united the whole world. Her crusade against the West would be a holy war of deliverance, one that would see the emperor – by means of his armed forces – take Japanese-ness to the entire conquered planet.

After invading French Indo–China in 1940, Japan was confronted with a US financial freeze and an oil and scrap metal embargo, which threatened to cripple her industries. She was faced with the prospect of backing down, withdrawing from China and Indo–China, or striking at the American fleet and British and Dutch possessions to get control of the Pacific and access to oil. She chose the latter: Tojo and the war cabinet did it for the emperor, in the name of the imperial house and in pursuit of Japanese distinctiveness and destiny. They knew they could never defeat the United States, but they expected that their show of strength would persuade the soft and decadent Americans to withdraw from the field and leave them to their mission. If not, they were prepared to take the huge gamble: the Yamato spirit demanded no less.

For a heady six months, it almost looked as if they had succeeded, until April 1942, when Lieutenant Colonel Jimmy Doolittle's carrier-launched B-25 bombers raided Tōkyō. In May of the same year, in the Battle of the Coral Sea, the Americans gained a bloody but significant strategic victory over the all-conquering Japanese forces, turning back the invasion of New Guinea; in June, the Battle of Midway was a decisive US victory – the tide had turned. It would take three more years to roll back Japanese gains in the Pacific and East Asia, with the deluded ideology of the kokutai and world domination discredited; yet not before millions more lives had been lost, including those six tokkōtai pilots who flew to attack the *Illustrious* that day in April 1945.

Sakura: falling cherry blossoms – they were the blood sacrifices of a suffocating belief system whose chief exponents – especially Emperor Hirohito – would largely escape the consequences of their criminal acts. Yet none of the old European colonial powers would return to their former dominions in the same imperious manner. Japan had sent the colonists packing – even if in the case of Britain in Hong Kong the final piece took some time to fall into place in 1997, when control was handed over to the Chinese Communist regime. Immediately post-war, with great swiftness, the Dutch were gone from Indonesia, France was kicked out of Indo–China, and the British had to surrender India and Pakistan as well as many other colonial footholds. Even America, acting *in loco parentis* for these fading ghosts in Vietnam during the 1960s and 1970s, was finally ejected: she still holds her place in Okinawa, but that too will go. While Japan's intentions in this war of conquest were never benign, she did leave a lasting legacy by attacking Europe's agents in East Asia – but not that of hakkō ichiu, the moral leadership of the emperor uniting the entire world. Japan would regroup and rebuild: she would colonise the West commercially instead.

Meet the new boss: General MacArthur and the emperor at Allied GHQ in Tōkyō, 17 September 1945. Gaetano Falliace (1904–1991), MacArthur's personal photographer, captured this image. WIKIPEDIA COMMONS.

Twenty years after the war had ended, in the early 1960s on the West Coast of the South Island, schoolboys such as me could stand on the wharf at the port of Greymouth and watch the exotically named Japanese colliers tie up and load metallurgical coking coal, hewn from the Paparoa Ranges where our fathers laboured underground to supply their former enemies. Japan had by then reverted to the peaceful option, after first risking everything in an attempt to take what she needed by force of arms. My family history intersects once more with great events: predicting the coming clash of arms – and abused as a warmonger for his troubles – was my great-uncle Hector, that famous semi-mythical writer and naval expert our Nanny recalled to us in our smoky Blackball miner's home.

We only half-believed her at the time, but she had his books, including the one that had made his theories a worldwide talking point: *The Great Pacific War 1931–1933*. There was nothing notable in the title itself – except the book had been published six years earlier, by Constable of London, in 1925. Of course she was proud of her famous younger brother; since his death in 1940 he has been largely forgotten, in spite of the fact that his dark prophecies were fulfilled the following year when Japan attacked Pearl Harbor. It was not until 1990, while working as a bookseller in Kent, that I came across a new title in a publisher's catalogue: *Bywater: The Man Who Invented the Pacific War*, by William H. Honan. That made me sit up: the next time the Macdonald's publisher's rep came in, I asked for and was given a copy. Honan was a *New York Times* journalist and author whose wife had found a copy of Hector's prescient title languishing in a New England second-hand bookshop; knowing her husband's nautical bent, she purchased the old book and took it home.

He was amazed by its contents and wrote an article on the book and its author for the *Times*. Deeply intrigued, he decided it was worth a full-length treatment and spent the next few years reading, researching and hunting down long-lost relatives on the Bywater side (both Hector and my other great-uncle Ulysses had children, my mother's cousins). As well as writing history, he was undertaking family history research for me: once I had his name, I contacted the publisher and we were soon writing back and forth. He was delighted to have smoked out another relative and we agreed to meet when he came to Britain in September of 1990 for the book's UK launch, coinciding with the fiftieth anniversary of the Battle of Britain. We met in London and, with his long-suffering family in tow, Bill took me on a tour of Hector's London haunts, including the building in Whitehall (now a hotel) where my great-uncle was recruited into British naval intelligence in 1908 by the mysterious 'C' – Sir Manfield Cumming, head of the Foreign Section of the British Secret Service. He took me to stand outside the very room where that transaction took place; Nanny had told us Hector had been a spy in the Great War. I saw now that she knew exactly what she was talking about.

# KOKUTAI NO HONGI: JAPAN AS THE EMPEROR'S BODY

With Bill Honan (left) on the Embankment, London, September 1990: the author of my great-uncle's biography gives me a whirlwind tour of Hector's London haunts.

Much of what follows comes from his book. Hector Charles Bywater was born in Tottenham in 1884, the son of a peripatetic Welsh world traveller, my great-grandfather Peter Daniel Bywater. As a boy, he lived for four years on the East Coast of America, in Cambridge, Massachusetts, near the Charleston Navy Yard. Where, much as later, I became obsessed with flying machines and books about them, so Hector at a tender age fastened onto his lifelong fascination with ships, navies, sailors – and writing about them. He was a mere ten years old when his first article – about the Japanese surprise attack on Russian shipping in the decisive sea battle on the Yalu River in February 1894 – was accepted by a newspaper, only to have the offer withdrawn when his age was discovered. This precocious debut was tinged with some prescience: having witnessed at such a young age the rise of Japanese sea power and their willingness to attack without warning, using speed and skill to defeat more ponderous opponents, he never lost his respect for Japanese derring-do and seamanship. He remained thereafter years ahead of most of his contemporaries in his appreciation of naval skill, daring and tactical acumen, regardless of race or creed.

Hector's boyhood passions blossomed into a career, and his polymathic linguistic prowess, as well as his ability to read the writings of other naval experts – especially those in German – ensured his value to the British authorities. His later willingness as a newspaper correspondent and author to employ experts in Japan on the ground in that country, in the build-up to World War Two, was symptomatic of his cosmopolitan character and hunger for accurate detail. His father returned to Britain in 1900 to complete his children's schooling; Hector and Uly also spent time in Germany where both became fluent speakers (they would later both work for the US Consulate in Dresden prior to and during the Great War, with false American citizenship provided). Returning to America at the age of seventeen, Hector worked for three years as a tram conductor and later a clerk for a railway company whose workers were mostly recent German immigrants. Between polishing his idiomatic German and spending all his spare time at the Brooklyn Navy Yard, he was slowly but surely preparing for future careers in espionage and journalism – while cultivating an ability to discern the larger picture in naval affairs.

In 1904 he landed his first reporter's job, working for James Gordon Bennett on the *New York Herald*; this man was a convinced Japanophobe, sure that Japan had become America's great Pacific rival and that war was one day inevitable. Hector had arrived at the right place at the right time, and his scoops on the naval battles that took place between Japan and Russia in 1904–05, with the crushing of the latter, began to be recognised as a brilliant and persuasive commentator whose writing was both intelligent and stylish. He was on his way. A move back to England and then Germany saw him involved in chronicling the naval armament race that took place between the British and the Germans prior to the outbreak of hostilities in 1914 – and his secret-service engagement, which led to many dangers faced and foes outwitted in the course of the war that followed. Over all this time, he never took his eye off Japan and the wider picture; he was preparing mentally to write the book that would first make his name: *Sea-Power in the Pacific*, published in 1921.

Hector Bywater was one of the first commentators in the post-WW1

Bill Honan's signed copy of *Bywater*, complete with D4Y-3 Suisei model.

era to realise that the defeat of Germany had made much naval writing and analysis irrelevant; he saw how myopic – and racist – many of his contemporaries were. As Honan notes in his biography, 'unlike so many of his contemporaries, he gave no credence whatsoever to the disparaging stereotypes and caricatures of the Japanese prevalent in England and the United States'. He was prescient also in observing that the typical Japanese sailor displayed 'courage and contempt for death' and demonstrated this heroically in Japan's war with Russia (shades of what my father would experience later in the Pacific). He refused to portray them as fanatics, noting also that discretion and prudence were obvious in Admiral Togo's tactics in defeating the Russians. Like all professional military writers from whatever nation, he respected a potential enemy – real or imagined – and concentrated on analysing the facts as he saw them.

More than this, he could see how the balance of naval power had shifted radically to the Pacific from the Atlantic; even in World War Two, the German Kriegsmarine – except for the U-boat fleet – was never a serious threat to the Royal Navy, boxed into Channel ports for much of the time, threatening largely in their potential. Hitler was not a navy man: while the large battleships *Bismarck* and *Tirpitz* had propaganda value, their contribution to the deadly and effective submarine Battle of the Atlantic was virtually nil. The Pacific was different: here, the aircraft carrier, the new kid on the block, was about to change the whole concept of tactics and overall strategy. The Japanese were amongst the first to understand this development; the Americans were not far behind.

While Hector was never convinced about carrier warfare – and to this extent was wrong about how the naval battles in the Pacific would play out – he was nevertheless right about the main issues. He saw clearly – in the light of recent history and strategic realities – that Japan would one day decide to attack America, seeing her as the major stumbling block to her expansionist plans in Asia and the Pacific. He saw – a good twenty years before the strike on Pearl Harbor took place – that she would almost certainly do so with a surprise attack in advance of any declaration of hostilities. It was 'reasonable to infer', he wrote in *Sea Power in the Pacific*, 'from their conduct on previous occasions, that the Japanese would act with swiftness and energy once a rupture had become inevitable'.

The book appeared to rave reviews in America, and his career over the next two decades as one of the world's foremost naval authorities was launched; it was not only in the US and Britain, however, that notice was taken. The Office of the Imperial Navy General Staff in Tōkyō was soon busy mimeographing copies for the top naval brass, distributing the work as 'material for strategic studies'. By 1922, demand for the book was so great that a translation into Japanese, *Taiheiyo kaiken ron*, was undertaken, and made available to a wide number of senior naval officers (although it was never released to the general public – a sign of how seriously Japan's naval planners took its contents). It was soon required reading at the Imperial Naval Academy and the Naval War College. Bywater's analyses and authority were compelling to the Japanese. Here was one of the West's greatest naval writers taking them seriously: as a people, as a navy – and as a threat.

He had also mapped out a strategy by which Japan, in a series of bold island-hopping moves, could neutralise America in the Western Pacific and shore up her own East Asian empire while capturing vast resources – especially oil. His discussions of tactics emphasised the effectiveness of the pre-emptive strike, in a fresh portrayal of Japan as a world power acting decisively in her own interests. This was a picture of the Japanese on the offensive – heady prospects indeed for a nation that was used to the kind of 'lure and ambush' strategy employed so successfully by Admiral Togo at Tsushima in 1905. Yet that same strategy was essentially defensive, waiting for the enemy to come to you: Japanese planning had proceeded ever since that time in the expectation of warding off and defeating an American blow. Here now was a thinker who foresaw Japan doing to America what it had done to Russia – but on a far greater scale, against a much more formidable foe.

Most Japanese naval officers at that time – intoxicated with the prospect of conquest – ignored the book's sober conclusion, however. If such a war came, the Americans with their vast economic strength undoubtedly had the legs to win the race in the end. This was the strategic balance to the equation that Japan would have consciously to risk acting against: America had more manpower, materiel and resources. The gamble would be with the likely US response to an attack – would she reply in kind against Japanese aggression, and keep coming? One of those reading this analysis, whose job it would be

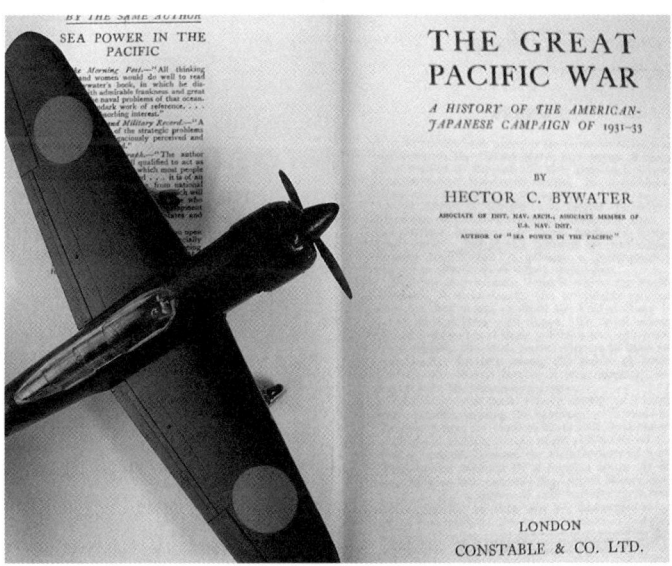

*The Great Pacific War* (1925), Hector C. Bywater's prophetic study of the coming clash of arms between Japan and America.

in the 1930s to advise on these considerations as a prelude to the decision to go to war, was a young naval officer born in the same year as Bywater, 1884 – Isoroku Yamamoto, the man who would go down in history as the major architect of the attack on Pearl Harbor. As a naval attaché to the Japanese embassy in Washington in 1925, he was well placed to be party to the great controversy stirred up by the book that really did make Hector's name: *The Great Pacific War 1931–1933*.

Yamamoto returned to Japan two years after the book's appearance and delivered a lecture in which he had adopted Bywater's theories as his own. What was it about them that excited such interest? The British expert's writings were already well known to the Japanese. In 1923, he had publicly sparred with the then Assistant Secretary of the Navy, Franklin D. Roosevelt, over the possibility of a trans-Pacific conflict between America and Japan: he saw war as a strong possibility, while Roosevelt did not. As to what would spark such a conflict, my great-uncle foresaw from his readings in translation of contemporary commentators in Japan the rise of a militarist tendency there. Japan's colonial ambitions in China would place her on a collision course with America – something that came to pass, just as he predicted. His book – a *guerre imaginaire* – belonged to a genre of future fictions, dramatic prophecies of what was to come based on a knowledge of present circumstances. Where it differed from earlier examples was in Bywater's magisterial command of naval strengths and strategies and his ability to create a convincing narrative style that persuaded the reader they were reading a genuine historical account.

The book opened with the Japanese attacking the US fleet in Manila in a surprise attack and sinking the majority of its capital ships, with the loss of 2500 US sailors (the casualties at Pearl Harbor in 1941 numbered 2638). The American tactical response – a naval attack with overextended supply lines, at the limit of its fuel resources – was soundly defeated. The Americans then adopted an incremental island-hopping strategy made clear in the book (with maps and diagrams), working their way back into a position to launch a sustainable attack on Japan's naval forces and, eventually, the mainland (which was what happened from 1943–45). The technique was not in favour at this time, after the apparent failure of the amphibious landing tactic at Gallipoli in 1915. Bywater did not share the conventional view that such landings were no longer tenable: he knew that the Dardanelles campaign was mismanaged, and might well have succeeded with better leadership.

As well as being a strategic thinker, Hector was also a ship model-maker; this meant testing naval tactics on Keston Pond in Beckenham, South London, with elaborate working models that could be guided into action and even launch salvoes at each other. Boys' toys, indeed – but these were games played with deadly intent. War gaming was used to leave nothing to chance: he spent long hours trying to solve the problem of how the Americans could lure the Japanese fleet into battle. Finally he came up with the idea of an attack on the Japanese possession of Yap, with the apparent intent to capture it and establish a forward base; Japan would have to respond from the Philippines, which they now held (in reality, in 1944, the Americans bypassed Yap and retook the island of Guam further north – but the strategy was prophetic, if not that particular tactic).

The book ends with an American defeat of Japan through the engagement of capital ships and little vital recourse to air power; at this stage of his thinking, Bywater, a capital ship man, was not persuaded by Jimmy Mitchell's bombing of stationary battleships. By the mid-1930s, however, he had moved on and foresaw that any attack would involve the strike power of Japan's new carriers. He also saw that torpedo bombers would be deadly, as Pearl Harbor proved, and his awareness of the Japanese temperament when it came to battle – and the prospect of losing – proved deadly accurate in forecasting the kamikaze phenomenon. Japanese airmen, devoted to the emperor, seeing attacks about to fall on their homeland, would not 'hesitate to ram when otherwise balked of their prey, *preferring to immolate themselves*' (my emphasis). So the book's war ends in a Japanese surrender, without the need for atomic weapons – not even someone as far-sighted and well-informed as he could have foreseen such an outcome.

*The Great Pacific War* was widely reviewed and praised in the West by the majority who studied it; the book created an intense and heated debate in Japan, where its conclusion that Japan came out as the loser was derided as insulting, and British government propaganda. Nevertheless, it was soon translated and appeared on the curriculum of Japanese naval academies, where it influenced the thinking of a generation of those who would be at the helm of the Imperial Japanese Navy at the outbreak of World War

# The Lost Pilot

Admiral Isoroku Yamamoto (1884–1943), from the cover page of *Gahouyakushin No Nihon*, February 1942, a few months after the Pearl Harbor strike.

Two. Mitsuo Fuchida, the pilot who commanded the aerial assault on Pearl Harbor, studied both of Bywater's books, as did that even more influential figure, Isoroku Yamamoto. Once again, a racist underestimation of Japanese creativity and valour in military matters was about to prove costly for those in the West who chose to ignore Hector Bywater's prophecies. In a world haunted by the slaughter of the Great War just past and a very present and disabling Great Depression, this response was hardly surprising.

While the West went back to its preoccupations after the initial furore the book created, Japan kept up its observations of what America was doing through a number of intelligence sources. The one that was to prove most useful was Yamamoto's role as a naval attaché in Washington during the 1920s, where he reported on American military matters to his superiors. It was during this posting that he read Bywater's writings and conceived his vision of a carrier-borne attack on Hawai'i. Yamamoto had discovered that the Americans were undertaking a $50-million-dollar dredging operation at Pearl Harbor. He saw immediately what this meant: significant naval forces would ultimately be based there and change the whole situation for Japan in the Pacific. In 1928, this rising star delivered a lecture at the Imperial Navy Torpedo School in Yokosuka; he was recalled in 1970 by a naval officer present, Ichitaro Yoshida, as saying this: 'Japan will lose if she adopts the traditional defensive strategy. Japan's only chance of victory would be to attack American forces at Hawai'i.' He went on to predict the replacement of battleships by aircraft carriers as the primary naval weapon of the near future, and that an attack on Hawai'i would be made by naval aircraft.

Both of these significant thinkers were to meet on two occasions: briefly in 1930 at a naval conference in London; then again there in 1934, when the now Vice Admiral Yamamoto was sent to head the Japanese delegation at the preliminary Naval Limitation Conference. The two men spent the evening of 3 December cloistered together – Bywater with a bottle of Scotch – discussing the world situation in an interview published the next day in the *Daily Telegraph*. A photograph taken at the time shows a confident fifty-year-old Yamamoto posed in a three-piece suit with his left hand minus the two fingers lost at the battle of Tsushima in 1905. Here was the tough-minded gambler who would turn the world on its head in seven years' time, arguing for a common upper limit of naval tonnage (an idea he had got from my great-uncle) – and about to have his proposals rejected.

In the event, Japan could not get an agreement to be treated equally in terms of tonnage with Great Britain and America and the meetings ended in a stalemate. Japan was to pull out of the main Naval Limitation Conference in 1936 and begin an unfettered programme of naval expansion that had its consummation in December 1941. A binge of supership building ensued, giving rise to such monsters as the 72,800-ton battleships *Musashi* and *Yamato*: peace was now a forlorn hope, as the militarists took charge and drove Japan towards war. All this – along with the expansion of German naval power under Hitler – was faithfully chronicled by Hector, the now grand old man of naval affairs, in books and his reports in the *Daily Telegraph*. By 1938, a naval arms race was universal as the world counted down to the inevitable clash of arms that was to come.

Along with Winston Churchill and a minority of other Jeremiahs, Bywater was using his public platform to tear strips off the Chamberlain government in vehement denunciations of its inadequate responses to German naval rearmament. Sadly, his employers supported the policy of appeasement and by the end of 1939 – proved right, surely – he was off the payroll, officially due to 'ill health'. Unemployed, his drinking escalated, a dependent relationship with alcohol that had existed throughout his professional career. He wrote some more articles for the *News Chronicle*, including one about the loss of the *Glorious* – a sister carrier to my father's *Furious* – in June 1940. In July, he wrote his last article about Japan, clear-eyed as ever, where he made it plain that Japan would eventually take advantage of the Allies' entanglement and losses in Europe to make her claims on French Indo–China and British possessions in the Far East. On 16 September 1940, the day after the Germans had been decisively bested in the aerial battle over Britain and the strategy of bombing the airfields was abandoned, as wave upon wave of bombers droned overhead to attack the new target, London, Hector Bywater lay dying in suburban Richmond. The next day, aged fifty-five, he was dead. His physician wrote on the death certificate: 'Consider death due to Alcoholic Poisoning.'

Hector C. Bywater (1884–1940).

Later speculation by one of Bywater's colleagues that Yamamoto – now planning the strike on America – had him killed, because 'he knew too much', is almost certainly far-fetched. By now the Commander-in-Chief of the Combined Fleet, he had seen his intuition that Hawai'i would be used as a forward base for the US Pacific Fleet come true in May to June of 1940, when its operations were shifted from San Diego to Oahu in those islands. He would carry through his orders to create an attack plan right up to its execution on 7 December 1941, when the West learned once more how deadly and efficient Japanese surprise attacks could be. In an echo of Bywater's prophecy in *The Great Pacific War*, Yamamoto had told the Japanese Prime Minister Konoye in September of 1940 that he could 'give them hell for a year and a half', but guarantee nothing after that. This is almost exactly what happened. Yamamoto had lived in America: he knew that Japan could damage the US tactically for a period, but that strategically – as Bywater had foreseen – the Americans had the ultimate advantage in a protracted war. War needs both manpower and raw materials: Japan had the former, not the latter, while America had both.

It was to bring this ill-advised war to an acceptable conclusion – a negotiated peace – that Japan would turn in its extremity in 1944 and 1945 to the desperate and doomed tactic of the tokkōtai squadrons. By April of 1943, Yamamoto was dead: his plane intercepted and shot down by American fighters sent to meet him after a code-breaking coup revealed his journey from Rabaul to Bougainville. The rot had set in – after the major Japanese defeat at Midway, by the following year the Americans were on the move north. They were advancing on the Philippines in fulfilment of another of Hector Bywater's predictions: island-hopping towards a final attack on the Japanese mainland. Shortages of men, materiel, fuel and food – along with the overwhelming US superiority in all these areas – soon had the Japanese high command and some of their experienced airmen on the front line considering the possibility of suicide attacks, to slow the American advance and forestall the expected attempt at invasion of the homeland. By late 1944, the first kamikaze attacks would be launched against the enemy from the Philippines: the imperial body, convulsing in its death throes, had begun sacrificing more of its expendable members at the cold behest of the head.

# 4

# Fubuki: Falling Blossom, or Human Sacrifices?

Our bodies are fully resolved to do battle and we cast away any frivolous needs.
Do not cry for us insects of the grass, for the sake of peace in the Orient,
What sacrifice is too great?

*'Roei no uta' ('The Song of the Camp') – Yūji Koseki, 1937*

I knew the tokkōtai pilots would die like dogs. When I was selected to be one of 36 tokkōtai out of 200 trained to be tokkōtai pilots, I sank into the depths of despair . . . of course we could not say what we really thought and felt. So we had to lie. It was taboo to express our true thoughts (hon'ne).

*Shinta Masamichi, tokkōtai pilot, at the point of writing his will*

I am desperately trying to find my true self without any ornament. I no longer have a self.

*Wada Minoru, kaiten submarine torpedo kamikaze, died 25 July 1945*

When I received [my] order, I felt like the earth were cracking [and] swallowing me, as if my blood were flowing backward.

*Warrant Officer Takeo Tagata, 14 August 1945*

# Fubuki: Falling Blossom, or Human Sacrifices?

Corporal Yukio Araki, holding a puppy, with four other pilots of the 72nd Shinbu Squadron at Bansei, Kagoshima, 26 May 1945. Araki died the following day, aged seventeen, in a suicide attack on ships near Okinawa. Three of the five are seventeen years old and the other two are eighteen and nineteen years old.

With Japan plainly on the back foot by 1944, those who had led her into a disastrous, unwinnable war were now confronted with how to extricate themselves from its consequences – in particular, the Allied demand for an unconditional surrender. Japan had never suffered invasion and occupation, and even while facing military defeat, her leaders could not contemplate such a shameful outcome. The emperor's body – the people of Japan – would have to make more sacrifices. Kamikaze attacks – which began in an ad hoc fashion – would become a tactical imperative, designed to ensure that the Americans would give up the idea of invasion, on the basis of the unacceptable losses it would entail, and so come to the negotiating table. Unaware of the atomic weapon option America would choose in order to avoid the expected massive loss of Allied lives that invasion would surely incur, the kamikaze attacks seemed to Japan's rulers and tacticians to be a wild card that might just gain them the face-saving escape they were seeking.

As with any extreme military tactic or operation that enters into legend, the young men who made up the tokkōtai (special attack) units were from the very beginning a kind of blood-ready blank canvas upon which their own people and their enemies could project their needs and fantasies. Nurtured inside the culture, society and traditions described in the previous chapter, they spent their last weeks, days and hours in anticipation of an end decreed for them that they could no longer avoid. Any searcher on YouTube today will find endlessly reprised the last moments of those whose deaths were caught on film — often the same clips, recycled to bizarre musical backgrounds that reflect the political and aesthetic prejudices of those posting them. From a comfortable distance, we can view Japanese schoolgirls brandishing sakura branches in mournful salute as the planes lift off Kyūshū for the last time. We see comrades waving hats and samurai swords: then plunging planes, diving sailors, torrents of anti-aircraft fire, the broken bodies of burning aircraft cartwheeling into the seas off Okinawa, billowing smoke and flame as the same carrier is hit over and over and over again.

Watching these funereal processions, what strikes is not only the mesmerising pyrotechnics of human sacrifice viewed long after the event, but prior images of the faces of the departing men, close up. Certainly there are gung-ho shots of clean-cut figures mounting their Zeros, Oscars and Judys, but much of the footage is less successfully stage-managed, and at times the actors seem to fumble their lines. One that appears often is a motley group resembling a bunch of farm boys, their shoulders slumped, heads down, as they receive their final orders and the officer's handshake. Horror and despair seem to lurk just behind the control they are managing to keep on their sad facial muscles; they look depressed and cornered, as they surely were. To Western liberal perceptions, this group seems a far more realistic vision of what it must have meant to stand there on your last day, the engine of your death chariot roaring in the background as it warmed up to ferry you into destruction.

There is a face behind these faces, unseen: the Emperor Hirohito in whose name they were flying away to die. How much did he know and approve of the adoption of these tactics? By June of 1944, Admiral Chester W. Nimitz's naval armada had landed marines on Saipan, and mainland Japan was now within reach of the high-altitude B-29 bombers, already raiding

## FUBUKI: FALLING BLOSSOM, OR HUMAN SACRIFICES?

Cover page of a weekly magazine, *Manshu Shuhou*, published in Japanese-occupied Manchuria, northeast China. A caption (cropped) reads: 'The intensity of the battle has been increasing. All pilots must go for kamikaze attack.'

Kyūshū from bases in China. Hirohito and his advisors now realised that regular and deadly air raids were unstoppable. Civilians would have to pay on their doorsteps the price of their masters' imperial adventures overseas. A decisive naval battle in the Philippine Sea saw the end of Japanese sea power; a despairing naval officer, Captain Jo Ei-ichiro, sent a message to Admiral Onishi Takijiro, which came to the attention of the emperor:

NO LONGER CAN WE HOPE TO SINK THE NUMERICALLY SUPERIOR ENEMY AIRCRAFT CARRIERS BY CONVENTIONAL ATTACK. I URGE THE IMMEDIATE ORGANISATION OF SPECIAL ATTACK UNITS TO CARRY OUT CRASH-DIVE TACTICS.

Special attack – tokkōtai – became known in the Allied camp as kamikaze; the tactic was born out of desperation, in the face of the failure of conventional arms.

Since 1943, earlier studies had shown that crash-dive tactics could sink more shipping per man-loss, but Japan had not yet reached the point of believing her overall strategy was bankrupt. By late 1944, her armed forces were everywhere facing defeat on the islands they had overcome, her navy was a spent force, and both the army and the naval air arms were rapidly overwhelmed in a war of attrition fought with newer, superior American planes and fresh, well-trained personnel. Bywater's predictions were being fulfilled in a measure even he could not have fully conceived. The romance of the kamikaze pilot as samurai was intoxicating; flying in combat for Japan was becoming increasingly hazardous for old and new pilots, with shorter training periods and flying unreliable, obsolescent aircraft against a vastly superior enemy. It was only a further step in logic to conclude that the kinds of losses the Japanese air arms were already sustaining in air-to-air battles would be more decisively directed in kamikaze tactics that would almost certainly reap rewards.

Hirohito had discussed the pros and cons with his advisors: some were wary of what such a taint of fanaticism could do to his public image in any post-war arrangement, while others felt the pressures coming from below – petitions from pilots themselves dispirited with the fifty per cent casualty rate they were suffering with little real effect in slowing the American advances. No decision was made at first; the emperor was elsewhere encouraging civilians on Saipan to commit suicide, rather than face dishonour in surrender to the all-conquering invaders. The people of Saipan had been promised equal spiritual status in the hereafter with soldiers who died in combat – over 10,000 chose to kill themselves and their children. It is plain that it was not out of a concern for his subjects that Hirohito did not immediately approve of the tokkōtai tactic of crash-diving onto enemy shipping. Guam was next to fall and then Tinian – the latter transformed overnight by the Americans into an air base from which B-29 atom bombers would later fly to Hiroshima and Nagasaki.

The fall of Saipan coincided with the emperor's withdrawal under pressure from the war cabinet, and Prime Minister Tojo was deposed shortly afterwards. With him went the resistance to the use of 'special attack units' at the highest level. General Koiso Kuinaki became prime minister, along with Admiral Yonai Mitsumasa; in a meeting of the new cabinet in August 1944, Hirohito, who was now back at the table, approved of the production of the Ohka, a rocket-propelled piloted missile dropped onto enemy shipping from a mother ship bomber. Kamikaze tactics were about to become official policy. In the defence of the Philippines, the Sho plan called for the salutary sacrifice of 300,000 soldiers and sailors to show the enemy what kind of resistance Japan would put up in the home islands. Air forces were ordered to be more conservative, and save themselves for that final battle. The Americans, however, were reading from a different script.

## Fubuki: Falling Blossom, or Human Sacrifices?

In early October, Admiral William F. Halsey's huge battle fleet attacked Japanese air bases in the Ryukyu Islands, Taiwan and Okinawa, supported by B-29 bombers from bases in China. Over 500 Japanese aircraft were destroyed – the air forces that were supposed to protect the homeland. Halsey then turned his attention to supporting the re-conquest of the Philippines. The general staff in Tōkyō was well aware of what this meant: it was one more proof of how the Allies could defeat Japan at will using conventional tactics. The Japanese public was never told the extent of this reversal; Hirohito, however, was well briefed and persuaded his advisors that now the remaining planes should be used in tokkōtai tactics of suicide missions. On 17 October 1944, the emperor sent a convinced kamikaze strategist, Vice Admiral Onishi Takijiro, to the Philippines to present the alternatives.

Two days later, this emissary addressed the few remaining pilots at the air command centre in Mabalacat, Manila, saying that using their Zero fighters carrying bombs in suicide attacks was the only way to maximise their strengths. After a long silence, one of the veterans agreed: there was far more chance of sinking or disabling an enemy carrier with tokkōtai tactics. They slowly agreed, and volunteers began to come forward; soon there were more recruits than serviceable aircraft. Here was the birth of the kamikaze suicide squadrons. On 25 October, the Imperial Japanese Navy sent its remaining oil-starved battleships and carriers on kamikaze-style final missions designed to inflict maximum damage on Halsey's invasion fleets. At the same moment, six of Onishi's pilots were receiving final orders near Davao, on Mindanao, with this blessing: 'You are now all gods, without earthly desires . . . I shall watch your efforts to the end and report your deeds to the Throne. You may rest assured on that point.'

The first six human sacrifices were not chosen as the best and the brightest. They were average pilots, seen as expendable; their ranks over the next ten months would swell to four thousand souls. They were those deemed fit sacrifices for Japan, as the emperor procrastinated over ending the war and the fatal week in August 1945 drew near. They drank their sake and pure water: bowing to each other, with the hachimaki head cloth of the samurai wrapped around their heads, they made ready for the end. At 7.40 a.m. on 25 October 1944, the six Zeros spotted the American escort carrier fleet Taffy One, striking, damaging, but not sinking two vessels: USS *Santee* and USS *Suwanee*. The divine wind had begun to blow: a second attack launched from Luzon crippled the carrier USS *St Lo*, which foundered and sank – the first success of the kamikaze tactic. There would be no turning back – nine Japanese pilots had killed 100 Americans, damaged three carriers and sunk another. This Pyrrhic victory would spell doom for thousands of young Japanese men, including the cream of their universities – the student pilots whose diaries reveal what so many of the later conscripts really thought and felt about dying for the emperor.

A message of congratulations was sent to Onishi from the emperor, which included the somewhat ambiguous wording: 'Was it necessary to go to this extreme? The men certainly did a magnificent job.' Even here, Hirohito seems to have an eye on posterity and Japan after the war: the apparent expression of distaste, yet a response which cannot hide his pleasure. Yet not all of those flying and fighting for Japan were so minded: the famous air ace Saburō Sakai, who survived over 200 combats in the Pacific War, wrote in his bestselling account *Samurai!* an assessment of the kamikaze tactics after hearing of the Philippines mission:

> As a fighter pilot I was never inclined to approve of suicide missions . . . [yet] I had to acknowledge the fact that suicide dives appeared to be our only means of striking back at the American warships. [. . .] Again, however, it was a case of too little too late. Not even the stupendous toll reaped by the *Kamikazes* could halt the terrible power amassed by the Americans. [. . .] It is difficult to believe that many of those who flew the *Kamikazes* did not recognise the hopelessness of Japan's position in the war.

There is more to Sakai's position: he lauds these young men for giving him and other Japanese renewed courage to carry the fight to the Americans, and does not see their deaths as suicides, as lives given up in vain. In dying for their country, they were giving life to those who remained. He was eventually required to undertake kamikaze missions himself in the attacks on US shipping off Saipan, but ran into a tropical storm and returned to the base on Iwo Jima with other pilots, so surviving the war. He has stated in various interviews that it was not thoughts of glory, revenge and honouring

## Fubuki: Falling Blossom, or Human Sacrifices?

Saburō Sakai (1916–2000) was a legendary World War Two Japanese fighter pilot who survived to write a bestselling account of his exploits: *Samurai!*

the emperor that were going through his mind as he flew out on this mission, but of his family, his sweetheart Hatsuyo, and his fallen comrades. The diaries left behind by the dead kamikaze tell the same story.

There are no such records available of the private thoughts of those men who died attacking the British Pacific Fleet in the following April, as they became part of the kamikaze story. The First Air Corps had been based in the Philippines, and were forced to withdraw to Taiwan, where they formed the Niitaka Squadron equipped with the fast and effective Yokosuka Suisei (Comet) dive-bombers on 8 January 1945. The 701st Air Corps – to which they belonged – set up the 102nd Tokkōtai at Tainan air base in late March 1945, later becoming the Chusei Squadron that would fly out to attack my father's ship in April.

This account has come full circle: there are no words left behind by these six men, except for the private messages they sent to their families – postcards, letters from the bases, their wills and final words. Others, however, have left their own stories. Many such messages are now posted on websites, freely available; they tell stories that would certainly echo those of the last weeks and days of the *Illustrious*'s attackers. Of all the resources open to those who care to read them, none convey more moving accounts than the diaries of student pilots that have come to light for English readers

# The Lost Pilot

Lt Yoshinori Yamaguchi's Yokosuka D4Y-3 Suisei dives onto the carrier USS Essex, 25 November 1944. The port wing tank is trailing fuel vapour and smoke. WIKIPEDIA COMMONS.

over the past decade. This has come about through the work of a Japanese-American Professor of Anthropology, Emiko Ohnuki-Tierney, with her book *Kamikaze, Cherry Blossoms, and Nationalisms* (2002), and the more intimate follow-up to that study, *Kamikaze Diaries: Reflections of Japanese Student Soldiers* (2006). Anyone wishing to grasp what it means to be chosen to die, counting down to the day of one's death, can find all they need to know here. The account which follows – and the excerpts from the pilot's diaries – is deeply indebted to these pioneering studies.

In the last nine months of Japan's war with the West, almost 900,000 Japanese lives were lost, along with those of their kamikaze defenders, when it was obvious to their leaders that the fight was unwinnable. Yet they concealed from their own people the losses and defeats after the battle of the Leyte Gulf when the Philippines fell and the first kamikaze strikes were made. Even while resistant to the idea of defeat, most Japanese civilians were well aware that their own propaganda could not be true; that defiance at the cost of the last man, woman and child standing was a romantic and desperate gesture. The public and the private domains, however, as in Japan today, were held in separate, tight compartments. Behind closed doors, inside the privacy of their own thoughts, many knew the writing was on the wall. A post-war poll conducted by the US Strategic Bombing Survey revealed a rise from two per cent of pessimists despairing of winning in June 1944, to almost seventy per cent by the first week of August 1945 when the atomic bombs fell on Hiroshima and Nagasaki.

Many recruits to the tokkōtai units were increasingly filled with doubts concerning the cause into which they were conscripted to die. Between October 1943 and the war's end, fresh faces were drawn from schools and universities: intelligent and capable of absorbing new knowledge quickly, they could be rapidly trained to fly in an adequate fashion – then sent to their deaths, often in unreliable and antiquated aircraft using poor-quality aviation fuel. They were a readily available pool of reinforcements, the best and brightest, unable to refuse the call – the finest young minds Japan could produce. It is not surprising that those highly trained intellects turned towards analysing their own positions and that of the country they were called to die for. These intimate thoughts were kept in their diaries – a cultural tradition with strong roots in a country where it was unacceptable to speak one's true feelings publicly – leaving a unique record of the unnatural and cruel position into which they were forced.

Higher education has a way of introducing conflict between all received values and cultural norms – the family, the school, and the 'common sense' of society – with a competing tradition of critical thinking. Many a young provincial has entered university study with a mindset that would be changed completely upon graduation; the Japanese students of the 1930s were no exception. They were raised at a time when experiments in democracy were flowering and fading almost together, with confusing speed – in a society that promoted Confucian reverence and debt to one's elders, all this too amidst the newly minted Meiji Restoration doctrines of imperial divinity and obedience to authority – creating inevitable tensions. Young men in their late teens and early twenties, multilingual, exposed to Marx, Shakespeare and a huge range of Western learning, were conscripted from their studies and called upon to die as kamikaze.

Those that had been trained to think critically were now expected to accept and act upon that 1882 Imperial Rescript for Soldiers, and devote themselves to their 'most important obligation of loyalty to the emperor ... [to] realise that *the obligation is heavier than the mountains but death is lighter than a feather*' (my emphasis). Once drafted, they were brutalised into obedience by officers and NCOs alike – often happy to have the chance to humiliate their betters – while donning uniforms bearing the militarised symbol of the cherry blossom, signifying the Japanese soul. Fallen soldiers were fallen cherry blossoms, and the kamikaze units would adopt and transform this symbolism as they fell upon their enemies, apparently despising their bodies – while their souls flew to the national shrine of Japanese militarism, Yasukuni. Bushidō – the way of the warrior – had become a key element in national identity. State religion had captured the soul of Japan with a doctrine that death was preferable to life, and obedience to divine authority was the highest good; this was bound to cause conflicts in minds fresh from the study of Plato, Goethe, Nietzsche and Aldous Huxley.

As draftees, student soldiers were invited to volunteer. Almost nobody refused and stories abound of those who did refuse being 'volunteered' anyway – they were blackmailed and manipulated into doing so, unable to bear seeing their comrades going off to die while they remained behind. If anything, they died to protect their families, with few genuinely believing that their first loyalty lay to the emperor. Most knew the war was surely lost: the Americans were bombing their cities with impunity, burning Japan's urban centres to the ground. If their deaths had any meaning at all, it was to prevent whatever horrors a full-blown Allied invasion might mean for their loved ones.

There was also a fresh tradition of loyalty to companions in these small, bonded groups: those who had gone on before the living to their deaths as kamikaze (a similar tactic is used to create solidarity in terrorist cells today). It was impossible for other group members to ignore their courage; any refusal to emulate such a sacrifice was a betrayal of the group code. So they wrote to their families, wrote to their sweethearts, speaking of love and obligation, leaving behind the kind of self-censored wills Shinta Masamichi was pointing to when he wrote of the tokkōtai pilots dying as 'inujini' (a meaningless death): 'the death of a dog'.

How can we begin to imagine what their last days and nights were like before that final mission? An account of observations by Kasuga Takeo, written in 1995, forty years after the war, has a ring of truth that gets beneath the censorship and propaganda. As a naval rating, his task was to look after the student pilots at Tsuchiura Naval Air Base; he was able to see close

Imperial Japanese Navy Kamikaze Corps naval emblems: anchor and sakura.

up how they reacted on the night before they flew out to die. There were parties where sake unleashed the kinds of primal emotions suppressed until that final evening. Chaos reigned: light bulbs were smashed with swords, chairs were thrown through windows, tablecloths were torn; some shouted in rage and others cried, some danced in frenzy, others sank into despair as the wills were written. He remained haunted by these memories until his death. Japanese kamikaze were not alone in such behaviour – bomber crews in England have been reported wreaking similar havoc under the crippling stress of too many missions and seeing their comrades nightly failing to return – but few other combatants were forced, as these young men were, to live with the knowledge of the exact day they were to die.

The surviving families – those the pilots had died trying to protect – suffered agonies of loss, unable to come to terms with the wastage of their precious children. This was the next generation whose role it was to repay the filial debt to their parents and care for them in their old age – and now they were gone. All that was left were their letters, the last postcard home

– and their wills. For a fortunate few families, there were the diaries that have become so vital in revealing the humanity of these men, some of which have been published, allowing others to glimpse the thoughts and feelings of a doomed generation. Few of these have appeared in English translation until recently; Professor Ohnuki-Tierney's work has now opened the world of these young men to Western readers.

Even armed with an awareness of the background discussed here and in the previous chapter, few might imagine that a kamikaze pilot could be inspired by reading Karl Marx, and so go to his death in the hope that Japan reborn and cleansed of the virus of capitalism might arise from her purgation by destruction. Sasaki Hachirō was twenty-two years old when he died as a navy ensign on a tokkōtai mission, 14 April 1945 (he was in fact a volunteer). A brilliant student, widely read and politically engaged, he was convinced that wartime defeat was 'turning the disaster into a fortunate event' and Japan could thus be 'a phoenix which rises out of ashes'. He was well aware that he and his comrades were 'sojō no koi' ('carp on the cutting board'), but death for them could still be honourable if the result was the creation of a new Japan. One wonders what he might think of the Japan that has emerged post-1945; certainly there was no left-wing revolution, despite there being socialist political parties in the political spectrum. Capitalism and cronyism, state welfare involving the fattening of monopolistic zaibatsu corporations that had profited from the war – all were nurtured by the American occupation rulers.

Sasaki was a mix of apparent contradictions: an anti-war patriot who despised the joy expressed publicly at the early easy conquests, but one whose romantic view of an idealised Japan did not prevent him from fighting for that vision, and sacrificing his life for his country. Yet he was ambivalent, torn between living selfishly or dying for Japan: 'Sometimes my chest pounds with excitement when I think of the day I will fly into the sky [. . .] I think my life and death belong to the mission. Yet at other times, I envy those science majors who remain at home.' His romanticism and his idealism looked backwards to a primordial Japan, to the Yamato spirit uncorrupted by capitalist modernity; when this cherry blossom fell, he was spared any of the inevitable compromises life forced upon the post-war generation. The decision to volunteer as a tokkōtai offered some kind of relief for

# FUBUKI: FALLING BLOSSOM, OR HUMAN SACRIFICES?

Postcards sent home by Chiharu Nagata.

these tensions, and to that extent at least, partakes of the psychology of conventional suicide where conflicts are avoided and resolved by the taking of one's own life.

Another Marxist – and a volunteer – was Hayashi Tadao, a naval ensign shot down over Shikoku on 28 July 1945, at the age of twenty-four. An economic historian and a student of French and German literature, he too struggled with the question of the life of the self and one's duty of service to society. He was also anti-militarist, especially in regard to the effects service life had on the human spirit: 'The military kills passion and transforms a human into a cog in a machine.' In his idealism – like Sasaki's – he was calling for the defeat of the old Japan; in his patriotism, he was prepared to defend her potential for renewal in defeat. A lover of poetry, he also wrote his own: 'Why should we hesitate to give our lives [to] / Stupid Japan. / Indecisive Japan. / You, although quite foolish. / Us, who belong to this nation, / Must rise for your protection.' Hayashi was a sensitive and intelligent individual drowning in the overpowering currents of the times;

with what choices he had, he chose to fight and die, at a time when every decision was a matter of life and death.

Nakao Taketoku was a student pilot draftee, who died at the age of twenty-two on 4 May 1945, leaving an extensive diary over 700 pages long. He had read widely in the literature and philosophy of West and East, especially Buddhism, as well as the sociology of Weber and Durkheim and the anthropology of Malinowski. He was a lesser critic of the government policies than Sasaki or Hayashi, but he was deeply committed to social justice. He was also well aware, after reading accounts of military life in the First World War written by German student soldiers, of the horror and futility of war: 'Combat between human against another human, blood against blood – what else but cruelty. In the battlefield, daily witnessing friends being killed, observing grotesque slaughtering, feeling the imminent approach of one's death ...' Written in 1941, this hardly reads like the thoughts of a suicidal fanatic, blindly willing to die for the emperor's honour.

How is it, then, that such a sensitive and reflective individual would be prepared to clamber into the cockpit of a kamikaze aircraft for a one-way trip to inflict such slaughter – and die? Nakao was also something of a fatalist, aware of life's brevity: 'how lonely is the sound of the clock in the darkness of the night', he writes, a line prophetic of the anguish tokkōtai recruits experienced as they listened to the timepieces in their barracks ticking away on the walls as they struggled to sleep. He was also a patriot, but one made ambivalent by the realities around him: he had witnessed a 'victorious return' ('gaisen') at Kyōto Station, where the repatriated 'remains' of soldiers in boxes draped with white cloths bore the inscription 'We shall meet again at Yasukuni Shrine'. He was later moved to observe: 'Do soldiers utter these words without hesitation when they die in combat?' More often than not such boxes contained only a piece of paper representing the remains: obvious in the case of kamikaze pilots, but true too for the hundreds of thousands of Japanese troops who were dying unburied in the vicious island-to-island warfare that led to Okinawa, and the final surrender.

In the end, however, the idealism of his commitment to serve society overcame such struggles and he too would return to his family in just such a box. Another likewise tormented soul was Wada Minoru – a kaiten submarine torpedo kamikaze – who also shared the common longing for life, in conflict with his patriotism and a felt responsibility to defend the Japanese homeland. His death in July 1945 at the age of twenty-three when his torpedo sank and he died slowly of suffocation was one more tragic waste of life in an ocean of wastage and suffering. Again, there exists the tension between a passionate patriot, highly critical of the mechanical thinking and censorship involved in military life, and the volunteer who as his mission approached got so drunk he drank water from a flower vase and ink from an ink bottle. His *cri de coeur* could speak for his generation:

> Only one month is left to sum up my life. The second hand on the clock is moving... Up to now I have kept a calm face. But now I am frantically searching my past. I am desperately trying to find my true self without any ornament. I no longer have a self... I am seen as the bravest of pilots in my own view and that of others.

His experience of depersonalisation ('*I no longer have a self*') is a key to the way state propaganda in a time of mass warfare robs individuals of the conviction that they have the power to choose – that they are in fact autonomous human beings. This sense of unreality – in the case of the kamikaze pilots, an extreme version of what was felt at times by many conscripts in the Allied forces – is beyond the ability of civilians to understand, simply because of its extremity in the scale of human experience and endurance. No matter what external constraints were operating on men like Wada, eventually a crack would appear and release the force of pent-up contradictions: thus the smashing of clocks, the drunkenness, the drinking of ink, the admissions of despair – behaviours such as those observed by the orderly Kasuga Takeo. A final example illustrates the tensions at work between the self and the group that emerged in this extreme period of human history: a kamikaze who was a Christian, Hayashi Ichizō.

Hayashi, a twenty-three-year-old navy ensign, died on 12 April 1945 off Okinawa, a week after the attack on HMS *Illustrious*, part of a massive wave of kamikaze attacks on the American and British fleets. He came from a Kyōto family of devout Christians, parents who had converted as adults – an event very rare in Japan. As a young man, he and his friends actually went to an air base to dissuade other youngsters from volunteering – an exceptional (and dangerous) activity. Yet when he was called up as a university graduate, he joined the navy against his mother's wishes, so as to avoid the army. It was this decision that saw him eventually drafted as a tokkōtai – at which point he reflected sadly on not having followed her advice. A Christian and a patriot, Hayashi was bound to experience the conflicts already observed in other kamikaze – but with the added twist of his belief in a foreign religion that forbade him to take his own life.

He was a patriot who wanted to defend his homeland against the American bombing; yet he was unable to convince himself that he should die for the emperor. On an emotional level, his deeper conflict lay in opposing his mother's will, while affirming his own honour. The psychological and spiritual dimensions of his choices may seem bewildering to a Western mind, especially to evangelical Christians. Here is a man who promises to plunge into an enemy ship singing hymns, and citing scripture to the effect that 'For me to live is Christ, and to die is gain' (Philippians 1:21). He carried his bible and his hymnbook in the plane, along with his mother's picture on his chest, an amulet she bought him from a shrine and a Japanese flag she had also sent. He begs her to pray for him, and agonises over whether this kind of death might debar him from entering God's presence, and separate him from her forever: 'I cannot bear the thought of going to a place where you would not join me later.' In other words: hell. Hayashi is terribly conflicted; he must have endured some deeply painful moments alone on his final mission, bound for an appointment with death – and eternity.

The day before he took that flight, Hayashi had been singing hymns with friends at a nearby school; he credited his inner strength to daily bible readings, which led him to feel his mother's presence. How could he reconcile that dimension of his existence with a fatalism that said his end was decreed: 'Today, death is given to me'? In the end, death proved an escape from such contradictions: here was a believer, a pacifist at heart and yet a patriot who loved Japan, a young man who saw this course as honourable. The loneliness of such a conflict seems to lie just beneath the surface in a poem he wrote to his younger brother: 'Cherry blossoms are blooming and I am going'. However much we might try to analyse the imponderables of such a life, in the end there is only the sad truth of the poems and the last letters home.

## Fubuki: Falling Blossom, or Human Sacrifices?

USAF B-29s bombing Japan in 1945. TACHIARAI PEACE MEMORIAL MUSEUM.

A trainer of such pilots, a veteran of long years of warfare, Warrant Officer Takeo Tagata described in 2003 his own feelings when he too got his orders in 1945: 'On August 14th I received orders to commit a suicide attack, and finally I understood how kamikaze pilots were feeling. When I received [my] order, *I felt like the earth were cracking [and] swallowing me, as if my blood were flowing backward*' (my emphasis). He regained his composure and felt a new peace of mind. This is a graphic account of what many must have felt as the death sentence was delivered. The following letter from Corporal Kiyoshi Oishi is true of many unbearably poignant last messages to families and loved ones: 'My Dearest Sei-chan! It's time to say goodbye. Your brother finally makes a sortie. When you are receiving this letter I will be under the sea of Okinawa. I am sorry to leave you alone after the unexpected deaths of our father and mother, but please forgive me.'

He writes of his bankbook and the watch and sword he has sent her; sell them, he says, to get money: 'Your future is more important than my mementos.' Then this: 'The propeller is already rolling. Well, it's time to go. I am going. Don't cry, Sei-chan. I am wishing you good luck!' No trace of fanaticism here – rather, a shared humanity it is difficult to ignore. If the testimony of these men does nothing more than persuade us that what we have in common is greater than what separates us – that they were human beings in a similar predicament to my father and his shipmates, seized by the power of total war – then perhaps they have left a bequest for their former enemies, as well as their own families.

For the kamikaze, once airborne – and for those on the waiting Allied ships – it was kill or be killed. No quarter was given and none asked. Yet those who know, like the tough old ace Sakai, have claimed it was not the name of the emperor that was on their lips in those final dives, but that of their mothers – the same name in death so often heard in the mouths of their enemies, our fathers. As Hayashi Tadao wrote in his last letter home, dated 30 May 1945: 'My ageing mother to whom I cannot offer my love. I cannot bear the thought of you – my poor mother.'

There are also other sources of testimony: accounts by surviving kamikaze that emphasise our shared humanity with these men, stories that reveal

Gunsight in the cockpit of a Zero fighter – the last vantage point of the diving pilot.

them not as some faceless fanatical Other, but make obvious their likeness to our fathers who fought them. For this evidence, we can look to the impressive work of the film-makers Risa Morimoto and Linda Hoaglund, who premiered in 2007 a remarkable documentary, *Wings of Defeat*. In this deeply human document, Morimoto, the niece of a former tokkōtai pilot – recently deceased – returns to Japan from America on the trail of the kamikaze. She has become intrigued with the image of Japanese suicide pilots in the public imagination in the West, in conflict with the reality of the gentle and sensitive man she knew her uncle to be. How could such a person be a fanatic?

Her visits to Japan over a number of years – making contact with those few kamikaze who miraculously survived – form the subject of the film in a series of revelatory interviews that follow, transcribed here and used with permission. What is remarkable is the way in which these four men gradually undermine the idea that they were blind and willing sacrifices; that they were possessed of a fanatical zeal; and that they were in any way different from their enemies, when it came to the will to live and their response to a call that meant certain death. This fate they clearly saw as futile and empty, in view of Japan's desperate situation. Yet they flew out to die – and somehow came back. They had almost no choice – but fate, and in two cases sheer survival instinct, gave them another chance. The atomic bombings of Hiroshima and Nagasaki ensured that they at least would not have to die. Their post-war isolation, the loneliness, rejection, shame and guilt – as well as their anger and courage – summon up the true nature of war's effects on those combatants and civilians who survive.

In the film itself, the interviews are thematic, switching from speaker to speaker: their recruitment, training, the tokkōtai culture, the mission, survival, and the post-war experience. The following transcriptions are presented as each man's entire account, so there may appear to be overlaps, especially where two of them (Nakajima and Hamazono) were a single crew and flew out together on their attack. Many of the interviews were conducted at different times and places – for the sake of clarity, the men's testimonies are given here as a single interview. A number of sections have been italicised, as of special note.

*Wings of Defeat* DVD (2007): transcriptions. Narrator and interviewer: Risa Morimoto. Pilots: Ena Takehiko, Ueshima Takeo, Nakajima Kazuo, Hamazono Shigeyoshi.

# ENA TAKEHIKO: STUDENT PILOT

COURTESY RISA MORIMOTO.

**Ena Takehiko was drafted into the Imperial Japanese Navy in December 1943. He was assigned to the Kamikaze Corps in March 1945.**
[He meets R. M. in a park, with a shopping bag, containing documents.]
'It's difficult to explain in words. I'm a human being so it was impossible to think about my death in a casual way.

'This is the photo they took of each of us before we went on our kamikaze attacks.

'I was twenty-two when I took off. You can see the shadow of death on my face. You see, it is my funeral portrait.

'It might seem that the kamikaze attacks were very bold and courageous, but for the individual pilots, it was a very grim and painful order. It was an order that we followed out of a sense of responsibility that we had to sacrifice our lives for our country.

'In those days, we knew it was our mission – that we must fight for our country. We were driven by a sense of mission. There's no doubt that the public opinion was politically manipulated, but there's also no doubt that we were surrounded.

'Once Japan was really backed into a corner, the military was especially short of pilots. The student military deferment was ended and in October 1943 the student mobilisation was implemented and it meant we students had to join the military.

'But we didn't go with joy, or relish it.

'Japan had lost all her aircraft carriers in the sea battle at the Marianas. There was a gigantic gap between America and Japan in terms of war equipment and the performance of equipment.

'When the leaders decided that the kamikaze attacks would become the central military strategy, *I couldn't accept it*. But I also knew Japan could no longer muster a conventional attack.

'We were pilots with very little flight time or experience, to begin with. But we trained ferociously day and night. We trained for actually crashing our torpedo planes into the target. Unfortunately, our planes were extremely antiquated, so even during training, there were many breakdowns.

'Even standing at the depths of despair, all of us wanted to plunge into an enemy ship heroically. That's how we felt taking off.

'The command post is where we gathered and the commander would give us our orders. "Now you will take off for Okinawa and crash dive into a transport ship." There was a severe shortage of fuel for the planes . . . some commanders decided "they don't need fuel for the flight back anyway – just give them enough fuel to make it to Okinawa".

'When Hamazono was taking off for his mission, he downed about five cups of sake and raced to his plane. The commander who saw him off couldn't believe it: "That man is a samurai!"

'The planes were waiting nearby. We would board the planes smiling; wave our final farewell to those who were seeing us off. But the reality was when you're about to go off to die, you hardly feel like smiling.

'The first time I took off was on April 28th [1945], and then I crash-landed in Chiran with engine trouble. *I felt that my life had been spared*, for at least several days. *But at the same time as relief, there's an even greater anguish, because there's the next kamikaze attack.*

'Instead of dying at once, I'm like a prisoner twisting on the rack with more time for suffering. On May 11th, I took off again from Kushira on a kamikaze mission. This is what I wrote about taking off at that time:

After a final toast at the command post, I encounter my final hours. My doom looms, wretched and unjust. I turn towards my family's home, bidding a final farewell.

**First Light**

*I step off this earth
betraying no uncertainty
and climb into the cockpit
soon to be my casket.
A desperate warrior's will
rousing my body
I entrust my pitiful life
to an 800-kilo bomb,
then ascend, leaving only
a wake of dust.
I will plunge headlong
into a fiery hell, an
abyss of carnage.*

Kamikaze strike: USS *Essex*, 25 November 1944, off the northern Philippines.
COURTESY CHIRAN PEACE MUSEUM.

'And then our engine failed. We dropped our bombs, headed back and crashed into the sea. We weren't far from Kuroshima. We swam one thousand metres and struggled ashore. The island was totally isolated. There was almost no food to eat, the islanders were near starvation, but because we were soldiers, they let us eat their reserve sweet potatoes, so we didn't have to starve. I stayed there eighty-two days, so I had no idea how the war was going any more.

'Every day, enemy planes were flying over the island and sometimes they'd drop bombs for fun. Eventually, in the final battle for the mainland, we knew the enemy would land here too. I had to defend the island and a sense of mission as a soldier was born in me.

'On July 29th, a submarine stopped by the island – I was rescued by them. When I reported back that I was alive, we were ordered to return to our base at Hyakuri because our whole unit was in kamikaze status for the final battle for the mainland.

[Author's note: Government propaganda posters were saying, 'Everyone a Kamikaze' and 'Let's All Die Together'. The entire country was mobilised to repel invasion. The first atomic bomb fell on Hiroshima on 6 August 1945.]

'On August 7th, I arrived in Hiroshima around 10 a.m., and that's where I witnessed the devastation of the atomic bomb. I walked through that for one half-day – *in that place, my warrior spirit simply withered. It was as though I was baptised in the deep conviction that I must never engage in warfare again.* That's when I learned my lesson. For humankind, war is . . . the greatest crime of all.

'We were still extremely anxious, how the victors, the Allied forces, would treat former Japanese soldiers. We were instructed to hide the fact that we had been [kamikaze] pilots.

'We had hoped that if we sacrificed our lives, somehow our imperilled country, Japan, could survive. After the war, Japan has sworn never to engage in war again. That is why we believe we owe the peace we enjoy today to the enormous sacrifices of our fellow pilots who died in the war. This is why it is so important to me . . . to honour their memories until the end of my life. [He returns to Kuroshima, the island that saved his life, on an annual pilgrimage.]

'We do have a responsibility to tell our stories, but we have to prevent what we lived through from happening again. So we have to speak about it with great humility.

'I feel a real urgency for human beings to create a way to resolve our conflicts other than through warfare. Unless we abolish war, I believe this planet is doomed.'

## Ueshima Takeo: student pilot

COURTESY RISA MORIMOTO.

**Ueshima Takeo was drafted into the Imperial Japanese Navy in December 1943. He was assigned to the Kamikaze Corps in March 1945.**
[Shows R. M. photos.]
'They were all in my class. They all died in kamikaze attacks. I collected their photographs and made it into an album fifty years ago [i.e. in the mid-1950s].

'When the kamikaze pilots were taking off from Hyakuri, we all sent them off. It was so sad. But each of us was thinking, "It is my turn next. We're all in the same boat."'
R. M. 'Did you cry?'
U. T. 'No.'
R. M. 'Were you crying on the inside?'
U. T. 'Yes, we were crying on the inside. On the outside, we just kept smiling. I never told my parents, my mother and my father, how I really felt. I've barely talked about it with my friends. In other words . . .'
R. M. 'Why not?'
U. T. 'It's not very pleasant to talk about it. No one is going to boast, "I was a pilot, I was a kamikaze." Certainly, I rarely tell my own sons about it.

'Those of us who graduated from universities and became officers knew all about America's productivity and were aware of its industrial might. Japan doesn't have natural resources – there is no way a country without resources could win a war against America and its huge productivity.

'But we were ordered from above to go and fight in that war. *We couldn't refuse. Our hearts were filled with sadness.*

'I'd never flown a plane, so I didn't know anything about flying. There was a flight manual which we had to learn. After we were transferred to the air base, the next morning we put on our flight suits and goggles and were told to get on the plane.

'On the first day, an instructor sat in the front seat, and students like us sat in the back. Before I knew it I was up in the air . . . It felt wonderful the first time I flew up in the sky. I thought, "Oh how wonderful to fly in the sky . . ."

'On April 4th, I put all my uniforms and clothes in a suitcase and came home to Tōkyō. I returned all my belongings to my home, to leave them behind. I am only one son and my mother was evacuated from Tōkyō. I couldn't see her [to say goodbye] but I could see my father.

'And overnight, we stayed in my house. And I couldn't tell my father I am a member of the tokkōtai, no. But my father told me, "Please, keep your life very safely, and come back. Please come back to my house." *That was a very sad night* [breaks down, restrains himself].

[He changes the subject, speaks of his comrades.] 'I just waved them goodbye, thinking, "Next time, it's me." Watching my friends take off ahead of me, I kept wondering if I'd be able to take off like they did.

'Each of our planes was equipped with a high-quality radio, an all-wave radio. They [the Americans] announced how many kamikaze planes flew to Okinawa and crashed into the sea or were shot down. We heard this immediately from American broadcasts. But their reports were very different from Japanese government reports, so we knew something was very wrong. But of course, we couldn't say that out loud.

'When the Okinawa battle ended, I thought, "Oh, I made it . . ." But then, the American aircraft carriers started approaching Japanese waters, so we had to attack them. We trained every day. Our superiors ordered us to train. *We didn't want to take off but we had to. It was like that every day.*

'When the war ended on August 15th, I was shocked.'
R. M. 'Really, why?'
U. T. '*Oh, I'm alive. Still I'm living, still I'm alive* [repeats this in English].'

R. M. 'You were sure you'd die?'
U. T. 'I was sure I would die – so I didn't know what to do.

'To this day, I feel bad towards those who died, *that I survived*. That's true. But it's also true, I couldn't go with them [swallows hard, emotional].'

Ueshima Takeo poses by his Suisei dive-bomber.
COURTESY RISA MORIMOTO.

# Nakajima Kazuo: Wireless Operator/Gunner

COURTESY RISA MORIMOTO.

**Nakajima Kazuo joined the Pilot Cadet Academy in May 1942. He was assigned to the Kamikaze Corps in March 1945.**

N. K. 'None of my neighbours know that I was a kamikaze pilot.'

R. M. 'Why not?'

N. K. 'They don't know – I've never told them. It's nothing to boast about. It'd be one thing if the kamikaze strategy had been effective, but mostly they died in vain.

'And then in the end, we lost the war. *What the hell did they die for? They treated people like waste paper.*

'Look at this list of how many pilots died, in just navy kamikaze attacks [shows lists]. They all died on kamikaze missions.

'I love Japan, but that Emperor, that Emperor... *because of that Emperor, we pilots were tormented and all those men had to die.*

'So I feel conflicted about the Shōwa Emperor – by conflicted, I mean ... why couldn't he have ordered the war to end sooner? Even six months earlier. If the Emperor had said, "Enough, I'll take the blame." If only he'd said, "Let's put an end to this", tens of thousands of lives would have been spared, right?

'I saw this graffiti, "Until now, it was someone else's problem. Now I have to go, God dammit!" It was about becoming a kamikaze.

'About a week later, we found out Hyakuri training air squad was being formed into kamikaze units. They didn't waste any time. They said they would announce the flight assignments and finally they posted them.

'I couldn't believe my name was up there too. It said my pilot would be Hamazono [they were a crew]. *I thought, "I only have a few days left to live."*

'I was just a pilot trainee – I never dreamed they'd send us to the front. But Hamazono had flown in battle many times as a pilot. He had combat experience at the front. Luckily he made it back alive and was a flight instructor on the base.

'Before my kamikaze mission, I flew from Hyakuri to Kokubu and I looked down – everything was bombed out from the firebombing. I thought, "At this rate, Japan will never last."

[To his landlady, he said:] '"Japan is going to lose." [She said:] "Don't say that, do your best." [He replied:] "Japan has nothing left."

[His host family made him a doll to take on his last flight – this was common.] 'The family that looked after me poured their heart into this doll, making it for me, so I fastened it to my waist and took it with me [swallows hard].

'We all headed for the airfield. I checked my guns, Hamazono checked the bombs. We all lined up on the airfield. The commander poured sake in our cups, and said something like, "I pray for your success."'

R. M. 'How did you feel that day?'

N. K. 'I thought, *"Oh, I'm screwed!" I have to die, too, when I have so many things left to do. But if my death will benefit everyone, then I guess I had no choice.*

'Hamazono and I took off from Kokubu at 2.05 p.m. Our three planes headed for Okinawa. When we took off from Kokubu, it was a gorgeous day. I filled six magazines with ninety-eight bullets each. Our mission was hardly to fight in a dogfight and come home alive.

'I heard two explosions. Anti-aircraft fire must have hit the other two planes in our unit. With crackling fire ahead of us, I yelled, "Fighter planes!" Hamazono responded, "Roger!" As we nosedived, he dropped all the bombs.

'Rat-a-tat-tat! He slid the plane away and said, "OK, fire!" and all their fire flew to the side of our plane. That's when I realised my leg was shot up.

My face was all banged up from the ammo casings. *We totally lost our will to continue our kamikaze mission.* Hamazono said, "Let's head home", and I said, "That's a great idea, let's head home!"

[He sees Mt Kaimon on the southern tip of Kyushsu.] 'I thought, "We're gonna make it!" Then we saw army planes heading out. "You'll never make your target – you'll just get shot down. Go home, go home," is what we wanted to say to them. *Not that I had any special goal in life, but I wanted to live. I didn't want to die.*

[Returned to his unit, he hears of the atomic bomb attack on Hiroshima.] 'A few days later, another one fell on Nagasaki. I knew then that now there was no question Japan would surrender and the war would be over. When I heard about the terrible devastation later, I truly apologise to the people of Hiroshima and Nagasaki, but I thought, "Now, I can live" [laughs].

'*Because, you see, the desperation I felt when I was sent off on my Kamikaze attack and during the dogfight – I couldn't wait for them to end the war* [tearful].'
R. M. 'How were the kamikaze pilots treated right after the war?'
N. K. 'We got nothing [tearful, angry].'
R. M. 'What do you mean, you got nothing?'
N. K. 'We got nothing. Not even a thank you.'
R. M. 'Were the other pilots given anything?'
N. K. 'They got nothing. They got promoted in ranks and they built them memorials, saying they were military gods or something, but that was it.'

# Hamazono Shigeyoshi: Fighter Ace/Instructor

COURTESY RISA MORIMOTO.

**Hamazono Shigeyoshi joined the Imperial Japanese Navy in May 1942. He was assigned to the Kamikaze Corps in March 1945.**
'I'd been in seventy or eighty dogfights in the Zero fighter plane ... I was really confident I could beat most guys. I'm still that way today. I think most pilots back then had that kind of pride.

'I took off at 2 p.m., April 6th 1945 [Author's note: The same day as the attack on *Illustrious*]. Already I had my doubts. If all our eleven planes flew in formation, one could make it through and crash into an enemy ship. But over two thirds of our pilots had just graduated. The awful truth is that they didn't even know how to fly in formation.

'I wanted to become a soldier because at the time [1942], the whole character of the country, including our education, was focused on risking our lives to protect Japan. We knew this, even as small children.

'Because our instructors had the shit kicked out of them at Midway, they felt that they had to make up for that. We were trained on their vengeance.

'The training was hell. Someone was always bleeding. If we weren't bleeding, we were collectively punished, by racing, holding push-ups and starvation.

'Everyone from the commander on down thought only a third of us needed to graduate. That was their challenge. The other two thirds, they could beat to death.

'Those were the times. In order to bomb or sink an aircraft carrier, better to have one motivated pilot than three half-baked pilots. And all that strict training led us to the cockpit.

'At first I was stationed at Rabaul Air Base . . . every day we'd have dogfights with fifty or sixty American planes and we'd shoot down about fifteen to twenty planes. I thought we were better pilots than them, but looking back on it now, I was wrong. They were getting hands-on front-line training, that's what they were doing.

'Day after day, at the same time, from the same direction, thirty to fifty American planes would appear in the skies. We'd shoot most of them down, but the next day they'd be back, with ten or twenty more planes.

'From the moment I enlisted to be a pilot – before there were kamikaze – I knew that at any moment I might have to happily face death. But once kamikaze began, I knew that unless we died, no one else could save Japan.

'But long before that, I was filled with doubts. Most importantly, in America, their engineers were completely overhauling their systems, day and night.

'One time a housewife's association came to watch us train. When we took off and we flew back, they surrounded the airfield. They were all weeping, and I thought, "Oh, they understand." They were grateful for us risking our lives.

'In Okinawa, the Americans had set up a line of defence. They had the whole situation in their grasp. As soon as they shot down one squadron, the next one comes. The Americans would just shoot us all down.

'In those days, the maintenance soldiers fuelled the plane, added oil, and saluted the pilot to hand over the readied plane. I said, "Thank you", and shook his hand. Then, he started to cry. This is what he said, "Man to man – they can court-martial me tomorrow – I gave you a full tank of gasoline, so if you have trouble, come home. It's a defective plane." I said, "You're right, it's a bad plane."

'Once we passed Mt Kaimon, suddenly there were lots of clouds and it started to rain. On the western shore, I thought we'd find at least 1500 to 2000 transport ships.

'I think they came ten seconds later [after Nakajima his gunner spotted the American fighters]. They were above and behind us, but they were in Corsairs, we were in a bomber. It was no contest. I dropped the plane straight down ninety degrees.

'In one descent, we fell 2300 metres. The Corsairs had us in their radar. We escaped, but there was no way we could elude them. They formed a single line and started shooting away at us. *I was flying for my life. I didn't mind dying but I couldn't stand to lose.*

'After thirty-five minutes, the lead plane pulled way ahead of us and flew directly at us. "Here it comes, here it comes!" But their fire never came. They never fired. Maybe they ran out of ammo . . .

[He decided to turn back.] 'We're running out of fuel and oil. The plane was falling apart. I didn't think we could make it home. Then Mt Kaimon came into view.

'We crashed into a forest; we totally lost consciousness. I felt the strength of God and my ancestors. If I had been all alone when I was dying, I wouldn't have lived.

[Speaking of his dead comrades.] *'To die in an instant, in their youth, not knowing the bitter or sweet of life, I just feel so sorry for them. They were so talented and so alive.'*

**Over 4000 kamikaze died. Sixty US Navy ships were sunk and over 400 damaged; 6800 US sailors died and almost 10,000 were wounded. The British Pacific Fleet lost seventy men with thirty-four seriously wounded; no ships were lost.**

A troubling question emerges from these representative accounts: do they really sound like potential suicides? I've been thinking about this issue of suicide, suicide bombers and kamikaze now for some time and it seems obvious that the subject is clouded by a lack of precision in the language we use. What are we talking about when we say a death is a suicide? Is there some point where the voluntary passes into the involuntary and we can say this death is not a 'true' suicide – that is, an adult decision to take one's own life? A self-inflicted death, chosen because, for whatever reason,

Samurai sword belonging to Hisashi Nishida, showing sakura rosettes.
COURTESY HIDEAKI NISHIDA.

continuance of that life is felt to be against one's best interests – that life is no longer worth living?

Most of us would agree that a suicide is when adults take their own lives, having decided that there is no further point in living. Their reasons may seem irrational to us, but if it was un-coerced by others in the immediate vicinity, we can say it was some kind of free choice. What then of so-called 'suicide bombers' today, so often likened post-9/11 to Japanese World War Two kamikaze: are the children captured by the Taliban and sent into crowded marketplaces in Afghanistan and Pakistan true suicides? Is a thirteen-year-old kidnapped from his village anything more than an abused child, a victim enslaved and brainwashed into believing he will not be harmed when his hidden freight of explosives is detonated, and that his martyr's death will earn him a special place in the hereafter?

It is plain that these children are not suicides in any sense of the word: rather, they are tragic cannon fodder used by cowards whose theology is as bankrupt as their psychopathic tendencies towards power and control. The 9/11 bombers were no less sociopathic, but their deaths move closer to the realm of genuine suicides – with one exception. They were not principally acts of self-destruction designed to resolve a personal crisis, but acts of war where the combatants chose to use their own lives and the lives of others – passengers in civil airliners – to kill other civilians going about their lawful business. In the process, they gave their lives in order to further the aim of declaring global war on America and her allies.

You could say that the difference here is that while they may not have wanted to die, they were prepared to die for a cause, in the way that many other revolutionaries have done in the past (without being seen as suicidal). Such sacrificial acts are often lauded in the West when performed by those fighting for a cause we approve of. Even the solo suicide in their lonely room or on a bridge somewhere is never without some level of conflict, the underlying stress of whether to take that ultimate step. Is there, has there ever been, a 100 per cent suicidal impulse that could push aside the survival instinct and the remains of a live conscience? I doubt it. Which raises the question: were the pilots of the Japanese army and naval air arms who crashed their aircraft into Allied naval units from October 1944 until August 1945 truly suicidal?

Each of the 4000 men who died in the prosecution of this tactic were individuals with a unique history – in terms of age, background, military service, and the point in the conflict at which their mission was despatched. Think of Japan's situation when the attacks were launched en masse between Taiwan and Okinawa in early 1945: with their backs to the wall, defeat being inevitable, drastic measures seemed called for. A culture that found itself caught between the twin poles of duty and honour was facing unthinkable shame: defeat, invasion, occupation and subjugation – a kind of living death. We are familiar with post-war Japan, shorn from that pre-surrender moment by two other great forces and their scars: the atomic bombings of Hiroshima and Nagasaki, and the severing of the imperial line from the headship of national destiny. In the Japan of 1945, Hirohito was still regarded as a being of divine descent; and while conventional bombing by B-29s was killing far more civilians than the A-bombs ever would, there was still an integrity to be defended. The Yamato spirit, the ancient force of Japanese identity, was bowed but not broken.

The kamikaze – with an average age of nineteen – dwelt inside this fishbowl culture. Most Japanese had never been outside Japan, they spoke no other language, and their view of Asia and the Pacific was dominated in greater part by an insularity that could be matched in some degree by the way Britain looked at continental Europe from its island fastness: down

Those about to die: 102nd Tokkōtai, 701st Air Group, Hinschu, Taiwan, 1945.

its nose. There are some similarities between Japan's situation in 1945 and Britain's in 1940. It is possible to make an argument that the so-called kamikaze suicide units were little different in their military position than was the Royal Air Force in the summer of 1940 when the air battle began in earnest as a prelude – so Goering promised Hitler – to a speedy invasion.

Young males of my generation were brought up to view the Royal Air Force in 1940 – The Few – as glorious defenders of England's freedoms; yet, conversely, to see the kamikaze pilots of Japan as fanatical suicides, flinging themselves at Allied ships in a doomed attempt to slow the inevitable defeat of their homeland's armed forces. Yet they have many things in common: a smaller force outnumbered by a larger, better-equipped enemy; battle-hardened veterans versus young men barely out of flying school, bereft of any real combat experience; an island nation with its back to the wall, throwing everything at the oncoming enemy in an attempt to forestall a seemingly imminent invasion; a war of attrition in terms of men and materiel; acts of courage and skill which are still remembered; and finally, the reverence in which both groups of combatants are still held in their homelands, by those who do care to remember.

None of this can allow us inside the psyche of an individual tokkōtai pilot or crewman – even to sit down with them, and ask them why, could never offer to an outsider their unique experience of facing death. The excerpts from their diaries and these interviews are all we have now. Yet a deeper awareness of Japanese history and culture can help us step back, to try to understand what was behind the decision to use this tactic. Why was it that young men who had so much to live for felt compelled to die – even when these and other well-documented cases show that everything in them at some point rebelled against the futility of their deaths? If we ask these questions, then the personal will always loom up to unsettle and challenge impersonal stereotypes – that last postcard home which ends: 'I must go, my propeller is turning.'

### The departed

*there are bullet holes in the silence*
*of certain selected homes*
*black and white photographs*
*of departed kamikaze*

*grief for them is hidden deep*
*you cannot see it from the street*
*not even in the cries of the crows*
*is it possible to trace that sound*

*only perhaps in this old woman*
*who passes bent beneath*
*a protein deficiency in her bones*
*shined hollow by a life of rice and fish*

*in one house in particular*
*there will be a portrait of the old*
*emperor and in another wrapped*
*in cloth behind the shrine a ceremonial*
*sword   its golden sakura blossoms disguising*
*the blade asleep within the scabbard*

*there are certainly sword strokes and sobbing*
*deep in the night but impossible to tell*
*from where they come*

# 5

# Japan Calling

When the photograph of the attack began talking to me, I had no detailed history of tokkōtai culture; yet an awareness of Japan had long been present in my life, mostly through comics and films. Everything was seen through British and American eyes, in the shadow of a war that had ended only ten years earlier. Japan was under American occupation administration when I was born in 1947; the country was used as a base by the Allies during the Korean War, when my father – now serving in the Royal New Zealand Navy – was going ashore at the former Imperial Japanese Navy base at Sasebo, on leave with his new-found Kiwi shipmates. While away on HMNZS *Rotoiti*, he called my mother in Devonport and we spoke to him on the telephone: he promised my big brother he was bringing back 'an electrically operated motor torpedo boat' – a fabled promise never to be fulfilled. When the frigate did return, and wives and children crowded the wharf at the naval base to meet her, what we got were tinny little jeeps and wind-up seals with rotating balls on their noses.

We were pretty disgusted with these torpedo boat substitutes, but were soon charmed away by trips to the galley with mountains of ice cream served by bearded, tobacco-smelling giants. What we were really seeing, however, as tinny toys made from US Army surplus beer cans bumbled around the deck, bouncing off anchor chains while fathers played with their offspring, were the first shoots of a post-war Japanese industrial revival. During the 1950s and early 1960s, 'Made in Japan' was a byword for cheap junk, while 'Made in England' was the mark of quality (twenty years later, the reverse would be true, especially if you were buying a car or a motorbike). Our comics – especially the American ones – were full of racist stereotypes of buck-toothed banzai-charging Nips.

Dad (right) and shipmates: '1.7.52. Fleet Club Hong Kong. "Just a quiet run".'

The spate of war films that flooded the 1950s – the majority here, British – were concentrated on the European theatre of operations: *The Dam Busters* (1954), *The Cockleshell Heroes* (1955), and *Carve Her Name With Pride* (1958). There were some American movies, and my father did take us to see two that had a Pacific focus: *Mister Roberts* (1955) and *Away All Boats* (1956). Both these films showed me something of the war against Japan

– especially the latter, the story of an amphibious attack transport, launching landing craft against Japanese-held islands. I would certainly have seen but cannot remember the realistic depiction of kamikaze attacks on the ship, without really knowing in my ninth year what in the world they meant. In *Mister Roberts* – a Broadway stage success that made it to the big screen with a stellar cast including James Cagney, Henry Fonda and Jack Lemmon – a kamikaze attack near Okinawa kills the eponymous hero, off-screen. While this meant little to me at the time, it is clear from this distance how deeply the tactic had embedded itself in the American view of the war.

Books were my real education, taking me beyond the elementary, the visual, and the ever-present propaganda of an understandable anti-Japanese sentiment. In 1958, Lord Russell of Liverpool published his exposé of Japanese war crimes, *The Knights of Bushido*, a companion chamber of horrors volume to his 1954 account of Germany's atrocities in *The Scourge of the Swastika*. These books had a profound effect on me as I entered puberty: this was a world where human depravity seemed to have no end. It was this kind of documentary material that led me to doubt the aforementioned Reverend Loveridge's attempt to shift onto the Devil the blame for humanity's propensity to do evil. A kind of horrified fascination took hold of me as I stared at the grainy images; I would later try to capture this time in a poem about the pornographic quality of man's inhumanity to man: 'It was all there: the heads, the bits of blasted / bodies, horror my father was dumb to speak.'

There is little doubt that these books were determining my attitudes towards the Japanese military in World War Two; it didn't stop me in my first high-school year joining up with a campaign to write to overseas pen pals. I had one in Utah, in Zion National Park, and another in Japan, in Shiga Prefecture, east of Kyōto. I can't remember either of their names now: we exchanged letters, postcards and small gifts for two or three years until I lost interest. My Japanese friend sent me beautifully drawn maps of his home area, communicating in textbook English – he would be over sixty now, my first real Japanese person. Our geography classes in the fifth and sixth forms covered most of Asia, so I was able to learn a little more about our former enemy. Sixth-form history took me into the rise of fascism in Europe, a fascination I fed privately, buying and devouring William L. Shirer's *The*

The cover of Saburō Sakai's story *Samurai!* (1978 edition).

*Rise and Fall of the Third Reich*. Encountering books like Joseph Heller's anti-war novel, *Catch-22* (1961), and A. J. P. Taylor's *The First World War: An Illustrated History* (1963) began to teach me that war was neither heroic nor morally divisible into good versus evil, winners and losers.

I fed my long-term fascination with anything that had wings on a slew of wartime flying memoirs and technical books: *I Flew for the Fuehrer*, *Samurai!*, *Stuka Pilot*, *The Big Show*, *They Fought for the Sky* and *The Dam Busters*. Saburō Sakai's book *Samurai!* gave me a Japanese point of view on the air war; another by the French Spitfire ace Pierre Clostermann, *Flames in the Sky*, published in 1952, included an entire chapter on the kamikaze phenomenon. He had earlier written *The Big Show*, a huge international success selling over two and a half million copies and praised by no less a luminary than William Faulkner: 'the finest aviation book to come out of World War Two'. Faulkner had tried his own hand at writing about flyers, barnstormer pilots in the air-racing novel *Pylon* (1935), having trained as a flyer in the Royal Flying Corps in 1918.

Clostermann made the argument that it was not good enough to explain the behaviour of the Japanese pilots as 'Oriental fatalism'; he explored the background of the culture that could produce such a tactic, including the influence of Shintoism, the inculcation of warrior values and obedience to imperial authority. While his account is mostly a discussion of the engagements that followed the adoption of the tokkōtai tactics, and hardly revolutionary by the standards of present analysis, it was controversial enough at the time for the American authorities in Tōkyō to attempt a ban on the book. As a pilot who had experienced combat, the French writer was willing to consider examples of Allied pilots who in desperation had deliberately crashed their planes into enemy aircraft. Yet this was still not suicidal in his view, 'while a glimmer of hope still burned, however faintly' in their hearts. He was careful to distinguish such acts performed in the heat of battle from what the kamikaze pilots were doing; there is no mention at all of the conscription of unwilling men.

There was also the example of the 'Hurricats' used in convoy protection: Hawker Hurricane fighters launched from CAM-ships, converted merchantmen equipped with catapults to fire off the rocket-assisted fighters on a one-way mission to intercept marauding Focke-Wulf 200 Condor bombers that were wreaking havoc on the convoys, sinking thousands of tons of unprotected shipping. If the pilot survived the interception, he then had to ditch in the sea beside the mother ship and hope to be picked up: not strictly speaking a suicide mission, but close to it. The pilot had no certainty of his death, but the odds were well and truly stacked against him; not a kamikaze exactly, but a man willing to give his life in order to ensure his country's survival when Britain was at its most vulnerable. The pilots of 804 Squadron who flew these missions had earlier served on HMS *Furious* in Norway, with my father.

My world view was growing, changed by such reading and by chance encounters. It was those Japanese colliers spoken of in an earlier chapter that gave me my first view of the men whose people had attacked him: seamen on ships docked at the Greymouth wharf padding about the decks in their white T-shirts and sandals with white sandal socks. There were rumours that the Jap sailors (it was 'Japs' in those days) had brand-new pocket-size transistor radios they would sell to you (this at a time when bulky valve radios still dominated the market and largish portable sets were just beginning to appear). The first Honda 50 cc step-through motorcycles were appearing on the streets in 1964, as the Beach Boys sang the bike's praises in 'Little Honda': 'First gear, it's all right / second gear, lean right / third gear, hang on tight, / faster, it's all right!'

A new Japanese invasion was under way, one that would sweep away the oil-leaking British BSAs and Triumphs so beloved of my schoolboy mates, out in the workforce while I stayed on at school. It was high noon too for all those underpowered Austin and Morris cars that post-war Kiwis, short of the necessary overseas funds to buy one new, had dreamed of owning. In the next ten years, Datsun, Toyota and Honda would show us all that 'Made in Japan' now meant quality, reliability and sharp pricing. My time shearing in Western Australia in the late sixties was where I began to see it happen: returned servicemen who had fought the Japanese were set up by the government on soldier settlement farms around Frankland River in the southwest where I was working. War stories were common at that time: former POWs who spat on the early Datsun Bluebirds and Toyota Coronas, bitter and angry after the starvation and the sadistic treatment they had suffered at the hands of their captors.

Not all of them were so minded. Two of the former soldiers I worked for were driving Toyotas, and I got to try a 1500 cc Corona one of them owned. It purred along like a little clock: not quite the testosterone-inducing experience of my shearing mate's Holden Monaro V-8 with its five-litre Chevy engine and terrifying 120 mph top speed, but the shovel-snouted little Japanese car and its later iterations were about to shunt the Holdens and Fords off their macho perch. The economic zone that Japan had hoped to create through conquest was now brought into being through trade.

My next encounter with her productions was in 1972: this time, literary and linguistic, in my second year back at university, the year of Dad's death. Immersed in writing and reading poetry, I came across Matsuo Bashō's *Narrow Road to the Deep North*, a travel diary from the seventeenth-century poet and one of the major texts of classical Japanese literature. The sharp images, the economy of thought and pithy expressions, were alluring: 'another year is gone / a traveller's shade on my head / straw sandals at my feet'.

This discovery of a Japanese literary tradition was accelerated by a timetabling problem: I had taken an American Studies paper, history and literature, and loved it. Studying American writers had opened my eyes and I wanted to carry on with their stage two offering. Sadly, this was taught at 10 a.m., at the very time I was working a half-day over at Waltham in a dusty potato-packing shed, to earn enough money to pay the rent and keep my brand-new family. I couldn't resign that job, so had to find another paper in the afternoon or evening. I surveyed the available choices and settled on an introductory language course in the brand-new Japanese Studies programme: Dōzo yoroshiku! Pleased to meet you!

The staff were a mix of Japanese and English teachers. The two I recall most clearly were the head of the programme, Kinoshita-san, and Max Friedburg, whose transliterated name went something like 'Furidabaga-san'. He was interesting: of German-Jewish descent, I suspect, he had been in the air force during the war and after the Japanese surrender was a member of J Force with the New Zealand occupation troops. His linguistic abilities were recognised by his commander, who ordered him to learn Japanese so his superiors would have a translator of their own to deal with the locals. He applied himself so well that he was able to take up teaching the language on his return to New Zealand. I wish I knew more about him. He was a colourful, urbane and somewhat ironic presence in the provincial New Zealand backwater of his day.

Kinoshita-san was Japan-born and -bred of course – and, as it turned out, one of those rare birds, a Japanese Christian. I was interested in the teaching style of our Japanese lecturers: 1972 was a pretty heady time in student culture, with regular anti-war protests, experimentation with sex, drugs and psychedelia, hand in hand with an obligatory testing of the boundary fences we'd all grown up within. Not so for the students in Japanese One. It was sit down, take note, and don't talk in class – a bit like being back in primary school. The residue of a Prussian educational system and that typical Japanese respect for authority ensured that we behaved ourselves. We sensed they expected it of us, so we knuckled down and wrestled with the challenge of learning not just a new language, but a new three-part writing system: kanji, katakana and hiragana.

You had to work hard to keep up. For reasons alluded to earlier, that year was not the easiest for me to keep my concentration on study. The pressure of early rising, humping sacks of potatoes, then biking furiously from Waltham over to the Japanese department on Worcester Street didn't make for ideal study conditions – especially as Japanese demanded a good deal of work outside of class and I had two other papers to manage. After one term I decided to drop that paper and concentrate on my English and Religious Studies units. I went to see Kinoshita-san and explain; he was horrified (dropping classes did not seem to fit with the Japanese psyche): please, how could he help? I explained that having to work part-time meant I could not study full-time, and that I wasn't doing justice to all of my three papers. He pleaded with me to reconsider, so I agreed to think it over; in the end, we decided I would give up work and my wife would support me for the rest of the year.

The next time I went to the language class, Kinoshita-san called me aside into his office afterwards. He sat me down: he and his wife were very moved by my predicament, he said. In order to help with our toddler, he handed over to me two large brown paper supermarket bags full of baby clothes, explaining that his children were older now and they did not need them. As a Christian, he wanted to do something practical for me. I think he must have been praying too – I wish I could thank this kind and gentle man today. He was certainly my first encounter with the shared humanity I am now seeking with his fellow Japanese – the kamikaze. I see him now, a short, smiling figure, his round confident face beaming at me as I dig into the clothing bag, producing a Japanese Little League Baseball cap and bib overalls. 'We love baseball in Japan!' he explained; it was the influence of the Americans after the war, and now his people had taken it up as their own. Dear man.

I stayed on as a student of Japanese for the rest of that year, but alas, not a very good one: my father's terminal illness, his death in October, and the subsequent failure of my short-lived marriage had me by the year's end a valium-gobbling customer of Student Health. I couldn't concentrate on anything much – my world seemed to have imploded. The doctor advised me to apply for aegrotat passes in all my subjects, which I did – and passed. It always felt like a cop-out, and not going back the following year was the same; somewhere in the midst of my domestic chaos, the kindness of Kinoshita-san had settled on the riverbed of memory and would not be forgotten. I even retained a few greetings in Japanese, but lack of use saw most of them disappear, along with the kanji, the katakana and the hiragana. Bashō and Issa, and the history of Meiji Japan, however, were never completely lost: 'an ancient pond / a frog jumps in / the splash of water'.

During the 1970s and 1980s, the Japanese consumer revolution in our lives rolled on: Akai stereo systems, the Sony Walkman, and Canon and Pentax cameras became ubiquitous. By the mid-1970s I was working for the

National Panasonic transistor radio, 1965–68: here comes Japan.

West Coast Hospital Board as a social worker, driving a hot little Honda Civic: with its front-wheel drive and peppy 1100 cc OHC engine, it was the closest and cheapest thing on four wheels to a sports car. The board's Ford Escort was an underpowered dray by comparison: everywhere, Honda, Yamaha, Suzuki and Kawasaki road bikes were kicking British arse off the bitumen. Looking way out to sea at night from Hokitika, Greymouth or Westport and all the way up Coast Road, you could see the lights of Japanese factory ships, giant squid boats, working all the hours God sent to feed the home market's appetite for fish products. In the early 1980s, resigned as a professional helper, I would be working on the wharves in Greymouth unloading massive bluefin tuna that were laid in huge styrofoam coffins and iced up for the rapid airfreight trip to the fish markets of Tōkyō. Premium-quality tuna was sold by the matchboxful in Japan, the fishermen told me, each fish worth a small fortune.

We were becoming an extension of the Japanese economy: ever since Britain had entered the EEC in 1972, our place as an Asia–Pacific nation was clear. The transfer of our trade from the UK to Japan was simply the economic confirmation of geographical reality. The Pacific was Japan's fishing ground and her primary trading zone – a stepping stone to the rest of the world. We started selling New Zealand as a tourist destination: by the 1980s, Japanese tour buses began to cruise down the Coast Road, camera-happy groups relentlessly snapping pictures at every rest stop. In a few more years, the bolder travellers amongst them would be renting campervans, and finally rental cars, as they became confident enough to leave the group and travel solo. The next development to affect us was the booming second-hand car import trade: Kiwis who since the end of the war had experienced great difficulty in affording modern cars were now given the chance to upgrade, as savvy importers poured onto the New Zealand market containerloads of cheap late-model Japanese cars. A Japan laid waste in 1945 had, forty years on, become both symbol and reality of late twentieth-century consumer culture.

I had yet to go to Japan, but was already a fully paid-up member of the global economy she had been so instrumental in refashioning from the ashes of war. My journey towards this story had long roots: my family's involvement in one way or another had been pretty constant, since my great-uncle Hector had as a ten-year-old avidly devoured the accounts of Japan's defeat of the Russians at Port Arthur in 1894. This was not inevitable, of course, but in retrospect it is a traceable lineage. Much of this history has lain dormant, as family stories; the cultural and economic forces at work were all part of life's inevitable changes. It was not until my mother's death in 2005, and a decision to have that dramatic little snapshot of *Illustrious* and the explosion scanned and cleaned up for digital preservation, that I began asking myself the kinds of questions that would lead me to the people behind it – the dead and the living.

That photograph, cleaned up and enlarged, was framed and, with all the necessary details taped to the back, mounted above the desk in my office. I printed off a small image of Lt Yoshinori Yamaguchi's D4Y-3 Suisei trailing smoke as it fell upon the USS *Essex* on 25 November 1944, exactly three years before I was born – and blu-tacked it to the lower bookshelf at eye level. On 9 December 2009, I uploaded the scanned original to Facebook, and wrote in the Comments box: 'I've been thinking about the unknown faceless kamikaze pilots who tried to kill my father in 1945. They died, he lived – who were they? Did they leave behind children, like me?' The journey had begun: a friend replied and we exchanged thoughts; he'd lived in Japan, and he spoke of the carnage on Okinawa. Something was happening. I wrote up the proposal for a memoir and applied to Victoria University in Wellington for a residency – eventually, missing out. I was still finishing off the details for *Best of Both Worlds*, the book I'd been working on for the past two years, so I laid the kamikaze idea aside.

In early March 2010, that book was finally in my hands. On the twenty-first of the month, I wrote this:

*I was born to ye sea . . .*
*I wanted to tell my father's story, that's why – a movie would be good, you reach more people, but so far, he's ended up in a poem, that's all. And movies reach more people, but they fuck things up with sentiment and moralising. I want to tell his story, call it 'The Lost Pilot' – not that he was a pilot, but the kamikaze trying to kill him off Okinawa in 1945 was, and he missed, he got blown to pieces and my father stood on the carrier's bridge still breathing, still able to go on and survive, have children, have me, the storyteller here. What about the lost pilot, who was he? What might his children have become? That is war: the unbecoming of the unborn. I want this message to find his flesh and blood, somewhere in Japan – O my God, yes I do. Dead man, here is my father's story, a message in a bottle, to you.*

'I was born to ye sea': I found this phrase while living in London, written by an old sailor on a church door somewhere in England. It was such a striking statement that when I read it, I wrote it down for safekeeping – and now can't find it. It stayed with me as an epitaph for my father and all whose lives have been spent on the great oceans of the world. Here was an idea and a name appearing as if on schedule – 'The Lost Pilot' – the moment the previous book was released into the world. I opened a new document and wrote this: 'I have been haunted these past years by one particular photograph of my father's aircraft carrier HMS *Illustrious* being struck by a kamikaze aircraft in April 1945, near Okinawa . . .' and then began assembling a series of images to fertilise the writing. The carrier, the Suisei in flames, young kamikaze, my father and my mother – the keel of a book was laid down.

In October, with 'The Lost Pilot' as my project, I applied to the University of Waikato for the 2011 Writer-in-Residence post, and then forgot about it. You never expect to win these lotteries, but you have to keep entering; writing is work like any other profession, and you can't do it well unless you turn up every day at the coalface. For a major work of non-fiction, that means money. On the first day of November, with the *Illustrious* and the Suisei images looking on, my cell phone rang: it was John Calman, a Human Resources man from Waikato, telling me I had the residency for the next year. I hardly heard the rest of what he said: at last, the chance to do something about it – and some money, to go to Japan. With the university releasing a news story shortly afterwards, I had my first contact: an email from Philippa Stevenson, a former reporter with the *New Zealand Herald*.

She had once done a story about a former kamikaze pilot trainer – an experienced flyer, training those sent to die – who had been coming to New Zealand on peace missions since 1990. Professor Nobuya Kinase had made it his life's work to go to Japan's former enemies, his old adversaries in air combat, wherever he could locate them, seeking peace and reconciliation. He had been to America as well, and was last here in 2006; some further research discovered that he had stayed with an ex-RNZAF pilot, Keith Wakeman, and his wife Jane at Kaiapoi. Wakeman took the old kamikaze up for a spin in his private plane, a Cessna – Kinase-san was nervous about flying by that stage of his life, but he went along for the ride. The New Zealander has since died, but it seemed the professor – who has proved elusive – was still alive. This encounter encouraged me to believe there were former kamikaze pilots still out there: could I find one who would talk to me?

After the trauma of the violent 7.1 Christchurch earthquake of 4 September, the year was starting to look up again. On 19 November, the

Pike River Mine explosion cut through that euphoria: twenty-nine miners missing became twenty-nine miners dead. It was the Strongman Mine disaster of 1967 all over again – flashbacks for all of those who lost loved ones, and for any of us who remembered that terrible day. On 2 December, the nation stopped for a memorial service at the Omoto Racecourse near Greymouth. I had made up my mind not to go: there were miners still in the ground and it just seemed too soon. I chose instead to give my energy to whatever might be ahead in Japan. I spent time with Dr Kota Hattori, a postdoctoral fellow at the New Zealand Institute of Language, Brain and Behaviour on the floor below me at the University of Canterbury. He would prove a vital helper in the weeks ahead. I needed a Japanese speaker to make phone calls to Japan, to search the internet for clues – in Japanese. Here was my man: perfectly placed, from the southernmost kamikaze base island of Kyūshū and Fukuoka, its capital.

Once I'd explained the mission to him, he readily got on board, promising to email the various directors of the kamikaze museums in Kyūshū, the site of the bases from which most tokkōtai operations were launched (the attack on my father's ship came from Taiwan to the south). On 9 December, he emailed to say he'd been sent information from the director of the Chiran Peace Museum on the flights that went out on 6 April 1945, a day when 391 navy planes sortied. He'd been sent a PDF file complete with images: two photographs headed up in kanji, IRASUTORIASU – *Illustrious*. I was getting goose bumps. That evening he showed me a printout: an image of a Suisei flashing down like some enraged insect, blurred and menacing; another, the radome on the carrier's bridge, sliced in half by the wing of the plane. I could see men leaning on the signal deck where my father was standing before he dived for cover. The world had shifted a little: it felt like we were under way. Japan was beginning to talk to me.

A week later, Kota called Japan, and the director at Chiran gave him the names of some websites with details of the 6 April attacks; searching these, he came up with a site that had been created by Hideaki Nishida, the nephew of Hisashi Nishida who had died attacking *Illustrious*: more gold dust. His website has three pages on 701 Squadron and the Chusei Tokkōtai group that made the attack, with pictures of the men getting their last orders and preparing to fly. Just as precious, he has uploaded another

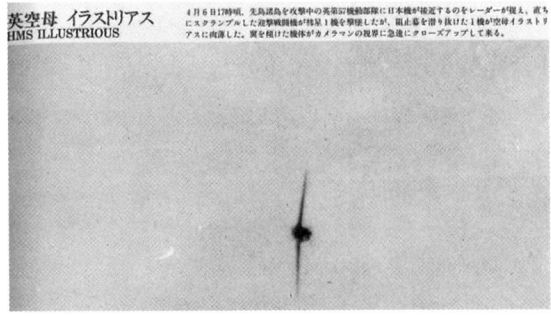

'Seven seconds to live': what my father saw coming. COURTESY CHIRAN PEACE MUSEUM.

page with the names of all six men who died that day in the attack on my father's ship. Kota, you're a genius! You've done for me what I could not do: this whole trip to Japan begins to hinge on the magic of the internet, and the willingness of a growing number of helpers to take ownership with me. There is an email address on the nephew's site, so Kota composes a message making contact – and we sit back and wait. I'm about to discover that waiting is going to be a vital tool.

Kota recommends that I post a small message on a Kyūshū social networking website, Fukuoka-now.com, using the connections link in the classified section. It's a dating site where the lonely seek partners, but is also used by those wanting to make contact with likeminded others. I write a simple message about the project, and my intended visit to Japan in April and May of 2011, to go to kamikaze museums and search for relatives of the pilots: could anyone help me? I also upload a small black-and-white image of me holding a picture of my dad on duty in the Pacific. The replies are not slow in coming: Ken, a Japanese-American living in Fukuoka, offers to help any way he can. There are many more, some curious, others practical, including an American video-maker who wants to film the journey. Neil, English, a language teacher in Kurume, makes contact; many of the foreigners residing in Japan make their living teaching the Japanese how to make sense of English. Both he and Ken will end up hosting me during my stay. I also get a reply to an earlier email, from Professor Emiko Ohnuki-Tierney, who has written so movingly on the student pilot conscripts and their diaries. She says she is no expert on kamikaze, but wishes me well and says to keep in touch.

The image posted. COURTESY ROEL WIJLAND.

By New Year's Eve, the trip has firmed from dream to possibility: I have places to stay and willing helpers. I know the names of the six kamikaze and have contacts with museums to follow up, so I can find their families. A colleague has sold me her old 1990 Mazda and the Interislander is booked: on 7 January, loaded to the gunwales, I hit the road for Picton, Wellington and Hamilton. The old car soars along on the narrow roads north and I sing; the only slight hiccup comes on leaving on Saturday morning, after the crossing. The old car coughs and dies as we pass Tawa on the motorway, shortly after I chant my mihi to Elsdon Best whose ashes lie nearby. Has the old taniwha stopped me for something I said about him in my last book?

A problem in the distributor, the AA rescue man tells me, winching the sick vehicle onto the back of his truck. He piggybacks me to Bowler Motors in Porirua, just in time to beat them closing. No chance of getting a replacement part till Monday, so I ring Roger Steele and he drives out from Wellington to pick me up; after a pleasant detour, Tuesday morning sees me and the Mazda back on track and heading for Kirikiriroa: auē, he piko, he taniwha, the great Waikato River with a chief on every bend! I make it to my board and lodgings for the next two months, at Ray and Ann Harlow's in Frankton, and begin to settle in.

Having an office and a regular pay packet at the University of Waikato is like a dream. There are no expectations except to get writing and produce something worthwhile, to validate the committee's choice of this project. Hamilton takes a bit of getting used to after the shaking we have lived through in Christchurch since last September: I keep looking at buildings as if they are about to fall down. I walk on the edge of the footpaths away from verandahs, feel edgy in lifts, and wonder why the people seem so unaware of Mother Earth's moodiness beneath their feet. Post-traumatic stress: it is going to take me a while to relax. My son and his family are visiting in February and so I book a trip home on the eighteenth. After a month in harness, with the writing under way, I'm feeling much better about the state of the world. The Japan trip is pencilled in, awaiting payment, when I fly back to Christchurch and meet the whānau at the airport the following day. Some sweet times are had with my Kiwi-French mokopuna who, at ten and seven, are just beginning to speak English with confidence.

We go to the beach, we explore the Air Force Museum; on Tuesday 22 February I am at home and they have gone to the Science Alive Museum. I have an appointment with Kota for lunch at 2 p.m., to catch up with him about news from Japan. At 12.51 p.m., I sit on the couch listening to a podcast on childhood attachment from Radio New Zealand's *Saturday Morning* programme with Kim Hill. Suddenly, the city is struck by a devastating 6.3 earthquake that topples buildings everywhere in the central business district and kills over 180 people. The house shakes as if rammed by a giant rockslide.

It is far more vicious than the 4 September shock of 2010 – because it strikes in the middle of a busy city lunch hour, with huge forces of acceleration smashing into weakened brick and stone structures, it is a killer. My son and his family are in that chaos somewhere. I try to save the television from going into orbit as glass crashes down from the broken lightshade onto the table. Getting a grip as the shock waves subside, I start to pick up the pieces, beginning with the broken glass. Well practised from September, I start taking photos of the damage for insurance claims. I comfort a weeping neighbour who staggers down the driveway. I'm feeling really anxious about my son's family in town and my wife out at the university.

Texts were erratic, but eventually, comforting messages came through:

they were all okay, and trying to get home. It would take over three hours, with flooded streets awash from the liquefaction, roads closed or choked with fleeing traffic, bridges down, and general chaos. My son abandoned their car in Gloucester Street, just across Fitzgerald Avenue, and they walked – or rather waded – back to St Albans. The sat-nav system they were using was useless in the emergency, for driving at least – but they managed to find their way home. My wife Jeanette hitched a ride, and by 5 p.m. we were all together again, and the city seemingly back where it started. Streams of refugees had been pouring out of the CBD on foot and those we spoke to, wading along the footpath, spoke of massive damage – they were sure there'd been deaths. That was the end of the family holiday: the boys and their parents left prematurely the next day for Hanmer Springs, after we had walked into town to retrieve the car. I couldn't blame them: we were getting used to it by then, but they were freaked out.

One of those who did die was an old friend, Te Taki Tairakena, Wally, my Ngāti Hāua mate who I'd known for thirty years; he was teaching English to Japanese students in a language school based in the doomed CTV building and died with his class (in the largest number of deaths on a single site). The building should never have been declared safe; this event had the negative effect of getting Christchurch onto the front page of Japanese newspapers and leading the television news. These were foreign language students who had come to safe, stable New Zealand to improve their English – only to die in an unsafe building.

It would not be long before Japan would have its own state of national mourning to grapple with. On 11 March, the massive 9.0 undersea earthquake and the following tsunami devastated Tōhoku, northeastern Honshu, and shook the whole island, sweeping away and drowning thousands in a terrifying display of natural forces that made what had happened to us look relatively civilised. Yet a life is a life: numbers don't matter to the person grieving; and somehow the two events would create for me an instant bond with Japanese I was to meet – as soon as they knew I was from Christchurch.

After the long weeks of finding and identifying the dead in Christchurch, it was time for the whānau to bring Te Taki home to Tauwhare Marae for farewell and burial. Back in Hamilton, I was able to be there, to be called on and join in the tangi amongst his Tainui iwi. We slept overnight and prepared for his final journey to the family urupā, carrying his poor human remains to his mother's marae where he was laid to rest: a prophet, and a caring brother in the faith. Ka tūtaki anō tāua ki tua o te ārai! / Beyond the veil, we will meet again. People were now questioning me as to whether I should go to Japan. I told them that Fukuoka was as far from Sendai as Dunedin was from Hamilton – of course I must go. But yes, now there was an edge to it.

The dates were set and I hit the Visa button: all that remained before leaving on 12 April was a trip to the University of Auckland to do some teaching, working with Michele Leggott in a course called Poetry off the Page. My brief was to talk about poetry in the community, specifically in this instance, the effect of the Christchurch and Japan earthquakes on my writing and what poetry might do in speaking back: 'everyone knows / one Japanese word / now: tsunami // cars: toys / houses: toys / ships: toys'. A new collection was taking place, lines rousing me in the early morning as my post-tremor wakefulness persisted.

I had another mission in Devonport too, where Michele and Mark lived beside the dead volcanoes I'd landed on in 1950. It was to go to Te Taua Moana sailors' marae for a pōwhiri arranged with the Tūhoe manager, Petty Officer Miru McLean; this would be a kawe mate, to carry the picture of my dead parents, a navy marriage, into the meeting house Te Whetu Moana. Carrying too an image of HMS *Illustrious* struck by the kamikaze, carrying the dead Japanese in there also to rest with my mother and my father. We will speak of this at the end of the journey.

This had now become a kind of dual pilgrimage: from war to peace, from quake zone to quake zone. Japan had turned into another kind of question mark, all about power supplies and travel arrangements. Back in Hamilton, emails from Ken and Neil, who by now had agreed to host me, were reassuring – Fukuoka was untouched. There were more aftershocks in Christchurch as I got ready to leave; I started to feel a kind of evacuee guilt, the sense of no longer sharing in the city's stress and suffering. And what was waiting in Japan? Would I find anybody willing to talk to me? There was no way of knowing: just live in the moment and press right on. Jeanette came north to join me; we caught a bus to Auckland and the Grafton Oaks Hotel at Grafton Gully. Japan: whatever you may be in my imagination, I'm coming to meet you in the flesh.

# 6

# On Kyūshū

**Day One: 12.4.2011. Leaving Auckland and being friendly: Mekkonen, driver, Discount Taxis.**
It's been a wakeful night with choppers coming and going into Auckland Hospital near the old hotel above the motorway: welcome to the Grafton Oaks, cheap, cheerful and noisy. I'm woken at 10.30 p.m. by a friendly farewell text from Tony Smith, *Press* sports guru – guess he's not psychic. That's what happens when you use a phone for an alarm call. Awake again at midnight, 2 a.m. and finally 4 a.m., at which point I give up and get up, say goodbye to Jeanette and head downstairs to the lobby to meet my 5.45 a.m. cab. The morning star Venus was huge and icily bright in the east over the city, seeming to move north over Rangitoto. My $35 Discount Taxi arrives early: the driver Mekkonen races through the dark city in his beat-up green Camry. He's pretty much silent, until I ask him where's he from. Africa – he's pretty monosyllabic. I press him further: whereabouts? Ethiopia. 'Ah!' I say, 'runners!' Now he laughs, 'They all say that!' – and so the real meeting, the exchanging of worlds, begins.

What did he do in Ethiopia? He was a primary teacher by training, then moved to Sudan and worked as a diplomat. I ask if he left there because of the fighting in Darfur: that was far away from Khartoum, he says. He left thirteen years ago to come to New Zealand, long before the genocide began. He tried to train here as a nurse, but needed money in a hurry to bring his family out to join him – thus the taxi-driving work. He hopes to go back and do some more nursing training; in the meantime, he works in community mental health as well as driving nights. Driver Mekkonen 3: one more highly qualified immigrant whose accent is thick, whose skin is not white. I can feel his native tongue in a wrestling match with his English: I have to work hard at times in the speeding taxi to make sense of what he is saying. He is highly fluent in English and I tell him that, which he likes.

He learned the language in Ethiopia and perfected it working in Nigeria, 'where English is the language of everyday'. He has a high regard for the English and their colonising genius, sincerely marvelling at how such a tiny island could create so great an empire. I muse on how some of my colleagues in the field of postcolonial studies would take all this: a poor downtrodden subaltern? I don't think so: this guy really likes winners.

So we talk about marathon runners (I have just read a magazine article about the young men of Ethiopia, running their legs off to find fame and fortune like their heroes). Some of the great names he rattles off are familiar to me (my West Coast inheritance here, Dave McKenzie and Eddie Gray, our local long-distance legends). He tells me of the famous Ethiopian grain called teff, which I weirdly seem to hear as 'fett'. He rhapsodises about this ancient cereal: how it powers the runners, how good it is for you when grown in the traditional way without modern fertilisers. I hear about the fine lean mutton of his native land, how our local variety is much too fatty. Somehow we get onto the thirty-four letters of the Ethiopian alphabet: how his people have their own script, not using the Roman style of the English imperialists (his people had the Italians as their colonial masters).

He's getting quite impassioned: we miss the turn into International and end up doing a few hairy manoeuvres to get back on track. He begins to recite the letters of his alphabet like tiny prayers: they burst off his lips, as exotic to me in their aspiration as an unfamiliar bird call in a new land. 'Sorry!' he says, 'sorry! I talk too much, I miss the way!' No way, Mekkonen, no way. He pulls up and says to me with perfect sincerity, 'Thank you for being friendly!' Is that all it takes: a few questions to a fellow immigrant? I give him $40 for the fare; he says it's only $35, fixed; I say, 'take it'. He's given me a sign for the journey: 'Thank you for being friendly.'

It truly is a glorious morning out there on the Māngere tarmac as we wait to go. The pure light is bathing the humped backs of the older veteran 747s and the 767-300 we'll be flying on, north. How different from our immigrant ship, RMS *Rangitiki*, leaving Southampton for New Zealand in May 1950 with its cargo of hopefuls. Jeanette texts me: there's been a new significant aftershock in Japan. What are these waiting travellers thinking, a small band of Japanese going home and this smattering of gaijin? There are plenty of seats, I notice, as the check-in operator told me, smiling: 'I'll give you two.'

The woman behind me in the departure lounge is tuning up some electronic device with its maddeningly repetitive bleeps; I have to move to another seat, just to think straight and write (a sign of how worn down I am from weeks of poor, broken sleep, my post-earthquake passenger). I'll have to get used to this in Japan (all forms of gadget chatter), so tiredness becomes a potential enemy. Me haere tātou! Let's go, get outta here! Taxiing out, I recall the words of that young kamikaze pilot written to his sister in a last letter home: 'I must go, my propeller is turning.' I can feel the shape of what's before me, the finding of a human face behind that picture. The turbines are whirring: time to go!

> *Power on! Kia kaha!*
> *Rolling out! Kia oma!*
> *Lifting off! Kia rere!*
> *Kei te piki ake ki te kikorangi!*
> *Up and into the blue!*

In the air, it was easy to see the plane was half empty; a flight attendant confirmed the reason. NZ99 is usually full both ways, with Japanese students leaving New Zealand, and those coming in. Air New Zealand normally flies the Boeing 777 on this run, a larger, newer aircraft – but with the drop-off in passenger numbers, we are back in this older 767. The earthquakes in both countries have killed off the travel market for now. Never once on this eleven-hour trip do I have to queue for the toilet – a small comfort, courtesy of the dead. I amuse myself playing peek-a-boo with a trio of rambunctious little Japanese kids and practising my greetings on the flight attendants.

Coming in over Japan, it seems more like a dream than ever: the haze over the coast, the khaki and mottled greens of the land. Seeing the white fringe of the waves breaking along the coastline, it is hard not to think of Tōhoku and that terrifying tsunami. We land without incident, and I'm whisked to my airport hotel the Nikko Narita, owned and run by JAL for those passing through – and in my case, not venturing into Tōkyō. I find my room, book myself in for an early-morning breakfast, and crash. It is still the same day I left behind in New Zealand.

**Day Two: 13.4.2011. Narita Airport, Tōkyō. Fukuoka.**
Partway through a broken night that included a wee wobble on the tenth floor of my hotel at 1.30 a.m., I was thinking of the woman I saw on the plane yesterday: a Japanese mother with three active boys who were all under six, I'd say – the youngest, and most difficult, a three-year-old toddler I'll call Sumo, for obvious reasons. He was big, tough and full of life. The older two were mild by comparison, absorbed in their electronic toys; Sumo, on the other hand, ran riot as she attempted to quiet, corral, feed and placate him. At one point he was trying to open the emergency door at 30,000 feet.

My late-night thoughts strayed onto how we can think of culture as something abstract that needs to be studied and analysed. Yet this dynamic, harried woman had given me an in-flight introduction to what it might mean to be Japanese – and in particular, a Japanese woman. She seemed to be experiencing in everything she did, not just her individual self, but an entire cultural inheritance as she marshalled, chivvied and cared for those boys over a long eleven-hour flight. Just thinking of the sheer energy she needed to carry out those internal messages of motherhood and politeness makes me tired. She was in constant motion, driven by invisible and inaudible imperatives, her plaintive 'sorry, sorry, sorry' to the other passengers framing each outburst, as Sumo howled his rage at some new frustration. The landing itself was an epic of her self-control (and prisoner restraint) as he struggled,

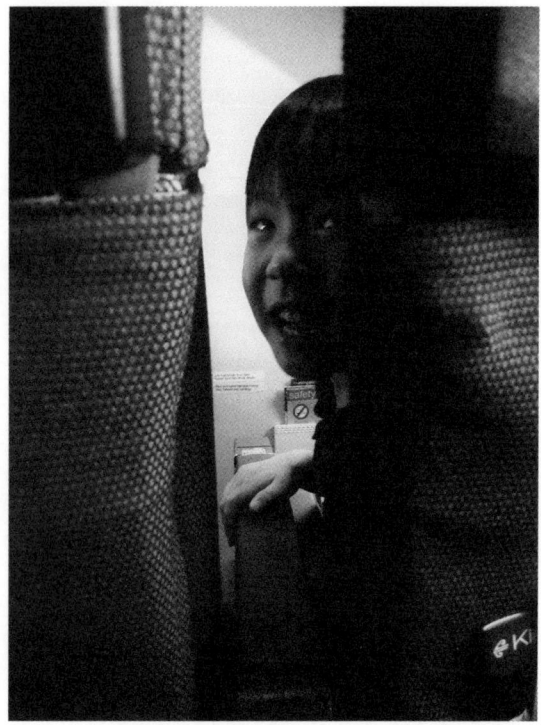

'Sumo' – my cheeky in-flight companion who tried his mother to the limit.

wriggled and bawled while we lined up the runway.

I had to say to her in the end, 'Please don't apologise, you are a wonderful mother. Travelling with three boys for such a long time is a real challenge.' I told her of my own mother's mission, bringing my brother and myself out from England in 1950: six weeks on an immigrant tub, with a two- and a four-year-old who, amongst other pranks, got up before her one morning and disappeared up on the deck, mid-Pacific.

Somehow this woman had become for me my first intimation of Japan: everything she was doing, I could expect to meet in other manifestations over the next four weeks. She was long-suffering and caring, attuned to others *in extremis*, the children and the other passengers. I never saw her do a single thing that seemed solely for herself, save for a rare break to recharge her sanity, and then only that she might be able to better deal with Sumo and his brothers. She was not simply a single self: it was as if she was carved from an invisible group, living out her role in that journey as one of a larger collective who knew how to make room for others. Culture is never simply conceptual: it is lived, demonstrated, embodied and personal – this poor woman was acting out before us a primal message from deep within about what it means to be Japanese.

I woke up to my first day in Japan. After breakfast, looking out on the swept gravel Zen gardens, it's back on the road and bussing to the airport. Immaculately uniformed security staff with their white gloves board the hotel bus at the entrance to Narita Airport and check all our passports; the approach of the personnel here is polite and low-key as well as firm – unlike some other jurisdictions. Checked in, I relax into a warm bath of Japanese politeness and honesty. I dropped a piece of paper on the way to check-in and was immediately shoulder-tapped by a fellow traveller, who handed me back my to-do list for the day. An exchange of bows, 'Arigatoo gozaimasu!', 'Ie, ie!', 'Thank you!', 'Don't mention it!' I pass a circle of All Nippon Airways employees having their morning team meeting and a pep talk. A nearby drink dispenser offers both 'Hot Drinks' and 'Cold Dorinks': in public signage, there's plenty to smile about in Japan's unique and sometimes hilarious relationship with the English language.

Airborne, in a window seat above the wing, I look out across its expanse to see embossed the red circle of a rising sun framed by the winglet at its extremity. Looking east, heading south: this was the direction in which the kamikaze took off from Kyūshū, heading for Okinawa and death. They too would have seen that once-feared symbol of their identity flashing in the rays of the sun. For me, expecting to land at this flight's end and live on, there is a special sight as we power on towards Nagoya. Fuji-san, the sacred mountain, is just ahead of us on the left of the plane. The flight attendant sits down beside me: she says we will soon see the volcano's snow-covered cone.

I have a perfect view, and plenty of opportunity to take pictures. The mountain gradually moves into sight: it reminds me precisely of Taranaki back home, except here there is a mountain range surrounding Fuji, not the green fields which set off our lone volcano in such stark relief. I manage to get a sweet shot with the 737's engine pod and the far-off snow cone appearing to almost touch, framed by the window. Soon enough we make the midday landing at Fukuoka, and at last I'm on the ground – on Kyūshū.

# The Lost Pilot

Fuji-san to the east: the flight south to Fukuoka.

Waiting to meet me at the arrivals hall in his promised red baseball cap is Ken Westmoreland, my email friend first met online at the Fukuoka-now.com website in late 2010. Ken's a slight figure, betraying a Japanese inheritance on his mother's side (but later says he can't fake walking like a Japanese, taking after his American father in the way he moves). He's already warned me about the lengthy subway and rail trek we'll have to make to get from the airport to his home in the older suburb of Kashii – towing my very heavy suitcase, I find out he's right. Thank goodness for his kindness and local knowledge: the ticket machines in Japanese, the new money, and finding the right rail line. He's taking a huge amount of stress off me by acting as my host for the weekend, my first Japanese tour guide.

On the trains we get talking: it isn't long before we've connected on many levels. Ken's several years younger than me, a man well aware of what it means to be an immigrant in a culture where he will never fully belong. He's the child of a Japanese mother who married an American GI based here during the Korean War in the early 1950s. He took her home to Nashville, Tennessee, where the poor woman, suffering from acute culture shock – and no doubt some post-war racism – had a nervous breakdown and had to come back to Japan. Ken was five years old when she disappeared from his life. He never saw her again: she died twenty-four years later.

He's had a lot of work to do and we find we have even more in common: there is much talk about healing and forgiveness on the journey. He's warm and friendly and very happy to have me stay with him. I'm here in Fukuoka till Saturday, when Neil Hall will come from Kurume and pick me up. Neil's already emailed me about their plan to drive me way down south on Sunday to meet the museum people at Kagoshima, so we can get the contact information about the families of the kamikaze aircrews. His wife and his brother-in-law have offered to drive me if I pay for the petrol and the road tolls. It's better to go with her as translator, he writes, as she is Japanese and knows the cultural nuances. I'm barely on the ground, but it's all on and looking very promising.

A historic area in the old city beside an ancient Shinto shrine, Kashii-gū was established around AD 200 as a mausoleum for an emperor; the shrine itself was begun in 724 and rebuilt in the early 1800s. It's included in the national list of first-ranked shrines, and is fully operational: every morning at 5 a.m., the priest beats a drum to announce a time of prayer as the new day dawns. Ken takes me walking in the shrine grounds as I try to stay awake from the broken sleep of the journey and arrival, adjusting to the three-hour time difference here in Japan.

The shrine and its buildings are serenely beautiful: they're very much everyday locations for worship and meditation, in a kind of parkland setting. The feeling is not at all like the confines of a church or cathedral – everything seems to be in nature, and of it, rather than standing against the surroundings as our churches often do. There are carp and turtles in the ponds, and racks of what appear to be clotheslines festooned with paper prayers and hung with ema: tiny prayer tablets decorated with the rabbits that are this year's sign. Great black crows wing from tree to tree giving

Ken Westmoreland showing me around the shrine at Kashii-gū.

voice to their thoughts, much as they have done for thousands of days over hundreds of years. Tied to a branch of blossoming cherry, there are more prayers to dispel bad luck; back on the narrow winding streets I receive the curious stares of the passing schoolkids. Who is this old gaijin? I couldn't have had a better welcome.

Ken takes me back to his tiny traditional home with its shōji paper screens and squat toilet. He rents it at a very reasonable rate, as nowadays most Japanese don't want to live this close to the past. We feast on salmon and rice for an afternoon meal, and then I climb the tiny stairs to an early bedtime. I borrow some of Ken's Rohypnol sleepers to knock me out just this once and they do the trick. I won't be repeating this: the drugs put me under for nearly eight hours, at a time when I've been subsisting on broken nights for weeks. Post-earthquake issues, pre-flight stresses – I'm damn near done in with the whole shebang.

**Day Three: 14.4.2011. Haruda: the Wallaby Language School and Dazaifu Shrine.**
Well, I made it: 4.45 a.m. on Thursday and I'm sitting up in Ken's bed (he's given me his delightful tiny Japanese bedroom with its screen walls). Wow: the Shinto drummer has started up over in the shrine at 5 a.m., which was

just what Ken said would happen. Sounds like someone banging a door, much amplified – and as dawn breaks, he's joined by the cawing of those great black crows. I eat boiled chestnuts while I wait for Ken to rise. Today he wants to take me to his morning English language class, so his students (prepared beforehand) can meet me and practise their English.

The day got well and truly going after I'd had an introduction to the traditional Japanese bath: a small tub into which you dip a ladle, wet your hair and body with warm water, then wash off the soaped mixture with more ladling. Sitting on a small stool, with no room to move, I get up close and personal with my own body. Well, it's one way of getting clean, and uses much less water than a bath or shower. His house is certainly old Japan, with something of a more rural feel in a style that the majority middle classes just don't want any more. The Japanese will knock down a perfectly good older dwelling to update on the same site with a new one: it's the land that counts, that's what's precious. Just don't get too starry-eyed about their love of tradition when it comes to being modern.

Ken's old-style house: Kashii, next to the shrine.

We have breakfast and head off to the train station for a trip through town and out into the country to Haruda, where Ken has his language classes at the Wallaby Language School (run of course by an Australian). I get to sit in on the raw beginners for one hour and the more advanced students for the second period. The four women in class one are pretty limited in their English; after introductions he patiently runs them through the drills. My job as guest foreigner is to answer simple questions and see if they can penetrate my Kiwi accent: konnichi-wa, Akina, Shoko, Hideo and Yaeko.

I try to explain what I am doing here, showing them the picture of the *Illustrious* under attack. Ken bravely has me read a couple of verses of 'As big as a father', to demonstrate the sounds of New Zealand English. We then spend ten minutes trying to explain the poem's central simile, and what it means to lose a father. I resort to Issa's famous poem for his dead baby daughter: 'the world is a dewdrop / the world is a dewdrop / and yet, and yet . . .' I am not sure if the ambiguities of Buddhist philosophy and the pain of transience are going to work here – I think they get some of what I'm trying to say. What they will make of my mission to the kamikaze museums is anybody's guess.

The next class has only two students: Fumiko, a retired pharmacist, and Shinji, a twenty-nine-year-old hotel worker. They are easier to deal with. I can tell my accent is a problem, so we do the old 'feesh and cheeps / fush n chups' Oz–Kiwi thing, to explain about Englishes and the various regional sounds of the language worldwide. They look at the picture of the ship getting hit and have to ask me some questions. Shinji is a little slower in forming his thoughts than Fumiko, who is pretty fluent – but you can see what a struggle it is for them to grasp the intricacies of English while forming their thoughts in Japanese. As a student of Māori, I'm in sympathy.

Class over, Fumiko offers to drive us to the Shinto shrine I want to visit at Dazaifu Tenman-gū, a very famous pilgrimage site where I have read you can buy those votive prayer boards: the ema. The patron saint and founder was, amongst other things, a poet and a scholar; it is very much a writer's shrine where students go to pray for success in their exams. The written prayers are then hung on wires (as at Kashii-gū), and if it all works out, the happy scholars return later to give thanks.

Fumiko zips us there in her little Suzuki Lapin (Rabbit), one of the ubiquitous 600 cc Japanese mini-cars that look like shrunken delivery vans: highly economical and practical in a densely populated country with little spare space anywhere in urban areas. Dazaifu is empty of the usual crush of pilgrims and tourists (both Ken and Fumiko express amazement at the deserted streets and quiet booths where everything is sold from food to souvenirs). It's the earthquake: the shopkeepers look forlorn as they call out to the few of us that walk by.

We enter the shrine, begun in AD 905 during the Nara period; it was built to honour and placate the spirit of the departed writer Sugawara no Michizane (now deified as Tenjin). Like the Kashii shrine I saw yesterday, it is set in ancient landscaped and manicured grounds (the precinct spans over 3000 acres); richly endowed with aged trees, willow-pattern stone bridges, carp pools and the shining statue of a bull much touched and rubbed for good luck – it is sublimely beautiful. At the shrine, I follow Fumiko in casting in some coins, bowing and clapping to attract the attention of the

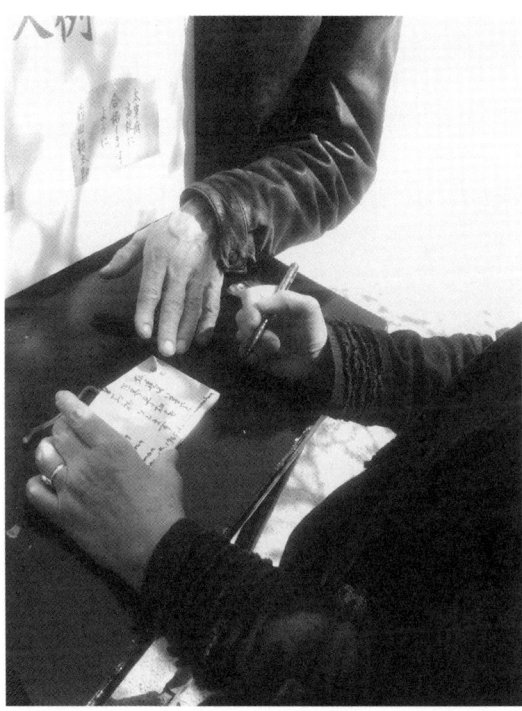

Fumiko writes a peace prayer on an ema tablet at Dazaifu shrine.

gods (in my case, a quick prayer to the Trinity: 'it's really you three I'm worshipping here!'). We wander around taking it all in and I buy my precious ema which I will carry to Ishigaki.

Fumiko kindly agrees to write a prayer on the tiny wooden tablet in Japanese: 'We pray for peace forever'; and I respond in kind with Māori. With the pressed cherry blossoms Ken has saved for me, I am well prepared to fly south to Ishigaki to sprinkle the petals on the sea and launch the ema. God willing, I will float this tiny wooden tablet covered in prayers on the waters of the East China Sea, just north of the Tropic of Cancer. I am seeking repose for the souls of those six tokkōtai flyers who died that day attacking *Illustrious*, for all the Fleet Air Arm men who died strafing and bombing the airfields on the Sakishima Gunto, for the families of those who died, and for my own peace of mind.

By now I'm famished: pilgrimage is hungry-making work. We head back into the village in search of a noodle house where they serve the famous Dazaifu speciality that Fumiko recommends: udon noodles. Turns out they're big, fat, chewy and filling. I have beef with mine, and it's not too bad. I'm shown how to slurp and drink from the bowl 'like a real Japanese' – which saves your mouth getting burned by the hot noodles as you suck them in, big time. Ahhh, that's better. We say goodbye to Fumiko after she buys us some manju – another local speciality, bean paste with plums – then drops us off at the train station.

I'm feeling whacked after the walk home from Kashii and lie down to rest. Japan is rich: yet in everything it has given me in two short days, I can't help feeling that these showers of blessing cascading down on this foreigner somehow emerge from the depths of a subterranean brokenness and pain. Ken and I discuss the meaning of freedom and order as I struggle to begin to understand why Japan happens the way it does, why those young men had to die in April 1945 – such futile deaths at the end of a war so plainly lost. The group rules here, he tells me: belonging, it seems, is more important than what we in the West might conceive of as the necessity of individual freedom. Enough of speculation: now for some of Fumiko's plum manju!

## Day Four: 15.4.2011. The Manyoshu Tanka Poem. Sakura and Mr Masuda.

After an average night's sleep and waking to more 5 a.m. Shinto drumming at the shrine, I go off exploring on my own. I tell Ken it's time I went for a walk down to the convenience store to get him some more coffee and bread – and some space for the two of us. For me as well, a breathing space away from his smoke – I'm beginning to smell like an old dried eel! I go up into the shrine first and take pictures: locals are selling plants, and the priest, fully garbed in white, plays a flute before a small shrine where offerings of fruit and vegetables have been made. This is one of the oldest Shinto shrines in Japan: Kashii, and Kurume where I will be going tomorrow, are two of the country's longest-settled sites.

Ducking the nana cars and the ever-present bicycles, I head down to Kashii centre and people-watch as I go. Nobody seems to take much notice of me, but you know they are clocking you. Japanese, Ken tells me, will avoid sitting next to a foreigner on a train: they are terrified you will ask them a question and they will have to speak English. In the corner shop-cum-dairy, there is no hesitation at the till; they talk to you in Japanese: 'Ohayoo gozaimasu / arigatoo gozaimashita – good morning, thank you, thank you', in the same run-together rapid-fire delivery. I buy a tinned coffee and bread, sorting the money as I come to the till. The smallest note is ¥1,000, which is around NZ$15 to $16, and it's easy to feel richer than you really are. I take a walk downtown into Kashii Sando, past the restaurants and the boutiques.

Strolling along, I see a sign pointing up to a monument that turns out to be the Manyoshu Tanka Poem memorial stone. A public acknowledgement of poetry, how civilised! I climb the steep track and there it is: a large upstanding obelisk, inscribed with lines from the Manyoshu tanka cycle. I've stumbled upon one of Japan's oldest poems, dating from the sixth century. There is a sign with an English translation and quotations explaining the Japanese – all this framed by cherry trees surrounding a small park and its pink sea of fallen cherry blossom petals: fubuki!

This is truly spectacular: a small, empty public square, hidden from the main road, surrounded by forest, blanketed with the thick fall of Japan's symbolic heart. I am deeply moved and take many pictures; coming back to the monument, I sit on a wooden bench and write my first poem in Japan.

# THE LOST PILOT

A woman arrives and photographs the remnant blossom on the freshets of cherry with her bright red cell phone. I stand before the stone poetry monument and pray in Māori for the souls of the Tōhoku dead, all of those swallowed up by that fearful March tsunami. While I am nodding away and talking it seems to myself, an elderly Japanese man comes by and greets me: 'Konnichi-wa!'

Sakura blossom fallen near the Manyoshu tanka monument, Kashii.

This is very unusual: he has approached a foreigner, and been respectful to this strange man. I get it right away – it's because he knows I am praying and showing respect to the poem, and I guess my sixtyish white hair helps too. 'Konnichi-wa!' I reply. This has been a very special morning. I walk back to Ken's home and tell him I now have a poem, dedicated to him. Nobody has done this for him before: he says he will get it framed (and he does). After a chicken lunch, we get ready to go into town. It's time for language class number three for 'a famous writer, who you can all practise your English on'! Ken's PR on my behalf is a bit cringe-making at times, but it's all done in good part.

This class included Mr Masuda, a former Japanese Air Force F-15 pilot. He'd also been lucky enough to survive his time flying the infamous F-104 Starfighter, notorious as 'The Widow Maker' for its habit of killing off any unwary pilot who couldn't handle its little idiosyncrasies. Google it: you'll soon see why. This tough-looking old jet jockey didn't have much to say for himself in the class, until I asked him what the F-15 was like to fly. Off he went: his English was actually very good, even though he presented as a man of few words, a man of action. The women were all pleasant and warm; one revealed she played the ukulele for a hobby to help her preserve her sanity while trying to manage her grumpy eighty-five-year-old father. We spent some time discussing what the English phrase 'set in his ways' could possibly mean.

I was asked many questions about Māori: Did they live in reserves? How could you tell them apart? Were they treated badly? Very interesting: of course, they were very familiar with the All Blacks and the 'Ka Mate' haka. Asked to demonstrate, I declined on the grounds it was for special occasions and not to be performed (badly) by random white guys overseas. They were very respectful of that. Ken had photocopied the title poem from my book, *As big as a father*, so they could hear the sounds while I read it aloud as they followed on the page.

That was interesting: try explaining a simile like that title, or 'death's head torpedoes' and 'the skiff of my father', to second-language learners. It was Ken's idea, not mine. Mr Masuda – like all the rest – said he could not understand the poem at all. When I explained carefully the concept of torpedoes and skiffs, as a hobbyist sailor his lights seemed to switch on. The others seemed to be getting some of it too. I would never have used such a poem in that situation; Ken, however, said it was good for them. They could take it away and talk about it later if they wished. He likes to bring in English speakers other than himself to break up the class routine. It lets him underline the point that it is normal to have difficulty in understanding people with other English accents, especially if you have learned your English solely from American English speakers in Japan.

Kyōko had brought some very nice cake, which we demolished with gusto; Mr Masuda then presented me with branches of double cherry blossom that I can also take to Ishigaki for the prayers at sea. They were such a lovely group, and so in farewell I sang the himene 'Tērā te manaakitanga, tērā te arohanui', and afterwards, translated the Māori for them: 'That is the kindness to strangers, the love and affection.' The ukulele lady began to sing along: it was a sweet moment.

We then took a short train trip into Fukuoka city for a meeting with

Ken's movie-making friends to end the day at the British Pub, where you can get genuine fish and chips (they were, too). It is popular with English-speaking expats and plenty of Japanese as well, by the look of the clientele. I met Ken's friend Eri, a graduate student, who works as a hostess in a bar with a second job as a nude model for life classes: she is Christian, converted by her former boyfriend. I wonder how long it will be before some zealot tells her she can't earn money by posing in the buff and flattering salarymen?

We get to chat to Mai, the waitress, another of Ken's unlimited circle (I tell her that she has a Māori name, which she thinks is very exciting); and then Kei, who works as a PA for an electronics professor at the university. It is a kind of subcultural soirée, an outing that Ken has with a group of semi-bohemian friends, young film-makers with high aspirations. More of his explanations follow: who I am, what I'm here for, and showing off my books, which he's tucked into his bag. I wish he wouldn't, but I can see why he does.

It's been another full day, and when I get home, I discover I have to sort out a slight misunderstanding with my next host, Neil Hall. It's all to do with a long, expensive trip on Sunday down to Kagoshima, and the kamikaze museum at Kanoya. Phew: emails can seem so cold and misreadings in tone are easy to create. The last thing I want is to upset my hosts – it's the same with them for me, I'm sure. An edited version of his excellent advice to me follows. I sleep well, and miss the morning drum: maybe they don't do Saturdays?


Neil Hall on dealing with Japan and the Japanese:

*Japan or rather the culture is difficult when dealing with the locals in certain situations. The Japanese themselves find it difficult too, which is why they don't speak directly for the most part. Things you will notice hopefully about Japan are:*

*Things are very tricky to do sometimes in Japan concerning talking and getting personal details. I know what to do because I just do. We will always try the 'easy way' first but things are never that simple here as you perhaps have had a glimpse of now. Getting the addresses of the two pilots was always going to be a 'royal pain in the butt'. I guess, I didn't convey that to you. There will be times when I will say something to you and it will sound really strange but there will be a very important reason for doing or saying it. That is what Japan is all about. Fifty per cent of their culture is identical to ours and fifty per cent is completely the opposite of ours. The problem is that they NEVER tell you what that 50 per cent is so you have to figure that out yourself. That alone took me five years! The other problem is knowing what to do once you have identified what that 50 per cent is.*

*Just spend today and tomorrow thinking about going to Kagoshima and I can tell my wife tomorrow. Just be sure because you CANNOT change your mind once you say 'Yes'. I have helped a lot of foreigners here so I guess I have a little experience in knowing how to go about helping you get the correct information. So, one such thing was going to pick up those contact details. The choice is go or don't go. If you don't go then you will not be able to get that info.*

*The Japanese are math people by nature, most of their speaking and writing ideals are very logical and well, math-like. Many times, my question will be very 'matter of fact' because that is how the Japanese think themselves. They are not sympathetic at all in their thinking. I can highlight that with you by using my wife as an example. Only this Kagoshima trip is difficult to know about. After this, it should be a lot easier. My wife was slightly surprised about them not giving that information out either.*

*I will be able to anticipate everything else for the most part so I will tell you beforehand. I have used this expression many times with other foreigners so I will use it one more time with you. The fastest way to do something in Japan is usually the 'slowest and most inconvenient way to do it' to us. If you try to do it the way we would do it back home, it will take three times as long. Please do not worry about anything. Once we sit down and work out a 'plan of attack' next week then things will be much easier. You will have an overall picture then we can work on the finer points as we go along.*

I'm about to find out how right he is.

## Day Five: 16.4.2011. Aftershocks back home. Farewell Ken, hello Neil and Ritsu.

Last day at Ken's for now: I pack slowly and we head into town to meet Neil at 7 p.m. On the way by train, I get a text from Jeanette: 'Just had a big one, still shaking . . .' My heart freezes a little and I feel sick: How big?

How is she? I text back: 'R u ok xx?', 'Sending prayers xxxx', feeling useless that I'm so far away. Not again! She replies: a lamp is broken, things fell off the sideboard, and the old eMac we were using to track the aftershocks has hit the floor and smashed its screen. The power has gone down in some parts of town, and the internet at home (the router fell off the table and disconnected itself). It turns out to be a 5.3. We text back and forth until things settle down and she's 'tucked up cosy' – which sounds reassuring. Will the lingering after-effects make it that much harder to trust terra firma again? Will it ever end? Will things ever return to normal? What in the world is that, anyway? Maybe this is the new normal. No more big ones here since I landed, but there are no guarantees. Even at such a distance, it shakes me up all over again. It's like the earthquake is inside me, imprinting its fingers on all my reactions.

I text her: I'll come home if need be, all the while chatting to Ken who is trying to comfort me, bless him. I start to feel really stretched, my selfish streak whining away, 'I don't need this!' Well nobody does, but here it is – so suck it and see, Jeffrey. I slowly get over myself and together we go to meet some more of Ken's friends before the handover, towing my heavy suitcase and jam-packed tote bag. It all feels very John le Carré – meeting a stranger at the Catholic church in Tenjin, this man who over the past four months I have only ever talked to by email. This must be the meaning of the kindness of strangers.

When we finally meet, it's fine: Neil is tall and talks *really* fast, towering over the smaller, slighter Japanese in the streets around us. He's brought along a Kiwi friend to meet me. It's goodbye to Ken and now I'm in new hands. It really is like being an immigrant: a kind of refugee – passed on and moved from one safe house to another. We climb into his new Prius Hybrid and head off to the very noisy Hard Rock Cafe Fukuoka to get introduced. Neil drives away to find a parking space, leaving Paul and me at the cafe: the town is packed out for a big baseball game in the Yahoo Dome Stadium next door to the restaurant. The Fukuoka Softbank Hawks are the local team and thousands of fans are packing the venue. Parking is non-existent.

It all sounds so American: yet the longer I'm here, the more I see how Japan makes over everything that comes in from outside the country into 'Japan style'. They may seem to copy imported Western culture and brands, but when you look at the people, they are resolutely from another time and place – and a very different philosophical base. The group, stupid, it's the group that counts: the very worst thing, Neil tells me later, is the crime of *not* belonging. The most un-belonging of all groups are the Yakuza, the criminals, but they are still a group with members. Not being a subtribe attached to the main tribe puts you beyond the pale in a way that Westerners cannot experience – simply because we cannot be Japanese. They are certainly different, more different than I will ever know.

Paul and I get acquainted, and Neil finally returns after parking far away. We order and eat, hardly able to hear each other in the din. My new host is a salesman by trade and preference, the London barrow-boy gene gifting him a not inconsiderable gab. He does an excellent imitation of Estuarese, the East London-cum-Essex Mockney affected by middle-class kids in the 1990s. I haven't heard anything like that for years, not since leaving England in 1997. He earns his living – as does Paul – by teaching English to Japanese students, but his heart seems to be in the buzz of buying and selling. He tells me he imports high-price, high-quality jewellery from the US, and sells it on to the mega-rich here in Japan. He's quite a character.

Neil's been in Japan for over fifteen years: he's highly fluent, and a close observer and critic of Japanese mores. It's not that he doesn't like Japan and the Japanese, he genuinely does; he just finds their unique way of doing

My Kurume host and guide: Neil Hall at Takata-machi.

things both absorbing and maddening. On the way home, I get the rundown on his wife Ritsu's special characteristics: she is not a typical Japanese woman (so it will prove, when she drives this strange gaijin on the 280-km, four-hour journey down to the kamikaze museum in Kanoya the following day). He's going to stay home and tidy the house – which he does do, often and repeatedly, I'm about to discover. By the time we arrive in suburban Kurume, I'm exhausted and overwrought – a brief introduction to his family and I'm really ready for bed.

But first, we must have the giving of the gifts: the Cadbury milk chocolate fingers for Ritsu that got me lost in Onehunga, trying to find the English Food Shop; the hair gel, the conditioner, toothpaste and deodorant for Neil – special products he just can't get in Japan. Some Kiwi lollies and Spiderman toothpaste for the kids rounds off the presentation. Despite his warning that his wife is not domesticated, when we arrive she is doing the ironing. Ritsu is a trim, no-nonsense woman: she greets me warmly, but tells me right off that the shirt-ironing ritual is a rarity! I like her straight away – she looks tough, and proves so, a country girl with a great passion for fishing. She works as a medical technician to make a living, but she'd rather be out on the Goto Islands near Nagasaki, night-fishing for kingfish. That's it, no more need for pleasantries. It's getting late and I'm well and truly past it. I fall into bed for the 4 a.m. start the next day, wondering just what is happening to me, just where I am – and why.

**Day Six: 17.4.2011. South to Kagoshima. Kanoya Air Base Museum.**
Rise and shine: up with the birds and by five o'clock we're on the road in Ritsu's big black Honda Inspire. She urges the V6 beast along the expressways with all the panache of a frustrated F1 driver who can't get past the car in front. Her English is excellent and she is seemingly not at all intimidated by this long car journey with a foreigner she has met only the night before. Easy to talk to, she drives like the wind: I lie back and watch the unravelling highway emerge from the darkness. Ritsu Hall (née Nishida) is a very unusual Japanese woman: she's actually liberated. With no desire to marry a typically chauvinistic Japanese male from Fukuoka or Kurume, she went to Australia alone in the mid-1990s to learn English. She stayed

for two years and met Neil there on a bus tour; they came back to Japan together and married. Even with their two kids, Aidan (11) and Kay (4), and a newish suburban house in Kurume, they are nothing at all like your average couple. These days, they can walk around the supermarket together without being followed by the curious citizens of Kurume – as it was when they first came to Japan together fifteen years ago.

Getting to the museum takes just over four hours of high-speed driving and plenty of chat. Kanoya is far to the south and with almost two thirds of the island to travel, the Hall family are proving to be deeply hospitable to a stranger they have barely met. By the time we get there – cruising through the gates of the Naval Air Base past the huge Kawanishi Type 2 flying boat (Allied code name 'Emily'), and the various post-war US-derived Neptunes and a rescue helicopter – Ritsu knows way more about me than I do about her. Waiting at the counter, the staff members are ready for our arrival and make us very welcome. Ritsu is straight into her new career as an interpreter for a kamikaze researcher; I can see right away she is deeply interested in this aspect of Japanese history, one she knew little of before I came on the scene.

Chiharu Nagata (19), official photograph. KANOYA AIR BASE MUSEUM.

They have all the information on the naval pilots ready and waiting, spread out before us. I see a picture of one of the young men lying on the counter, and suddenly I'm gone. I break down in waves of tears: in an instant, it is all too much. There before me is a black-and-white portrait of one of the six who died trying to sink the *Illustrious* and kill my father. I stand there sobbing and shaking: a deep grief rises from a reservoir within me I had no idea existed. It is like I have seen my own death in him. Ritsu carries on speaking to the guides as if all this is quite normal, organising our tour around the exhibits while they politely look the other way. It is the weirdest, the most cathartic experience I have had for a very long time. How can you cry like that for somebody you have never met? For a man who – had he been successful – would have made sure that I never existed, and these tears for him would never have fallen? Are they really for him, anyway?

I discover the man I was weeping over was the nineteen-year-old navigator Chiharu Nagata from Kashima-machi. The address of this family was one of those we had come so far to collect. I begin to understand why they would not give out family details over the phone, by email or fax: you have to come in person, to be seen and to see. Whatever they made of this gaijin weeping unashamedly, as if he had seen his father or his brother lying before him, I

Ritsu Hall and Nakamata-san: Kanoya Air Base Museum.

will never know. It seems in retrospect almost a set of credentials. Whoever I was and whatever this coming portended, it must have been clear to them that it mattered deeply to me to be there. Recovering a little, I give them a copy of the picture of the ship being struck for their records and they are genuinely grateful. We're assigned an individual guide, Nakamata-san: a retired naval engineer who proceeds to give us three hours of his undivided expert attention.

Guiding us from hall to hall, from the Zero fighter (immaculate) to the ranked photographs of the dead kamikaze in their thousands (heartbreaking), he kept up a patient commentary, most of which remained untranslated as Ritsu bombarded him with questions while I either looked on, or took photographs. She was making a host of notes and it somehow seemed irrelevant for me to keep interrupting her and asking questions, when it was no problem for me to work out what most exhibits stood for. I am able to ask questions, but after the emotional release of encountering Chiharu Nagata's image, I am content to look and listen. For a lifelong aviation buff like me with a preference for World War Two types and artefacts, this was a strange heaven entered through the blood of men. Ritsu didn't seem too far behind me in feeling that way either, given her intense engagement with Nakamata-san for the whole tour.

When we arrived in the Hall of the Departed (as I called it), the massed ranks of the dead aircrew were too much to take in at first. Wave after wave of faces, many of them hardly out of high school: in their sailor caps, their flying helmets; some in official portraits, others taken in the cockpits of their aircraft. Our guide walked us over to the twinned images of Yoshio Minami, the pilot of one Suisei, and Chiharu Nagata his navigator. Chiharu, a mere nineteen, a chubby-faced schoolboy under the brow of his anchor-crested cap; Yoshio, a tougher-looking twenty-five-year-old staring ahead, posed in the cockpit, fully kitted out with goggles and rabbit-furred flying helmet, conferring upon him the aspect of an ancient samurai warrior. Here they were.

In the end, overwhelmed, I had to skip all the later displays of post-war aircraft and leave my companions to it. The director, who could speak little English, came up to me as I waited in the foyer for Ritsu to finish talking. Out of left field, in broken English, he asked me how old I was (63); he then informed me very proudly that he was sixty-four! Perhaps I had made

# The Lost Pilot

Yoshio Minami (25), Chiharu Nagata's pilot. KANOYA AIR BASE MUSEUM.

a friend through my tears early on? When Ritsu finally emerged with a still fresh-looking Nakamata-san, they presented us both with framed pictures of the museum's Zero fighter; we posed then for a picture under the huge stained-glass memorial that dominates the entrance hall. With much bowing, they sent us on our way, replete and exhausted. In a word: unbelievable.

By now it is mid-afternoon and we're both very hungry, having had no real nourishment since early morning; we head into Kagoshima and park at the first available McDonald's. It's a compromise, this avoidance of the unfamiliar (not that Ritsu is complaining, as it's quick and convenient, with the long drive home in front of us). I order a teriyaki chicken burger, wolfing it down. On the road north, the gathering darkness blends with grey clouds of ash, a gloomy mist spewed by the active local volcano, Sakurajima. We skirt the coast, zooming through all of the twenty-plus tunnels at high speed. It's a sombre ending to a brilliant day; both of us are much quieter on the return journey. Tired and reflective, we are two separate islands of discovery and reflection, joined with little need to speak.

Back in Kurume there is an email from Kota at home in Christchurch: Nishida-san in Ōsaka (the nephew of one of the other kamikaze) will see me on 2 May. And now there is another Nishida-san who will also meet me on that day: the father, the pilot's brother. He is still alive! Ever since we first made contact online, I had assumed that only the nephew would be involved in a possible meeting. Suddenly, the kamikaze's brother comes into the picture. Bloody amazing, I feel like crying all over again – what will I be like when I see flesh and blood instead of photographs? Bugger it – I am crying now. Why am I mourning for total strangers? What is happening to me? Is it God crying through me? Tears on the keyboard – well, I don't care. That boy in the picture was nineteen – nineteen years old – when he died. What was my own son like at that age? What was I like? How their mothers must have wept behind closed doors and paper-thin shōji screens.

**Day Seven: 18.4.2011. Meeting the in-laws. English classes. A feast of sashimi.**
This will be my first day on my own in Japan, after the family got up and went off to work and school. They are so generous: Neil has been reduced to sleeping on a futon on the floor beside me, in his daughter's room, surrendering his half of the marital bed to her. I'm relieved to have a bit of space, to get showered in the quiet of an empty home, to catch up on emails and writing up daily accounts of the trip. I want to preserve the memories, to create a sense of immediacy when it comes to the writing back home.

After this housekeeping I head out for a walk to Lawson's, the ubiquitous local convenience store, to get some coffee. Elections are on here, and all about, mini-trucks and vans with loudspeakers invade the suburbs, shouting greetings and slogans – 'Arigatoo gozaimasu, thank you, thank you!' – but there is nobody around to listen. It's against the law – Neil tells me later – to doorstep voters. Instead, crammed vanloads of banner-waving supporters blitz the inviolable doors of suburban streets. People are not to be seen: the most visible life is when passing suburban trains set off the crossing bells and rattle on past. Kurume is an old country area, built up now, but shouldered by forested hills to the west, towards Nagasaki and the sea. Save for the different shades and shapes of the trees, it could almost be a New Zealand scene: Wellington or Dunedin.

Back home, I try napping without much success. I hear the grandfather, Tetsushi-san, bringing four-year-old Kay back from nursery school. She has been raised with the grandparents and is obviously deeply bonded. I come downstairs and greet him with a 'Hajimemashite / I'm pleased to meet you' – and bow. Sitting on the couch, he nods and smiles, cuddles his granddaughter closer, who hides from me on his chest. No English, little Japanese: there isn't much chance of any communication. After I try to reassure the little girl that her brother will be home soon, she bursts into tears. I retreat to my room to give them space, then hear his car start outside – he's decided to leave. It's sad that I could not talk to him: at seventy, he is now old Japan, a veteran of forty post-war years in the Bridgestone tyre factory (the major local employer), and tough as teak by the look of him.

Neil arrives to take me to his language class and save the day. We head off to meet the students at a local electricity company (they employ him to come to them, saving time and money). I try to imagine New Zealand companies doing the same here to teach their immigrant workers English (or their Pākehā staff te reo Māori). Neil has three students at various levels: Yanno-san, the sales manager, is the oldest and the most fluent, having done quite a bit of overseas travel. Warming up in a conversation about my country, he slyly prods me by asking if we eat raw horsemeat in New Zealand. No way! Apparently, this is his party trick with foreigners. Afterwards, he invites me out to dinner next Monday with the class members, to sample some ramen (pork and noodle soup, a Kurume special) – and maybe some raw horse (very funny)? Neil tells me this is honouring me so I must go, and go along too with Yanno-san's wit.

Back home, Ritsu has poured on the special treatment with a traditional sashimi feast, salmon (nice), octopus (uh-oh!) and seaweed (not bad). This is also an honour: fish (along with rice) is central to the Japanese diet (it's why they are so trim). It's especially significant that fresh raw fish is the dish du jour, as she is a big-time fisher who regularly gets her picture in the local fishing magazines with the big snapper and yellowtail she lands night-fishing out on Goto Island. What a feast: she is a truly excellent cook, and while thoroughly undomesticated in other areas, in creating the best of Japanese cuisine she will happily go for broke.

Neil, on the other hand – starved for English-speaking conversation and company – does the housework and complains about it, but he's really quite obsessive domestically. He couldn't stop cleaning up after her even if she was a household genie. He talks all the time he is with me and seldom stops for a breath. I do a lot of listening: he's the seasoned Japan-hand, the foreigner who has been here long enough to become as Japanese as it is possible for a gaijin to be. He's a kind of amateur anthropologist and very savvy, an autodidact deeply imbued with the philosophies and techniques of the neuro-linguistic programming school of psychotherapy. He credits NLP with saving his sanity and employs it tirelessly to order his world and that of others. Neil and Ritsu Hall: they are two great characters, perfectly suited to assist me in my mission.

After a superb meal, we get down to talking about tracing the pilots' families in Kumamoto to the south and in Yamaguchi. Ritsu debates with herself whether it is best to ring first, or just turn up – she says they might freak out, either way. She is keen first of all to arrange a meeting with the family of the navigator (Chiharu Nagata) south of Kumamoto; she's quite passionate now, fascinated in her personal awakening to the history of kamikaze. The first challenge is that there are three Nagata families in the area and she will have to call them all. What if the relatives, listening to a stranger on the other end of a phone call, just don't want to know? Well, we're here to go for broke: tomorrow she will ring and see what happens. I have this week and some of the following two weekends, then a couple of days before I leave – so we have to take some risks.

This far it's been pretty amazing and the feeling is that something good will happen. The visit to Ōsaka with Nishida-san and his father is starting to line up – we just need to finalise the date – but this is more complex. Whatever happens, we must get to see at least one family here in Kyūshū, for Ritsu's sake, for Neil's and Ken's. They have all done so much for me and I sense it would hurt her especially, if their guest went away from Kurume empty-handed. This area of Japan was the kamikaze base island – rural people, traditional, and old Japan is still in her psychology. Kurume is only eighty-five kilometres from where the second atomic bomb hit Nagasaki – Ritsu's paternal grandmother saw the strange light in the sky that day. They know something unique about war and suffering around here: the land of the rising sun where a new and terrible sun rose twice over to put an end to Imperial Japan. In so doing – by virtue of its awesome destructive power – it granted a reprieve to that remnant of doomed kamikaze, saved from squandering their lives in a lost cause.

**Day Eight: 20.4.2011. The Japanese Rail Pass. Riding the Japanese rails. Toto toilets.**

Rail Pass day! Today is my big adventure, trying to work the Japanese rail system with very limited language skills. I walk to the suburban connection and get smoked by a local grass fire burning near the train stop. The Yellow One Man Diesel Car rolls up after my ten minutes' waiting in the smoke and skiffs of rain: it is chilly for this time of the year, the locals tell me. They're right. I get on board and make my way to Kurume, asking at every approaching stop if this is the station: the usual stresses of the unfamiliar and trying out my Japanese makes for an interesting time. I want to relax and enjoy the ride, but it pays to stay alert if I don't want to end up going south instead of north.

At Kurume, I change platforms for Hakata as Neil told me to do, not bothering to pay the fare ('just tell them you want your JR Pass validated when you get there, just be the ignorant gaijin'). It's all plain sailing, right into the impressive brand-new multi-million-dollar station that took five years to build, because they could work only at night (the work was deemed too noisy to do in the city during the day). It is something special: floods of people streaming through the gates of the arrival platforms, and I really do seem to be the only visible foreigner. I find the exit gates and plough on through minus a ticket, after first sizing up a likely female attendant.

The gates give off a series of enraged 'beep beeps' at this illegal activity; my chosen official rushes over to reset them, as I wave my JR voucher and say I just want to find the office to get it validated. She doesn't bother asking where my ticket is (obviously, an ignorant foreigner), and kindly directs me to the Pass Office where it is all smooth sailing again. Now I have a spanking new passport to free rail travel in Japan for the next twenty-one days, complete with a Hokusai painting of what looks like a tsunami about to inundate Fuji-san on the cover.

Which reminds me: I have heard or seen almost nothing about Sendai since I have been here – except when individual Japanese people mention it, on hearing that I am from Christchurch. I may as well be blind and deaf to the local news media. The television at Neil's place is either switched on to kids' programmes, a diet of teen trash TV, or his UK football. I could almost forget the terrible devastation and loss of life in Tōhoku. Safe with

The coveted Japan Rail Pass for tourists, with Hokusai tsunami print.

my pass, I head off to locate the Shinkansen platform back to Shin Tosu where I'm meeting Neil later for another language class.

Eventually, I spy another gaijin, a tall white guy in a Liverpool shirt, but he's the only one in thousands: it really does feel at times like you have landed from another planet, an alien anthropologist seen and yet unseen. I know people are clocking me, but nobody stares, just the odd covert glance. I make my way to the platform: the shiny ivory worm of the Shinkansen rumbles in and halts with precision at marked gaps in the safety rails so the passengers can get off. The moment the last one exits, a team of cleaners invades the bullet train. I see the driver get out and ask him if I can take his picture. Sure: he poses and then asks to see, going off quite happy with the result.

Once on board, I drink it in: so much room in the luxury seats with their carved wooden armrests, which are actually very comfortable. We're off and I'm texting Jeanette about the experience. We plunge into a tunnel and don't come out till we're slowing down for Shin Tosu, a journey of only twenty minutes. In the dark, you can't tell how fast this thing really is, so I'll have to wait for my next long trip up to Ōsaka to see if they reach warp speed! Neil tells me later that they had to dig such a long tunnel because the land is so expensive to acquire (Shinkansen need their own wide track system, as they can't run on conventional rails).

I walk out to the exit and for the first time show my pass: a polite bow and I'm through and back on the rails again (like it used to be in New Zealand when we travelled by train and railcar). Neil meets me and we're off to the next lesson at a local power company. I'm beginning to wonder if I'm writing a book or learning to be an English language teacher in Japan. These are two more nice guys, Mori-san and Shinichi-san, who have to ask me questions and work away at their Headway books. Job done, we head home to the Hall house in Kurume, where I discover Ritsu has gone out and bought me a pair of traditional Japanese house slippers. She felt sorry for me that I did not seem to have any. How generous – and also a way of bringing me into line with Japanese domestic hygiene standards. Shoes for the world, slippers for the house: there are even toilet slippers, for exclusive use in the high-tech four-star Toto toilet that comes complete with both a seat warmer and a bidet.

In the kitchen, Ritsu has again turned on the cordon bleu afterburners and cooked superb lasagne, just to show she can do Western food too. We stuff ourselves with gusto. Afterwards, Aidan kindly brings me a special treat – his favourite dessert: green tea jelly balls. They resemble giant frogs' eggs and taste kind of, well, chewy. Not bad. I ask Ritsu about the calls to the families: today she rang a veterans' family association (like our Returned Services' Association), and talked to a man who will act as a go-between. He will ring the Nagata and Yamaguchi families for us. So, we must wait until tomorrow. She has a day off and is all set to take me to the Tachiarai Peace Memorial Museum nearby – the place where she first went to make the enquiries that led us to Kanoya, which have us now on the verge of contacting one of the families.


**Day Nine: 20.4.2011. Nagata's nephew: contact. Tachiarai Peace Memorial Museum. Paper darts.**
First things first: Ritsu calls her contact in the Veterans' Association; he

tells her he has spoken to the nephew of Nagata-san. He's told him why we want to come and meet them and the nephew's agreed to talk to his uncle, Chiharu's brother. Amazing: and now we must wait in hope until he calls back. Ritsu is excited too, even though she doesn't make a show of it. After lunch, we're off to the Tachiarai Peace Memorial Museum, a kamikaze shrine in Chikuzen town.

Tachiarai Army Air Base, close to Kurume, was established by the Japanese Army in 1919 as one of Japan's earliest air bases and Kyūshū's first. A pre-war training base for army pilots, it was used to train kamikaze and also to send bomber pilots on their missions. It was badly bombed during the war and the museum is on the old site. Ritsu introduces me to the director Isao Kitahara, who had been so helpful to her and Neil in giving them the Kanoya Air Base Museum contacts. He is very obliging and I thank him profusely – in translation of course. The tour involved hearing the history of the base, including the heavy bombing by American B-29s in 1945 (on hearing which, Ritsu spits out, 'Bastards!'). A classic Zero fighter and a rare

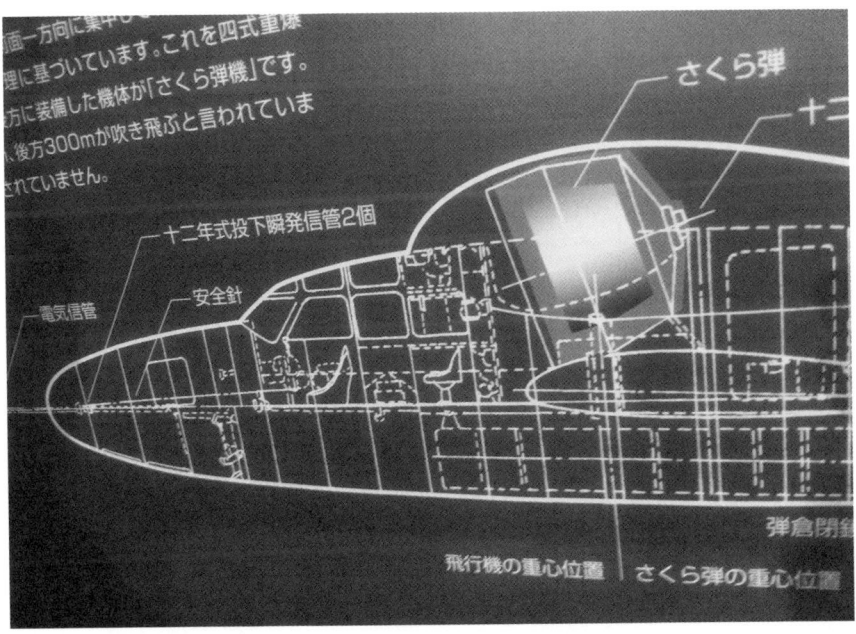

Hiryu ('Flying Dragon') Ki-167 bomber: showing massive explosive charge and detonator.

Ki-27 'Nate' fished out of Hakata Harbour were on display, but I had little time to ogle aged warbirds. I had to listen to her questions, to his replies, and then be ready with my queries.

Listening to long conversations between my hosts in Japanese, it was difficult at times to feel included and keep my focus. Kitahara-san pointed out images of the Hiryu ('Flying Dragon') bomber with its four-man crew; the version featured in these exhibits was the Ki-67-I Kai, a specially adapted kamikaze aircraft. It carried a huge 6393-lb explosive charge set behind the crew area; a long detonator rod extending through the bomber and protruding from the nose. A veritable winged dragon: this plane (Allied code name 'Peggy') was a massive flying bomb, taking its entire crew – pilot, navigator and radio operator – to their fiery doom. Their mission was to locate the American invasion fleet at Okinawa and inflict a terrifying level of damage on a scale not possible with a single-engine aircraft carrying only one bomb.

They called me over to watch a video: an interview with an elderly surviving kamikaze named Hanamichi, who lives on today in the city of Wakayama near Ōsaka. He was part of a Hiryu crew that flew down to Okinawa, only to encounter heavy cloud cover blanketing the American ships. After an intense debate the crew decided it was futile to waste the bomber on a blind plunge and kill themselves, all for nothing. They flew back to Kyūshū, landing first at the southern naval air base at Kanoya, almost out of fuel. When they finally landed at Tachiarai, Hanamichi-san confesses on the video that his legs were shaking uncontrollably, in expectation of some very severe discipline – or even death – for their shameful return.

Crews were not supposed to come back from a kamikaze mission. They were not exactly welcome in this instance but neither were they punished: harangued, ashamed, they were told to prepare for a return mission. Mercifully – for them at least – came the two atomic bombings and then unconditional surrender. Who can imagine the psychological and emotional stresses these men had undergone? Or their loneliness in the years thereafter, members of an elite band of survivors who were not meant to survive? Kitahara-san gave me the old man's phone number. I hope and pray I can meet this remarkable individual.

Back home I am making paper ninja darts with Kay and flying them with

# ON KYŪSHŪ

Hanamichi-san, survivor of a Hiryu mission, tells his amazing story on a video screening at Tachiarai Peace Memorial Museum, Kyūshū.

Aidan when the phone rings: it's the nephew of Nagata-san. He and his uncle, the surviving brother, will see us on Friday afternoon! Chiharu had five brothers, and this man, the youngest, is the last one left. What a result: Ritsu will drive me to meet them. Hallelujah! Her brother Yo-san and a friend arrive to go fishing off the Nagasaki islands; we talk and I show them my picture of Dad and the attack on the carrier. They ask Ritsu to ask me if Western people still hold grudges and resent Japan for the war. I say, no, not now: many of the old soldiers did, of course, but not my generation. We all want peace, I say. They can't grasp why I would have any feelings for the kamikaze – that someone, a gaijin, might be sad they had died so wastefully. Yo-san shrugged: they were kamikaze, weren't they? That's what they were meant for, to die – mission accomplished. Why be sad, what's not to like? asks Yo. Right there was the gulf between us.

So – I will get to meet my first kamikaze family, as Ritsu is taking the afternoon off. I want to pay her, but she says she gets paid time off work from the hospital. Without her as translator, I'd be sunk – strangely, it seems better this way than if I could speak Japanese. She *is* the culture: knows what to do and what to say, not just what words mean. Neil has also arranged for a translator in Ōsaka, a friend, so I won't have to pay a huge fee. I'm feeling overwhelmed: I cannot really express to Neil and Ritsu my sense of divine providence in all of this when they say how amazed they are at the speed with which good things are falling into place. I say I am blessed, very lucky, that kind of thing – and keep on thanking them, expressing my delight.

Another small series of miracles is my change of diet: fish, fish, fish! Rice, rice, rice! Last night I ate battered prawns: has anybody ever seen me eat a prawn? Quite delicious, served with élan by Ritsu, who would really rather be out fishing. When Yo-san came yesterday evening on his way out for a night of rods and reels, she was in another world; they sat on the floor inspecting hooks and lines, lost in the chase for the big one. This area (close to the Nagasaki islands) is like our Bay of Islands and has the best sea fishing in Japan. This morning a call came through: they caught five snapper; tonight, we will feast on snapper sashimi. I get an email from Kota telling me that Hideaki Nishida in Ōsaka has confirmed 2 May as our date to meet at the family home. I reply to this homesick Nihonjin marooned in shaky Christchurch with lavish descriptions of Japanese food, just to make him hunger even more for his native Fukuoka dishes.

**Day Ten: 21.4.2011. English football derby. Sashimi with the Nishida elders.**
Today was a hangout at home one, taking it easy. I went for a walk around 2.30 p.m. and took pictures of funny Japanese English signs: Janglish, I call it. It's kind of naïve, like a kid experimenting with language. It produces an unintentional freshness that's poetic – and hilarious. Whether it's the mysterious JoyWall, the WellBeing Mansion, or the Pooh Hair Shop, you're never short of linguistic curiosities. Like everything else here, English is promptly Japan-ised on importation.

Neil arrives home and the talk begins: a fount of local knowledge, he's making the most of having a needy English listener. He has no desire at all to be back in his native England (which he rejects) or America (which he loathes) – but can still get lonely here for the sounds of his birth culture. He needs to contact foreigners like me to allay the isolation. I listen to pick up what I need to know and avoid expending too much energy interrupting him. He's a really generous guy – between them both, I have the best possible help for a gaijin in Japan doing research on such an intimate level without the language. He also wants a mate to watch English Premier League football

# ON KYŪSHŪ

A Japanese feast: the best green tea in the country.

with him – I'm happy to oblige. We catch a sparkling three-all draw in the Arsenal–Spurs derby at White Hart Lane. Great goals, coaches having heart attacks, mass chanting – it's like being in Camden N7 all over again.

It works two ways: without them, I'd be sunk; being dependent gets me extra help and into places I would never otherwise get to go. Tonight, I get to meet both of Ritsu's parents, neither of whom can speak English. Tetsushi Nishida is from rural stock, six years old when Nagasaki was bombed and his mother saw the mushroom cloud. He has worked all his life at the Bridgestone tyre factory in Kurume, retiring as a manager, and is now a respected local elder. He is fit and lean, still working in his rice fields (they have land I'm told, so here, they are rich). Neil says the old man will be out there working in forty degrees Celsius as if it were a cool day. The hotter it is, he thinks, the better Kyūshū people like it. No wonder they've been complaining about these mild April temperatures being cold – or that the men were such effective jungle troops, in a war fought predominantly inside the torrid zone of the tropics.

His wife Asako-san is younger, a tiny old woman now; they both avoid making eye contact with me when they come in. She talks with Ritsu about the snapper sashimi for tonight's meal and he sits on the couch with his granddaughter Kay. Now I do feel the awkwardness of being without the language, so retreat upstairs to take a nap. Called for tea, I hope it will be easier – meals after all do make for intimate contact. Asako-san motions me into my place and sets up my chopsticks and plates, laying out the miso fish soup, the rice and green tea. Father comes and sits beside me: 'Itadakimasu' – 'I humbly receive'. It's time to eat.

When the sashimi arrives, I try to (i) eat my rice politely, holding the bowl correctly, and bring it to my lips; (ii) reverse my chopsticks when helping myself from the communal bowl; and (iii) pick up the slippery snapper slices without dropping them. This provokes huge mirth: Tetsushi-san is almost in fits and Yo-san is chuckling too. Being a clumsy gaijin is such an excellent icebreaker. Suddenly Father Nishida pats me on my Michelin Man tummy and chortles, 'Cholesterol!' Ha: he does know some English! I ask Ritsu to say these are my spare tyres – as a former rubber worker, he finds that very funny too. They translate for him about the earthquake in Christchurch, and so it goes: in our own awkward way, we eat and we bond. Whatever they think of my strange mission, we have an understanding now – food. He could never travel outside Japan, he says: more than three days away from Japanese food would be too much.

After the parents' goodbyes, Neil and I watch a bit of television and then I climb the wooden stairs to bed. There is a bonus with all this meeting and greeting: I'm so worn out each day by the work of communicating and being alert, I just crash. Even a small earthquake I feel at 3.45 a.m., then Neil's kitten getting under the sheets, doesn't disturb me for long or leave me wakeful for hours on end, as is the case back home. I still have to deal with symptoms of post-earthquake stress from Christchurch. Mercifully, I can drift back into sleep and get enough rest for my big day ahead: meeting the Nagata family in Kumamoto on this breaking Good Friday morning.

**Day Eleven: 22.4.2011. Good Friday at Kashima-machi.**
**Meeting the Nagata clan.**
So this is it: the big day. I finally get to meet the brother of a man who attacked the *Illustrious*. I spend the morning quietly preparing, getting all the photographs ready. Ritsu is coming back from work at midday to pick me up and then we'll be off. I relax a bit by watching television, a random activity

amongst the incomprehensible local channels. I stumble on a documentary about the famous Blue Impulse Japanese aerobatic team: a new generation of young flyers whose mission is to deliver high-tech entertainment. Now it's action stations: Ritsu arrives and prepares for the meeting by dressing up in a classy grey outfit, like she is meeting the emperor. The transformation from fishing fanatic to business executive is startling.

Neil has told me this meeting will be a big deal for her and she'll be stressed: she's never been to this area before. As well as driver and navigator, she's got a whole afternoon as my translator. Kashima-machi is about eighty kilometres from Kurume and we'll have over an hour's driving to get there. We buckle into the big black Honda V6 and hit the road running. First we need petrol and to get through the tollgates: then it's flat-out all the way, hitting 150 kph. To save freaking out, I just pray. It's wet, we're flying low and Ritsu is determined to get there by two o'clock – dead or alive. I start to think, 'Well, if I've come all this way to die in a Japanese highway pileup, so be it' – but it isn't easy to stay calm. I've got my own set of stresses about this meeting. Sometimes handing over control feels dangerous – and this time, it really is.

We have a short stop at a service centre with a mall, to buy the necessary gifts: two green tea cakes to respect the gravity of the occasion. I'm relieved when the off-ramp for Kashima-machi shows up and we can leave the speedway. We've passed everything so far, and now we have to join the slow traffic. She's a really good driver, but the other guy – you just never know. Now to find the house: we streak along as Ritsu drives and consults the map. What I don't remember until later is that because she's a smoker, she is getting even more stressed because she can't light up, which only adds to the pressure. By the time we finish down here, she'll have been nicotine-free and in withdrawal for six long hours.

She's having real trouble finding the house: keeps looking at the Google Maps printout and talking to herself – in Japanese, of course. Eventually, we find what should be the place but there's nobody there – we end up asking for directions at a small local bar-cum-shop. Next stop is a bunch of long plastic hothouses where the farmer should be but there's no sign of life here. We cross the river, searching all around: she's lost. I'm beginning to think we may not find them, but *nil desperandum*. We stop and ask some road workers if they know where the Nagata family live: Hai! Yes, they do!

They point to it – there's the house, back there, by the rice field! Arigatoo gozaimasu – thank you so much!

Getting in there proves to be a mission, too: another road crew is blocking the tiny track. We end up reversing in down a long curving grassy path. When we finally pull up at the farmhouse, an old German shepherd dog goes crazy on the end of his chain. A woman appears, a farm worker dressed with apron and gloves. Ritsu begins the complex explanation of who we are and the woman brightens in amazement: she is Tsuyako Nagata, the nephew's wife – sweet and helpful. She knew we were coming. She calls to her husband walking up the track towards us, a slim wiry man, his face lined deep by a lifetime's exposure to sun, wind and rain. This is Hideharu Nagata, named we later discover by the man who died on 6 April 1945 – his uncle Chiharu.

They ask us inside and I grab the green tea cake gift boxes. At the door, I'm careful to remove my shoes and place them in the middle of the foyer facing out, as Neil has taught me. This shows respect and also local smarts, it seems. We enter the first room and behold the portrait gallery of the ancestors: there is Chiharu, with his parents and another brother on the wall. At last: inside the home. Hideharu, in a flurry of bowing and greetings, removes the portrait of Chiharu his uncle from the wall and begins taking out the three images in the frame. No standing on ceremony here.

Named by his kamikaze uncle Chiharu before his final mission, Hideharu Nagata points to the parents in the family gallery.

First comes the heroic version of the young fighter: the silk scarf, half hiding his serious stare, goggles skew-whiff on his flying helmet – and the death sentence, his final orders, held beneath his chin. Then his official kamikaze record: a contemporary document, most likely sent to the family from Kanoya. And finally, a picture of a twin-engine Mitsubishi bomber on which he did some of his training. This family is not holding back – I ask if I can take pictures and yes, that's fine. Ritsu then disappears into the room next door and I hear a small bell struck and sounds of murmuring. It is the family shrine: she is in there, praying, paying respects.

Once more I have struck it rich with this amazing woman: she is fully at home in this rural, one-time peasant culture, yet she is also a sophisticated English-speaking world traveller, dressed as if for an imperial audience. Shades of the divine past: the old wartime emperor, Hirohito, and the empress gaze down from the opposite wall, facing black-and-white images of Chiharu's parents and another of his five brothers. It is like a smaller version of a wharenui back home on rural marae: the pōwhiri has begun. I have come into the body of the ancestor.

Hideharu ushers us into the family room where Tsuyako has been preparing tea and tasty treats for the guests. I look at the low table and the cushions and realise I have made it back to another Japan – neither Ken's at Kashii nor the Halls' of Kurume. Trying to sit on the cushions on the floor, my rusty knees won't fold beneath me so I have to kneel or sit awkwardly side-saddle. We sip the proffered green tea. I ask Ritsu if it is fine now to present the photos I have brought: the *Illustrious* picture, Dad on the bridge, and the ship's crest. She gives me the all-clear and I pass them over to Hideharu, while Ritsu explains what they are. Tsuyako takes one look at the image of the plane hitting the carrier and begins to weep. She gets up, gripping the picture, and takes it into the family shrine.

After all these years, they are faced with the moment two of those six men died. We cannot be sure it is Chiharu and his pilot, Yoshio Minami. There were no surviving Japanese witnesses, of course – but we can't be sure either that it isn't them. Somewhere within that time and space, this is an image of where those three planes went down, one after the other in quick succession. Families of the war dead never get to see the moment their loved one dies – many would not wish to. The emotion in the room is palpable. Ritsu keeps

# THE LOST PILOT

on talking as Hideharu nods and examines the other pictures while Tsuyako blows her nose and dries her eyes. This is why I came: whether they know it or not, they are my Japanese family, bound to me by the blood of that day.

There is a movement at the door: Tsuyako goes to welcome the next guests, Chiharu's brother Teruyuki and his wife Shizuko. They are tiny elderly people, immaculately dressed for the occasion, and full of bows as usual. They sit and we exchange pleasantries; Ritsu begins again the patient explanations. As I have come to expect, the verbal exchanges are between each Japanese speaker, not with me. They listen to her, staring intently and then replying. I only seem to get noticed when she translates something for me, which as the meeting warms up, gets more infrequent. A born-and-bred country girl, she speaks their dialect and they get on famously. There are laughs and smiles all around, no sense at all that this solemn meeting needs to be unhappy.

Teruyuki is a retired school principal, a teacher of Japanese; his wife is a calligraphy teacher. They are educated people, dressed neatly and with great

The family of Chiharu Nagata. Left to right: Hideharu (nephew), Tsuyako (his wife), Teruyuki (Chiharu's younger brother), Shizuko (his wife), and Ritsu Hall (driver and translator). They are reading Chiharu's postcards home.

208

style: in his sports coat and sweater, he reminds me of my schoolteachers, circa 1963, and she has the same classy but dated couture. I'm glad to see that after half an hour, he too must rearrange his legs, age getting the better of the supple posture that enables hours of squatting on haunches. His hair is iron-grey and neatly parted: he must be over eighty but looks forever young, slim and lean, like many older Japanese I see. They are an impressive couple, both mild and yet willow strong.

They examine the pictures, taking them in: Tsuyako goes to the shrine and retrieves the *Illustrious*'s picture so they can see the image of the strike. In a vain attempt to validate Chiharu's sacrifice and the family's loss, I explain to Ritsu that although the carrier was not sunk on the day, its side plates were so badly buckled by the tremendous force of the underwater explosion that she was slowed down to a mere nineteen knots. At that speed, vibrations would occur in the propeller shafts; the ship was withdrawn from the line, replaced by HMS *Formidable*. She was then sent back to Sydney, withdrawn from operations and sailed home to the UK on 24 May 1945; the ship took no further part in the war. I told her that from a Japanese point of view, you could say it was mission accomplished. Could she explain that to them?

I might have guessed Ritsu's response: 'That's not good enough!' Kamikaze were sent to sink our ships, to die: the job was not finished. In her eyes, it was a failure. I pointed out that had they hit the bridge and sunk her, we would not be having our conversation; she went ahead and translated my apparently illogical comments. As her brother Yo-san had said after seeing the same picture, 'Why be sorry? They're kamikaze!' I had her ask Teruyuki some questions that I can barely remember; it seemed to me any queries I might have had were hardly the point. What could I say?

In my heart I knew that simply coming here, the meeting and making a relationship, however brief – this was the answer, this was the meaning of the moment we were sharing. Teruyuki did speak a little of his lost brother, Chiharu, and Ritsu translated: his older brother was something of a local hero. He was a very bright student who had topped all the classes in the area, was a good all-round sportsman and wise beyond his years. 'A potential leader, then,' I suggested to Ritsu. She agreed: but as he was destined to inhabit that higher order of being, the kamikaze, his death was inevitable – and right.

Tsuyako got up and came back with a thick wad of postcards and a written scroll. It turned out that these were Chiharu's letters home from his time in the navy; the scroll was the funeral oration delivered by his navy friend the year after he died, when the family was able to have a service. Remarkably, these items had been found not long ago, behind the shrine (hidden by his parents, most likely). This occasioned a new bout of amazement and excitement – a conversation I was not privy to, as no explanation was offered. It was obvious what was going on.

They were so deeply engrossed in studying the postcards and the scroll that I could not bear to ask anything more of them. I took more photos and enjoyed the exchange as time moved on; I wondered if Ritsu really would want to go home. Then came the pièce de résistance: Teruyuki-san told her he had been in contact with Hideaki Nishida, the man I was off to see in Ōsaka soon. They had a mutual link, with the deaths of a brother and an uncle in the attack on my father's ship: Hideaki, it seems, had been diligent in making contact with other family members of the tokkōtai.

He called for special paper and began to write a letter for me to take to Nishida-san, writing my name in Japanese at the very beginning. I

Teruyuki Nagata writes a letter of introduction for me to Hideaki Nishida.

was witnessing a letter about me composed by the brother of the man who had died in the attempt to kill my father. I would bear it north to Ōsaka with a sense of wonder. Seeing this old man bent over a parchment, inscribing the kanji, the hiragana and the katakana that comprise the Japanese writing system, so elegantly, with such care, I could have been watching the penmanship of the poets Bashō or Issa. The letter written, he folded it into an envelope and handed it over to me.

We found out why it had taken so long to find the right house: the museum at Kanoya had the address of the family's ancestral home, the jikka. Hideharu had moved onto the farm and Teruyuki didn't live in the old place either. It wasn't surprising we'd had some problems finding them. The time was coming for the farewell: we'd been there for almost three hours when I saw Teruyuki stand up and put his sports coat back on. We bowed to each other around that tiny table and I asked Ritsu if I spoke a Māori proverb to them, could she translate it: 'Ko tā te rangatira kai, he kōrero – Conversation is the food of chiefs'? She had trouble grasping the words 'chiefs' (sounds like 'chefs'?) – and the concept that we might be chiefs or leaders. However, I made sure they all heard some Māori spoken – probably for the first and last time.

Ritsu translated and they all smiled agreeably: who knows what they made of such an unusual oration? It was time for group photos beneath the watching ancestors. I plucked up courage and asked if I could pray in the family shrine? Of course I could; so, for the first time ever, I found myself kneeling before an image of the Buddha. Tsuyako lit the incense and struck the bell, leaving me to pray – whereupon I prayed for the repose of the soul of Chiharu, for the other five men who died that day, and for this family whose aroha towards a foreigner was impeccable.

As we put our shoes back on for the journey home, waiting for us on the step were two huge boxes of strawberries. These were the fruit of the farm, with the name 'Chiharu Nagata' on the label: the dead kamikaze brother. What can we learn from these humble people? Almost everything. Ritsu was gasping for that cigarette now, digging in her bag as we scooted along the back roads to the highway. Did I mind if she smoked in the car? No, I don't think I would have minded at that point if she had lit them up six at a time.

The trip north back to Kurume was almost as fast as the one going south: not much was said until we got to the outskirts, when the intensely

Life's riches: posing with the Nagata family and Chiharu's final portrait.

practical Ritsu pointed out to me a series of neon-lit Love Hotels, where the unmarried (and the married who live with their parents) repair for an interlude of private sex. We then got on to the bizarre terminology for the prostitutes who will come to your hotel room, who go by the name of Derebu Health (Delivery Health). Japanese indirection at work again, meeting English, looks for a way out. The Soapland / Sopurando establishments she described to me – again rather matter-of-factly – left little to the imagination (sex parlour workers who masturbate their clients).

This conversation brought the day back down to earth, a day I won't easily forget. Details certainly, time will erode; and all that happened can't be written here. We can never recall everything, and boring it might be if we could. But those faces, those tears, and the answer to prayer: never. The night ended with a feast of tonkotsu ramen, divine pork soup, at Kurume's best traditional ramen restaurant. Slices of pork, ginger, noodles: heavenly Japanese kai – and just as down in Kashima-machi, there was no way I could get my feet under the table. Reaching home, I collapsed into bed and slept for eight glorious hours. Father, I think we have buried some ghosts.

**Day Twelve: 23.4.2011. Recovery mode. English practice and the dating game.**
Today it's time to take a deep breath and recover from the emotional and physical exhaustion of yesterday's highs. I try to capture on paper what it was like to meet the Nagata family, but it does seem a little like grasping a handful of mist: your hands are moist but you have no real hold on the gathering fog of yesterday. Writing is always past tense.

In the evening, for something completely different, Neil takes me to a social club gathering at Leona's Bar in Kurume town; Japanese – mostly women – who speak some English and want to improve their conversational skills. It's also a kind of hopeful dating agency: many of these women are in their late twenties, thirties and forties – unmarried, and approaching a danger zone in Japan. If you don't have a man by the time you're forty, Neil tells me, you're getting close to the exclusion zone. You might find yourself, and painfully so, outside the group.

There were some males present, albeit outnumbered. I spoke to Yūji, an older man, a retired company manager who had travelled overseas for an aluminium company and had lived in the US and the UK for extended periods. He had a university degree in commerce and was a very good English speaker. We were joined by Sawako, a woman who works as a care manager, in a residential home for the elderly. I ended up talking to them about Anzac Day, a pretty surreal conversation, after she said she wanted to go to Turkey, because it was 'exotic'. As for New Zealand, most Japanese people I meet seem to know about Christchurch because of the earthquakes, especially the 22 February event where so many language students from this country died.

This group just wants to practise their English – and in the case of the older women, meet a guy, foreigners in particular. It was exhausting. I went because Neil asked me to and it would have been rude to say no; I was pretty flat after the Kashima-machi trip. It was also very noisy. They meet in a small upstairs room in the bar: trying to listen to Japanese speakers of English while nearby a very loud American was spraying laughter at several decibels, it was a bit of a mission to concentrate. Somehow, we made contact – but I was glad to get out of there as, later on, more of the women attempted to engage my faded brain in chit-chat.

I left feeling sorry for some of them: Japanese women (with the exception of those like Ritsu who, as her husband says, is like a man in her attitudes) are often oppressed and downtrodden by their chauvinistic menfolk. Sawako, who has a profession and is independent (shock, horror), would frighten many Japanese males simply because she has learned to use her personal freedom (like travelling alone to Turkey). The price she may have to pay for this independence is that, having no man, she will have no family to care for, and as she gets older, no family to care for her. This will be their loss: she was highly intelligent, caring, and quite gorgeous. But too free and too old.

Neil, as a disciple and guru of neuro-linguistic programming, is something of a counsellor and a mediator to these people, especially the husband-hunting women. He's good at relating to others: he can read situations and be very useful in offering advice. Few gaijin here can speak Japanese, and even fewer choose to live in 'normal' suburban areas like Kurume, preferring the more cosmopolitan and foreigner-friendly Fukuoka. He's a bit of an oddity: he's bought into Japan on a deep level and his value to this fringe group is obvious. He too is an outsider who will always live on a certain edge in Japan. He happens to live in this area because it's where his wife comes from, but people like him are scarce outside the larger urban centres, more especially it seems in a place like this.

Kurume is quintessentially Japan: an ancient trading centre and country town that has sprawled since World War Two as the manufacturing centre of the giant Bridgestone Tire Company, now a huge global brand, famous for making high-speed rubber for F1 racing cars. Its name was apparently coined in 1931 by its founder Shojiro Ishibashi, when he reversed the English translation of his own name, 'stone-bridge'. They also had a presence in Christchurch, now sadly underlined by the recent closure of the Firestone factory in Papanui that had produced tyres in New Zealand since 1947. My father had worked for Firestone (later to be purchased by Bridgestone), on his discharge from the New Zealand Navy. It was largely the Japanese hunger for such raw materials as rubber (along with oil, coal and metal ores) that drove them onto the doomed path of a war that led me here – and, tomorrow, will take me to nearby Nagasaki.

# 7

# Ishigaki Pilgrim

**Day Thirteen: 24.4.2011. Easter Sunday. Nagasaki.**
Easter Sunday morning here in Kurume: awake at 5.30 a.m., everyone else asleep and I wish I were. It is strange to feel it is Easter – and Anzac Day tomorrow – in a country where, save for a tiny Christian minority, the day is no different from any other Sunday. I sit up and read a section of John's Gospel – Jesus before Pilate – and do not feel quite so alone. This whole experience underlines for me the power of a surrounding Christian culture: even if that culture is a museum experience for most people in New Zealand, it has deep historic roots. I feel instinctively that while many of those in Christchurch who are mourning the loss of familiar church buildings might only step inside them for weddings and funerals, church history in stone and brick is a bedrock element of our local identity.

Today I'm going to Nagasaki as a tourist, getting out from under the feet of the Hall family. Nagasaki is about as Christian as I'm going to get in Japan, with a church as its city emblem and a past where Christianity came into Japan through Kyūshū. The city has cathedrals and churches that recall this history. It's a day to strike out on my own and do a trip on Japan Rail with my tourist pass (it's use it or lose the value, really, at $1,000 for twenty-one days). I need some more practice navigating the rail system on my own in preparation for the Ōsaka trip on 2 May.

When Neil got up, we talked for far too long and I got away a bit too late for a full day trip to Nagasaki. The local train was on a Sunday schedule: I just managed to miss one by ten minutes, so had to wait over an hour on an exposed station in a chilly wind. I'd thought they'd be every fifteen minutes as they are during the week. Getting off at Kurume and taking the Shinkansen to Shin Tosu (the change for Nagasaki and Sasebo) was a breeze: the train actually banks like an aeroplane on some of the slower, curving banked tracks, which is a very strange and pleasant sensation.

The JR Kyūshū train was pretty slow, arriving at Nagasaki just on 2 p.m.; it was raining, which slowed things down a little more. The journey there was fascinating: lush green fields past Saga, the famous rice town area, with the seedlings pricking up in the wide paddies. Plenty of green tea fields too and other crops, where the country houses and small local businesses blend seamlessly in the typical absence of any waste space. I didn't see one animal till we got to Nagasaki, where a stray dog wandered about in the station. Not a cow, sheep or pig in sight as there would be in New Zealand once you leave town. Those that there are (and they must be here, given the pork, beef and milk), are all inside under cover.

It was a grey overcast day, making sightseeing from the train a little monochromatic. Still, there were many delights for the eye, large and small: ancient shrines hidden in copses and lines of trees, on those same sites for hundreds if not thousands of years, merging with the crops and the tiered-roof houses, the ubiquitous 600 cc mini-cars. The farmers in the distant fields look almost like those childhood willow-pattern characters I saw on my grandmother's china. The stature of the older Japanese raised on traditional diets contrasts strongly with my big-boned Caucasian frame. I hear two Americans talking loudly behind me, and get up and move several seats down the lightly populated carriage. I can't stand their magnified, seemingly opinionated chatter that fills the interior. I must be getting acclimated, feeling embarrassed for the Japanese ears around them.

In just over an hour, we slowly draw into Nagasaki, stopping at all the small stations; I get a chance to look out at the fishing boats on the wide flat bay, almost an inland sea. Suddenly we're there: buffers at the end of the line so it's out and into the rain. The station concourse is new, loud, bustling; I head for the information counter where a very helpful woman with good English gives me a map and writes directions and prices for the tram lines north and south. With my late arrival, I've given up on the idea of going on to Sasebo as way too ambitious; Dad was based there in the Korean War, with the Royal New Zealand Navy frigates. He's been in this part of Japan long before me: I wonder, did he ever come to Nagasaki on leave? I know he brought back a carved chest from Japan at that time – a mysterious object I often scrutinised as a child, now in my sister's house.

The carved chest my dad brought home from Sasebo in 1953. JILL CLARKE.

Time is against me – it's after 2.30 p.m. I have to make a choice between the Atomic Bomb Museum and Peace Park, or the Catholic Church at Oura, one of the oldest wooden buildings in Japan (one tram north, one south). The survival of such a historic wooden structure is unique: fire consumed Japanese homes on a regular basis in the past and the US firebombing of all the main cities was the same event on a far grander scale. It's Easter Sunday: I need a church to say hello to Jesus, preferably somewhere indoors. Standing close to where the second A-bomb fell, I make the choice to go to the Peace Park and start looking for a tram to Hamaguchi. It's always the same in a brand-new city: you never know which way is up. Every decision and movement has to be thought through or you end up on the wrong tram, train or bus, going somewhere else.

The trams are easy to figure out: for ¥120, I'm off, with the driver and his little white Mickey Mouse gloves piloting the old streetcar uphill. This area of Nagasaki is quite hilly: the bomb, exploding mid-air in the centre of a natural basin, had a deadly chamber in which to multiply its horrors. Getting off and walking up to the Epicentre Monument outside the museum, I see the first of many lines of schoolchildren on guided tours, each group listening intently to an explanation by the green-jacketed Nagasaki Peace Guides.

Memorial plaque in the Nagasaki Peace Park: the time of the blast.

I need to stop taking pictures, to be still and absorb the import of what happened. At 11.02 a.m. on 9 August 1945 the atom bomb that was meant for the Mitsubishi Shipbuilding Yards at nearby Kokura (now Kita-Kyūshū) was dropped instead on Nagasaki town, all because the American pilots of the B-29 *Bockscar* couldn't see the primary target due to cloud cover. An estimated 75,000 people died and about the same number were injured. The figures tell me something – and nothing. Who – standing here – can imagine what this spot was like at that moment? Who would want to try, were they even capable? I seem to have no emotion all. It is probably foolish to expect to feel anything.

Watching the Japanese, I am aware that, apart from two young Americans, I am the only gaijin here: what do these kids (many sneaking a glance in my direction) think when they look at me? One group has stopped in front of a brick column surmounted by what look like statues. The column, topped by Christ and his apostles, was once part of a Catholic cathedral that stood further up the hill; it stands today in the Epicentre Park as a reminder of the power of the blast. It is all way too much to take in. I follow a guide with his line of uniformed Japanese ducklings up the hill to the Peace Park. Before we get there, the rebuilt Urakami Catholic cathedral rises into view at the top of the rise. It's Sunday, and here is my church. Lines of students queue up outside to have a short lecture before the bust of Pope John Paul II – what are they thinking about him?

The cathedral is important because the original was almost completely destroyed by the bomb; that's why those saints on the brick column stand today in the Epicentre Park. They're a kind of resurrection, a rebuke to the enormity of nuclear sin. Urakami Cathedral was once the largest church in the Orient: rebuilt post-war, it was reopened in 1959. I join the line of Japanese schoolkids and enter, hungry to pray; there sitting to one side are

School party examines statues of saints and martyrs, Urakami Cathedral.

two Japanese nuns. I smile and greet them, and say I too am a Christian: they smile back. Even though the pews are roped off and the altar seems miles away, I get to stand there, to bow my head and pray. I even cross myself, as if to let the passing kids know I'm not a Buddhist.

Looking back, there was something familiar about the cathedral at first sight: its central gabled roof and the upright columns of the twin frontal spires on either side. It's not unusual – maybe I'd seen it in cowboy films, or Spanish Catholic influences in California? It turns out (I discover later) that this is the model the Māori prophet and healer T. W. Ratana used when he built his now iconic temple near Wanganui in the 1920s. Ratana had paused in Japan in 1924, his ship delayed by a dock strike on the return journey from England where he'd tried (unsuccessfully) to present his Treaty of Waitangi petitions to the English king. Ratana travelled to Nagasaki, where the great cathedral was almost completed (it opened the following year). He was also a guest of the Japanese Pentecostal preacher Bishop Nakada who would later join Ratana at a rededication of the completed Ratana Temepara in 1928. There it was declared that Māori and Japanese both belonged to the lost tribe of Israel (Ratana's association with Japan would later cause him problems in the war with that country).

On my way out of the cathedral I drop my hat; pursued by a polite Japanese gentleman, it's promptly handed back to me, helpfulness I've come to expect. On the walk back down to the Epicentre I have some unkind thoughts about lesson two for these schoolkids, starting with the invasion of Manchuria and ending with the Rape of Nanking. But that's for the Chinese and the Japanese to deal with. I'm here to discover what makes Japan tick, not to judge them – to learn why young men like Chiharu Nagata were willing to dive to their deaths in those final months of a war plainly lost. These kids in their sailor suits and Prussian uniforms are all in their early teens – he and his fellow kamikaze were only a few years older.

Back at the station, I grab some Japanese food for the journey, thinking the delicious-looking offerings of local kai in the station food hall might be some kind of meatball – no, they have little slices of octopus tentacles within. This is takoyaki (octopus dumpling balls) – a bit like chewing fish-flavoured rubber – I'm told it is very good for you. After two or three of them, my weak Western jaw is aching; I go back to the vendor and get them

URAKAMI - NAGASAKI
24-4-2011

The Urakami Cathedral stamp: all the kids were making a copy, so I joined in.

packed into a takeaway box. The return journey is a mirror image of the one coming here – I finally stagger home to the suburbs, having managed the last leg from Kurume Station by bus and foot, at around 8 p.m., where I swap the takoyaki for some of Ritsu's unimpeachable cuisine.

This is my last day here before my early flight from Fukuoka to Ishigaki tomorrow. We spend the evening talking, eating and discussing plans to meet my translator for the Ōsaka meeting with Nishida-san. Ritsu's mother and father arrive, and while I eat my evening meal Asako-san laughs gleefully with her husband about things I will never know; somehow, I'm glad I never will. This world is too big to encompass and there is so much of it to go around. Ignorance here is somehow bliss right now; I hope we will never again have to go to war with such amazing people. It's a good way to prepare for Anzac Day at home tomorrow: today I have stood on the site where a true weapon of mass destruction was set off. I tried to show a measure of respect for those who died that day – and later.

As a footnote to the statue of John Paul II at the cathedral, the next morning before I leave for his place at Kashii that night, I get an email from Ken. He makes some comments on a photo I had sent him of the Japanese students at the cathedral in Nagasaki. I had queried them having any idea at all about who or what a Pope might be. He writes:

*A brief digression: Urakami Catholic Cathedral is famous, and I bet the high school students actually find it quite interesting! They certainly do know who the Pope is, especially John Paul II (I saw him in a crowd of 100,000 in Rome shortly after he became Pope. Tiny little red dot in the distance on the balcony of St Peter's, but it was exciting). Though few are Christian, they have no particular antipathy or even any strong opinion about other religions at all. Both girls and boys often wear Christian crosses as necklaces and earrings – just a way of being part of the wider world outside of Japan as so many of their favourite Western singers and celebs wear them. Almost all weddings nowadays include both the traditional Shinto ceremony in kimono and then the white wedding dress / tuxedo ceremony presided over by a Caucasian in priestly garb. I have friends who do that as a relatively lucrative part-time job.*

Pope John Paul II: Japanese eclecticism in spiritual matters starts young.

*Japanese find it very appealing and beautiful because of all the movies with such weddings in them. And the British Royal Wedding will be watched by millions on Friday. They really loved Diana here, and Elizabeth as well when she got married. My dad pointed to references to Queen Elizabeth in my mother's letters to me as a young teen and thought it an indication of serious mental aberration. He just didn't realise that everyone was still avidly following all news of Elizabeth here ever since her 1947 wedding, and so my mother perhaps assumed that we were as well. Elizabeth was crowned queen in 1952 when my young parents were dating in downtown Fukuoka! The local American GIs were naturally less interested in such things, though they certainly recall Marilyn Monroe's visit to the armed forces here in 1954! Ah, how life is. :)*

**Day Fourteen: 25.4.2011. Anzac Day in Japan.**
It is Anzac Day back home and another working Monday as the Hall whānau get up and go their separate ways, leaving me in charge of the house and the cats. Tonight I will relocate to Ken's place at Kashii for the early flight to Ishigaki tomorrow. I take my time, making sure I don't leave the cherry blossom leaves behind (they have turned an autumn brown in their plastic sleeve). I walk to the post office and its ATM full of yen: Neil insists I have to get cash to go to Ishigaki. Japan runs on ready money, he says, and you can't afford to be caught out sans a wad of yen in your wallet.

Walking back, I'm getting used to being the roving gaijin zoo animal: drivers, bikers and walkers sneak a look at me as I go. Tourists don't come very often to Kurume and there are few local foreigners. Neil, tall and blond, sticks out like a giraffe in a deer park: when he breaks into his fluent Japanese, amazing the locals wherever he goes, suddenly he seems to blend in. He's a permanent outsider here, however, a state of being he accepts and wears as a kind of badge. Japan does seem a nation unto itself: despite Western prejudices about its propensity to imitate the West, that's only true on the surface. So, a gaijin is a gaijin is a gaijin: the price is a certain indefinable loneliness I sense both in him and in Ken. That may account for some of the volubility they display, talking almost non-stop. I'm one of the few chances they have to host a live-in English speaker who knows something of both their English and American cultures. Nuance takes on a fresh dimension here: who can Neil find in Kurume to join him in a Monty Python skit? Who in Kashii can quote Alan Ginsberg back at Ken?

I sit at the kitchen table drinking Neil's industrial-strength filter coffee and write up the day in Nagasaki. The recall and the typing of what seems so close – as it drifts out of reach – drains something deep down. This is a new kind of writing experience: it's almost a bodily effort to get to the end of the previous day and have it fresh, almost too encyclopaedic – knowing much of what I'm writing may never survive the editing later. It's all about trying to keep the journey alive so that when I'm back at my desk at home, I won't have to rehash dead memories or re-create what will certainly be lost. I'm here and now but always thinking of yesterday.

I call it a day on the page and write emails, trying to line up Kota in Christchurch to reassure Nishida-san in Ōsaka that all will be well – that we'll give him a time of day soon for the 2 May meeting. I'm completely dependent on Neil and the translators he's lined up. It will all be sorted for Friday when I come back from Ishigaki where I'm going to make my pilgrimage, as near as I can possibly get to the site of the strike on HMS *Illustrious*, 100 miles offshore from the Yaeyama Islands in the Philippine Sea. If you don't have Japanese and you're a new arrival, it's back to a form of childlike dependency and waiting at the mercy of powerful adults (it must have been a bit like this for the first missionaries and traders in New Zealand).

I'm ready and packed when Neil gets home. We walk to the local station with my bags to catch the Yellow One Man Diesel Car to Kurume, then the meal at a yakitori restaurant with his language student and company head honcho, Yanno-san. When we met at last Monday's class, he insisted on me coming along for this, and having the class while we all share a meal. I wanted to say no (my plan had been to go in to Ken's place in Kashii at midday, and take it easy), but I knew it would be insulting to refuse this middle-aged salaryman's invitation.

This meant meeting him near the station about 6.30 p.m. and then walking to the backstreet yakitori place, which proved to be over a mile away. Every step we walked, I knew I would have to get back to Kurume Station in just over an hour at the latest, to make the Tsubame Super Express for Hakata at 7.48 p.m. Yes, I could have got the next train and kept Ken (who has no mobile phone) waiting another twenty minutes, but I'd said I would be there on time. I didn't want to prolong the meal either – I was knackered before we even started down the street.

The yakitori house was all you might expect from a savvy Japanese manager who dines his clients three to four times a week. It was old, well-worn and well-loved, a tiny hole-in-the-wall entrance with a Mama-san who greeted Yanno-san like a long-lost family member, took our coats and served us right away in the small dining room off the main bar. Cross-legged on the floor for those who could: the endless flow of dishes began to appear and the golden tankards of Kirin beer. Raw cabbage was the appetiser, then plate after plate of grilled meats, noodles, and of course, raw chicken. Neil and I couldn't go that far (salmonella scares in the West), but he ate everything else and I had a go, too. Not a sign of Yanno-san's favoured horsemeat, for which relief much thanks!

Comes 7.25 p.m. and I get up to go, bowing profusely, exclaiming my great appreciation with hands pressed prayerfully, and more outward-bound bowing, backing out. Ritsu had informed Neil that my bows to the family at Kashima-machi after the visit to the Nagata clan were not deep enough, nor did I show my appreciation with the prayer hands. Did anybody tell me beforehand? Give me a practical demonstration? No, this is Japan: in such matters, the gaijin is meant to be psychic and then tut-tutted later when his mind-reading powers have once more failed. But I'm glad, deep down, to get the feedback – I think I'm going to need it up in Ōsaka when I meet the Nishida family.

I have to run with my two bags – the salarymen were amazed I didn't take a taxi, but they're not on my budget. I get there with much prayer ('Lord, please slow down time, like you did for Joshua') and a heavy sweat. The Shinkansen seats are heated; I have to perch forward for the twenty minutes it takes to reach Hakata, fanning myself with the printed flight schedules. Ken is there and we head for his place by suburban train and foot. I'm so tired – I wish he wouldn't talk and give me advice on how my every last pearl of wisdom belongs in the book. His proprietorial affection for my writing would be a little too much ordinarily; now, half-crazy with weariness, I almost snap inside as he takes forever running up and down the train, trying to find seats when there are plainly none to be had. I manage to keep my swearing in my head.

We finally make it to his place in Kashii and I'm ready to fall into bed. Politeness dictates we talk a while, so I tell him the story of the Kumamoto visit to the Nagata family. It's giving him shivers of recognition, recalling family reunions at the time he first came to Japan from America as an adult, never having seen his Japanese relations. It's going to be a 5 a.m. wake-up call and I need to hit the sack: I'm tired and he's withdrawing from nicotine. I excuse myself and climb the stairs of his tiny old Japanese home to the bedroom he's given up for me with its paper-thin walls. Sometimes it can be very difficult to like yourself, but the balm of sleep soon takes care of that.

**Day Fifteen: 26.4.2011. Flying to Ishigaki.**
The alarm wasn't needed. I heard Ken's go off, and we were up and away by 5.30 a.m., walking the dark and narrow streets of Kashii. We made the airport fine, but the woman on the checkout counter gave me a bit of a start when she said, 'Plane is full!' It took a while to realise that my request for an aisle seat had garnered that response. I would have to go down the back if I wanted one of those, with the school party heading to Okinawa. That sorted, we headed to have a coffee and Ken decided on bacon and eggs. I was ready and raring to go through security: sayonara! He wanted to eat and talk – and the more he talked, the slower he ate. I made up my mind to talk as much as possible, just so that he would keep eating and I could get through the gates and be on my own. Travel stress on top of sleep deprivation can turn you into a very selfish animal.

On board and off to Okinawa, the promised school party fills the rear of the plane in their sailor suits and trainers. One gets a bit of a shock when I speak in my limited Japanese to the flight attendant. As we begin our descent into Okinawa-Naha, having flown the same skies the kamikaze flew to their violent ends in 1945, I try to keep my mind on them and not the bucking of the plane in a serious dose of tropical turbulence. We descend, as did those young men: to lives we expect to continue on arrival, not to our deaths. So much bloodshed on these islands in 1945 – it's hard now not to sense the ghosts of those battles.

The landing at Okinawa was smooth, taxiing past a gaggle of USAF F-15s on the ground over to one side of the runway. The Americans are

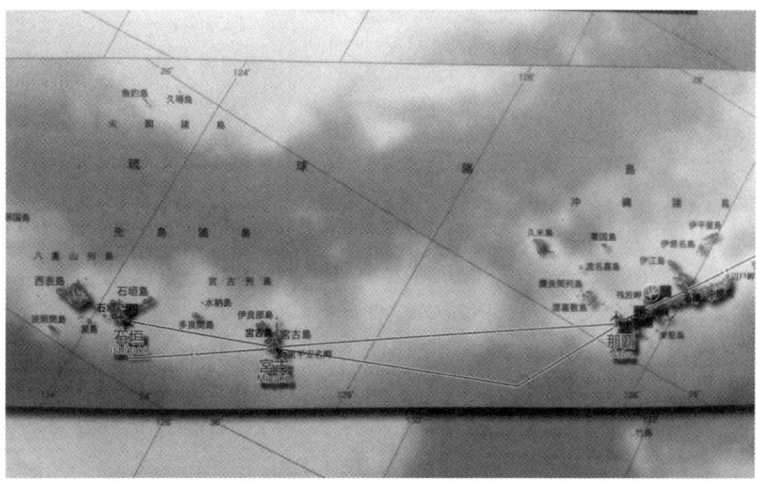

Airline route map of Okinawa and the Ryukyu Islands: Ishigaki, second left.

a hated and resented presence here now – but then there is the money they bring into the economy. Many Okinawans – not all – just want them gone. There were moments of anxiety waiting for the Ishigaki flight: an announcement that due to bad weather at the island, the plane might have to turn back. I asked what would happen if we did return? There were more afternoon flights and we would get on one of those if ours was turned around. When we did get airborne, it was easy to see why we might have to return. Almost the whole flight was blind through cloud, a nasty bucketing about in some very unsettling turbulence as we flew through a tropical storm. Over Ishigaki, the plane settled into a holding pattern for twenty minutes until the pilot and the tower decided we were clear to land.

Coming in on the final approach was even more interesting: long after the landing gear was down, there were still no visuals. At the last minute, we broke cloud and there was the ground, lashed by sheets of rain as we came in very fast. We hit hard and the speeding 737 jiggled; tensing up, I wondered what it would be like to skid broadside-on in the wet? The pilot got the brakes on smartly and we hauled up in a big hurry. I sometimes check how much runway is left after a landing like this – you can often see that when they turn off the landing strip and head for the terminal. In this case, not a lot: nicely done, Captain!

It was pouring down, so we were bussed the short walk to the terminal; umbrellas raised, we climbed down the steps, 1950s style. There were no shuttle buses so I took a taxi to the hotel for ¥900 – about NZ$15 – it was worth it for the convenience and the chance to look around. Not that you could see much in the murk. The Chisun Resort Hotel seems a perfectly adequate budget tourist choice; the room was fine, much like the one at Narita only smaller. I jumped into the delicious shower. The manager Takeshi came up in answer to a call for help and enabled the internet; with time spent overseas for fluency to develop, he spoke excellent English. I sortied downstairs for a meal – an overpriced hamburger mince sandwich, which was fine (note to self: eat out after the complimentary breakfast).

Ishigaki waterfront: the heat reminds me I'm touching the Tropic of Cancer.

Takeshi was a fount of local knowledge: he went over my options to get out to the islands and then to Denshinya, the military telegraph post strafed by planes from *Illustrious* and the other carriers. He could arrange a rental car for a reasonable rate and advised me on the ferries for Kohama, the nearest island. I needed to get out onto that sea where the kamikaze met their fate to perform my ceremony of reconciliation. He persuaded me to take the ninety-minute bus tour of Kohama as well, which would prove a winner. Takeshi was brilliant: three years working in Australia, he thought his English was a bit rusty, having few chances to practise it working on

Ishigaki. He was fine: after meeting many Japanese with little or no English, fluency in a Japanese speaker is easy to recognise – they don't sound like they're reading aloud from a textbook.

I walked down to the ferry wharf and watched some boats leaving: one had twin Hamilton jets – New Zealand technology so far away from the Canterbury rivers where it was perfected. I even felt a little bit proud. Weather permitting, tomorrow we will sail in one of them over to Kohama. It is very strange to feel I am now just miles away from where that amazing picture of the strike was taken: 100 miles south-southwest of Ishigaki, according to Royal Navy records. It won't seem real until I am on that ocean. Strolling about, there are souvenir shops everywhere, stacked with images of the shisha: a kind of lion/dragon/dog that is the local guardian deity. There are only two full days here, so I want to get the best from my time: tomorrow, Ishigaki is mine.

## Day Sixteen: 27.4.2011. Kohama Ferry: fubuki! Maseru and the origami grasshopper.

The day dawns fine: I decide it's best to do the ferry trip and the prayers at sea now and leave the drive out to Denshinya till tomorrow. After breakfast (what is that: octopus? manta fins?) I line up Takeshi to do some rental car research and find out the ferry sailing times. There's one at 9.10 a.m., so I head for the terminal and find another English speaker at the counter of a company with a ferry leaving for Kohama. I think I'm getting obsessed with who speaks English well enough to help me; this far south, it makes a world of difference for a non-Japanese speaker. I always compliment them, as a courtesy: I wonder how many tourists do?

There are plenty of fast ferries to choose from, plying the many outlying islands for both local and tourist traffic. Ishigaki is the scuba-diving capital of Japan and Takeshi tells me the surf's not bad either (he got the bug living in Newcastle, New South Wales). All sorts of people board the ferry, including a bunch of builders heading over to Kohama to do work, it seems (one has a tape measure hanging on his belt). I sit in the open rear section, free to scatter the sakura and launch the ema prayer board: most passengers go for'ard to the covered seating. Once we're under way and the big Hamilton jets kick in, I find out why. It's noisy and windy, but I love it: it feels like being on a motor torpedo boat under power, an adult vision of the promised toy Dad never brought home from Sasebo in 1953. Huge white spumes of churned water rooster-tail behind us as we streak past the slower ferries in the open water. Time to make my move.

White-water wake: fast ferry to Kohama, a perch to scatter the petals and prayers.

I have the decomposing sakura petals in their plastic sleeve ready to go, gifts from the generous bough Mr Masuda, the old F-15 pilot, brought along to Ken's language class. That's a nice touch: pilot to pilots. I'm in the very back row of the open-air seats under the rear canopy on the starboard side. Behind me is a chain, implying no admittance to the bucking stern area where the motors roar. The builders, three Japanese fresh-air freaks, look stolidly ahead, so I grab the plastic sleeve containing the sakura and steady myself near the side. One wrong move, one big buck over another ferry's wake and I'll be tossed into the sea at a good thirty knots. With the huge racket these engines make, the guys in front of me wouldn't even notice.

Here we go: I scoop out handfuls of the soggy brown petals and cast them onto the swirling white waters: 'Sakura! Fubuki! Kamikaze!' Blossom! Blizzard! Holy wind! What else was there to say? I clamber gingerly back into my seat: it's too noisy and windy to think, let alone pray. The act itself is an intercession. Time now to release the words on the ema, launching

Fumiko's prayers and mine out onto the sea my father sailed, waters the kamikaze dived down into at terrifying speeds.

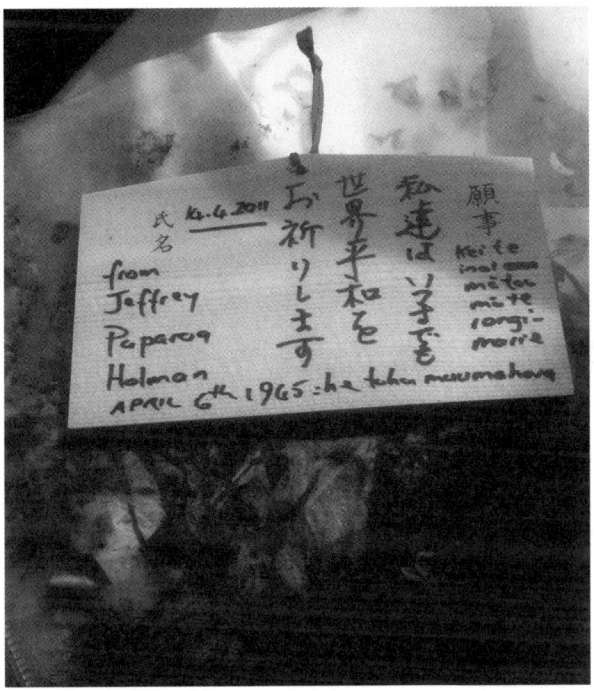

Sakura and the ema tablet: with prayers in Japanese and Māori.

The prayers are for the repose of their souls, for the souls too of the British and Kiwi pilots who died attacking Ishigaki, for the Yaeyama people here today, and the families of all those affected by the war. 'Mission Sakura' accomplished: the petals have fallen into the East China Sea, a rustling in the winds of the spirit realm. Murmuring to myself, I lean out of the roped-off gangway and fling the ema out to sea. Behind us in the white wake, the prayer board sails away forever. I'd given one of the builders my camera, asking him to take a picture of this moment. He pushes the wrong button and manages to turn it off. I pose again and he gets a souvenir shot of me: arigatoo gozaimasu!

As the ferry comes closer to the flat coral island of Kohama, I see waves breaking on the beach and the strip of white sand, a green fringe of tropical

Approaching Kohama, after launching the ema prayer tablet.

jungle filling my vision. This was the last sight many American marines saw as they landed on Pacific islands from the Solomons to Truk, shot dead by Japanese defenders as they ran up the beaches into a storm of fire. Today, it is different: except for a handful of right-wing über-patriots who worship the old bushido code and spirit, the Japanese people have no desire for war. The Pacific War and its aftermath killed that off. Kamikaze are revered today by those who remember them but nobody wants to see it all happen again: they've given birth to a generation allergic to militarism.

The island tour bus is waiting and my driver Maseru holds up a board in Japanese. I wave my ticket and we make contact. There are only two of us for the grand tour of Kohama, about ninety minutes in all, but it proves to be quite a hoot. Maseru and my companion, an elderly Japanese tourist with his 'Aloha Hawai'i' baseball cap, will keep up a steady banter of jokes, exclamations of surprise and cries of delight. The old man is not afraid to show how happy he is to be here. Maseru stops for photo opportunities (the same ones every day, I imagine, as he has to keep in synch with the ferry timetable). As we climb the hill, he points out the high point reached by the Great Meiwa tsunami of 1771 that killed 10,000 people here and on Ishigaki. Tōhoku and the recent carnage in Japan's northeast is nothing new in this part of the world, where typhoons wreak their yearly havoc. The sea is the master on islands like these: when it rules over its subjects on the day of a tsunami, it shows no mercy.

I think of my father out on that sea: how little I know of what he faced before the elemental forces of the world's great waters: 'they that go down to the sea in ships / . . . these see the works of the Lord / and His wonders of the deep'. What was sleeping within him years later in the coalmining town of Blackball, a place where nobody knew what it was like to sail these seas? Maseru stops us by a coral wall, and points out where the deadly habu snake sleeps in the cracks to stay cool: one bite and it's goodnight. We stop at a roadside stall for a local delicacy, a kind of round doughnut mixture, minus the hole. It's a bit like being on a tour bus journey in New Zealand (those taken by groups of elderly Japanese), stopping at set beauty spots to take pictures (of yourself, before majestic mountains), and then arriving for lunch at an appointed restaurant.

Except here, it all seems a little like an off-the-cuff imitation of the real thing, the hard-nosed commercialism of the mass tourism existing elsewhere. Maseru is a very nice guy who genuinely seems to like the company of his passengers; he proves this while hiking with us both in tow, up to the lookout on Mt Ufudaki, the highest point on the island. Scattering exotic multi-coloured butterflies in his wake, he strips a palm frond and begins to fiddle with it. As we reach the observation post, he presents me with an incredibly realistic origami grasshopper, created as he strode uphill. Amazing: this delightful folk art creature is definitely going home with me.

Then we're off back to the ferry terminal in a buzz of final jokes and chatter with Aloha-san. As soon as we arrive, there's a ferry docking from Ishigaki, disembarking a phalanx of middle-aged golfers. Gorufu – in this clammy heat? They have to be kidding: but no, slinging bags that are as tall and as heavy as themselves, the happy golfers crowd up the wharf to their waiting game. My guess is that Kohama has a cheap course: the game in mainland Japan costs a small fortune to play, and some smart operator down here in the tropical boondocks has got the word out. I find out later from Neil that this is exactly the case.

Back at sea for the last time here, I'm quiet, emptied and reflective. I have come all this way and now it is done. I don't feel deflated: poured inside

My guide Maseru's magical origami grasshopper, made from palm fronds.

out somehow, with nothing left to do but let the ferry and the ocean take me back to Ishigaki and into tomorrow. I keep looking out to sea, out to the east, as if in the hope I will see some shape on the horizon, the ghost of a fleet carrier or a flight of unidentified aircraft disappearing into cloud.

It's Takeshi's last day working there and so I make him a small gift: a copy of Dad's *Illustrious* picture. He gets to work organising a car for me to drive to Denshinya the next day. It's a humid twenty-eight degrees: where can I get a cooler shirt, Takeshi? He gives me directions to a local clothing shop called Toa (as it can mean 'shop' as well as 'warrior' in Māori, this is quite funny). On the way to the Toa store, I take a detour into the Shinei Peace Park to see the famous Peace Bell: there are two of them, large and small. Having little Japanese, I can't see if the public is allowed to sound the little one. I'd love to, but refrain. By now, the heat and humidity are really getting to me. I hide in as much shade as there is: finding the clothes store, I buy a lightweight and quite noisy Hawaiian shirt on sale for a mere ¥850, about twelve of our dollars. Back at the hotel, I shower and put it on: now I understand why the hotel staff are wearing their tasteful short-sleeved shirts. They are so cool, in that most physical sense of the word.

After a late snack, I write postcards and head out to the post office. There's a covered street market all lit up, just on closing time, selling a hundred different versions of the shisha, the Yaeyama guardian lion deities, Chinese imports from centuries long gone. From an ancient street vendor, I buy some more of those delicious doughnut balls sampled on Kohama. When I get them back to the hotel, they're not half as nice as the fresh ones we ate on the island tourist trap route. Ishigaki day one is done, and I'm serene.

**Day Seventeen: 28.4.2011. Denshinya Undersea Telegraph Station.**
A fresh adventure: driving in Japan. I'm nervous, but all the advice online says it's a breeze down here in these islands, with few roads and few people. Just take out the liability insurance they offer and don't hit cyclists be they mad or sane, as you'll be blamed. My man duly arrives at 9 a.m. and we head out to Orix Rentals. All up, it's ¥6,500 (around NZ$100) for a six-hour rental – and wonder of wonders, they don't swipe your credit card and load up a refundable damage cover, just in case.

He shows me to my chariot. It's a new Daihatsu Move, one of those ubiquitous mini-cars the Japanese favour that resemble tiny urban golf carts. After the explanations of the sat-nav system and a health check for dents, I'm in the driver's seat. I don't bother with the navigation aid, just turn the voiceover down so the picture shows and it tallies with my road map. After a brief familiarisation, I nose out gingerly onto the city roads. It's an easy ride, really: 40 kph is the limit and nobody hurries; a little bit like being amongst motorised rickshaws and ox-carts. Island life moves slowly: why hurry? There are only so many places to go and plenty of time to do whatever it is you're there for.

I follow Highway 208: press the accelerator, and with an urgent buzz the little Move lives up to its name, whizzing away to 60 kph like an angry wasp. I have to watch myself – there are 40 kph signs even on the open road. Just driving through the tropical greens, the pineapple and sugarcane fields, is a feast for the eyes. It does look a bit like the Coast back home, but the vegetation is even more lush. Technicolour butterflies float across my path, some as big as small birds; one or two suffer the same fate as any other unwary flying creature sucked into the grill. Ouch! I see what looks like a roadside shrine and pull over to check the map. There are shrines and graves everywhere here, town and country, cheek by jowl with factories and schools. The dead are never far away.

This one fronts a hilltop restaurant and tourist trap, filled with all manner of shisha lion-dog and local souvenirs. Pressing on, I reach the coast and Route 79 to Kabira, a left turn which goes where most tourists head – to the beach. I'm in search of a broken-down old building, a relic of the 1890s: the Denshinya Army Telegraph Station that once carried undersea messages from the Ryukyu Islands to Japan from its colony, Taiwan. It was pummelled mercilessly in 1945 by the strafing runs of Corsairs and Hellcats from HMS *Illustrious* and the other British carriers of TF57. The beach looks very inviting as I cruise the coastal road; way across the bay in the haze, I think I can see the far point where the old station should be.

With Takeshi's excellent instructions, finally, I find the sign and see the route down to the point: Denshinya. The local dairy farm cows keep up an unexpected lowing, an unusual sound in Japan. Here on Ishigaki, beef is important; I've even seen sheep in a small pen down the road. Now I've found the place, it's time to walk down the rough track to the station, leaving the rental behind in case I bend it. The road to the wartime site seems to have been sealed with concrete; the air is humid, the sea inviting, spread out behind the tiny building surrounded by dead trees.

I come closer and see that the site is also a memorial with an impressive plinth and a map of the Ryukyu Islands from Taiwan to Okinawa, showing the kamikaze strikes from Ishigaki northwards. I assume those near to this island are strikes on Task Force 57: a list nearby, under the headings 'S, I, D' (which I take to mean 'Sunk, Incapacitated, Destroyed'), points out the effectiveness of this last futile attempt to bring the Allies to the bargaining table. The military justification for continuing with the kamikaze attacks was to dissuade the US and its supporters from launching a costly invasion of the Japanese mainland, and thus avoid an unconditional surrender. I'm standing now before this forgotten evidence of my father's part in the death throes of Imperial Japan.

It is strange to see this image and these old statistics on the memorial, near to the tropical beaches where tourists swim, canoe, fish, scuba dive

The battle-scarred Denshinya Undersea Telegraph Station still shows the ravages of strafing by aircraft from carriers of the British Pacific Fleet in 1945.

and surf. The telegraph station ringed by its silent companions, the ghostly trees, is a graphic reminder of what it must have been like to sustain attacks from the carriers on which Dad served. It's a hollow, burnt-out shell: all of its surfaces are pocked with deeply gouged holes, the work of the Fleet Air Arm fighters that strafed the island daily with .50-inch machine guns. There is little to see inside: a stand on which the telegraph may have sat, looking out over the bay, a small cooking area that once held a stove in the living quarters, and what is unmistakably a traditional Japanese squat toilet with the hole going down beneath the small building.

Human life: a lonely outpost of Japan's colonial empire, silenced now for nearly seventy years. Who were the men that manned the telegraph on the day the Fleet Air Arm struck them from the bright sky, hammering the walls with their deadly machine-gun bursts? They had no chance against that kind of firepower. Did they have any anti-aircraft guns to protect them, or did they just hit the floor and hope to survive? Most of the heavier protective guns were sited on the main airfields at Ishigaki and Miyako, regular targets of the Royal Navy planes; many were shot down and their pilots killed on these repeated runs. It was this strategy designed to prevent Japanese air attacks from these airfields on the US invasion fleet massed off Okinawa that attracted the attention of the Taiwanese kamikaze squadrons from 1 April onwards. On that day, a great fubuki – a blizzard of attacks – announced to the Allied forces off the Nansei Shoto the reality of kamikaze warfare.

I wait in the silence for some revelation to come, and pray. I do a final tour of the ghostly site, pick up and souvenir a white plastic fishing net float and a tiny chip of rock from the telegraph station with its embedded fossil. On the float I write, 'Ishigaki: 28.4.2011' – then it's time to leave this desolate and storied place. Back in town, the man at Orix checks the vehicle, looking for new scratches and dings; he zips me back to Chisun Resort Hotel complete with bananas, a sandwich and chocolate biscuits bought at the supermarket. All that remained now was to close the chapter on my time in Ishigaki. Tomorrow it is back to Fukuoka and a much-needed weekend break, until Monday: then Ōsaka, and the mysterious Nishida-san.

**Day Eighteen: 29.4.2011. Return to Fukuoka. In-flight haiku. Tales of Okinawa.**
I misread the departure time, arriving at the airport three hours early, but the helpful check-in operator gave me an early flight to Okinawa. The flight to Naha was calm and stable going back north. The friendly hostess who had given me some wrong terminal directions after the Fukuoka–Okinawa flight on the way down was on the return flight from Okinawa, off duty. I let her see the origami grasshopper from Kohama: she was delighted and showed it to the rest of the cabin crew. I spent the Okinawa–Fukuoka flight writing haiku, based on seeing an egret stalking prey in a rice paddy near Denshinya.

On the ground in Fukuoka at the baggage counter, there she was again with her two companions, in their civvies: they'd hitched a ride down the back of the plane. She was smiling and waving so I went over and said hello. On an impulse, I took out the fair copy of the haiku series I had written and gave them to her, explaining that they were written on the plane (I'd already told her I was a writer, on the way down to Ishigaki when she had asked me why I was going there). This was a way of thanking her for being so kind, I said. 'It's poetry, the English might be a bit hard,' I explained, superfluously, bumbling on. She took the two small sheets of notepaper with their seven linked poems. 'You can take them home and translate them.'

She stared at them as her two friends looked on; not knowing what to do next, I spotted my bag on the carousel and said sayonara. Who knows what she will make of the egret, the frog – and the tsunami. Neil had told me to wait outside for him to turn up, so I headed straight there and spent an hour listening to the maddening chimes of the pedestrian crossing and watching the theatre of pick-ups and drop-offs at a busy Japanese airport. The choreographed actions of the impeccably dressed concierges opening taxi doors for passengers provided some relief, as every car but his loomed up, made the pick-up, and left. Finally, Neil's blue Prius emerged from the shoal of vehicles and I could escape.

On the way home, he wants to go to the only Costco in Kyūshū to get budget cornflakes and eat some pizza. We talk flat-out about the trip, and Okinawa comes up. He's been to the museum there and seen the exhibits that display in graphic detail the indescribable sufferings of the Okinawan people in the closing months of the Pacific War. The Ryukyu Islands have an ambiguous relationship to Japan, even today: the Japanese people do not recognise Okinawans as truly Japanese, but they claim Okinawa as part of Japan. It's the reverse of British-style colonialism in New Zealand, where it was obvious the country was not at all part of England, but they signed it up for the Queen and declared that Māori were now British subjects. The results for the locals have been unhappy in both cases, but for the Okinawan people from March to April 1945, they were a total disaster.

Spurred on by the emperor, told they were a bastion of Japan's home defences against the foreign invader, the already invaded Okinawans were used as a buffer to both slow, and hopefully prevent, the Allied invasion of Japan. Okinawa was where the US forces would be bled white, the Allied shipping devastated by waves of kamikaze attacks: that was the plan. The result, the Japanese high command gambled, would be a negotiated peace where the Americans and the British, realising that the cost of landing on the Japanese mainland would result in unacceptable casualty rates, would come to the table and allow Japan a measure of peace with honour. In this dream scenario, there would be no invasion.

The Japanese of course – like virtually all of the Allied populations – had no idea what had been created in Los Alamos, and what was to come at Hiroshima and Nagasaki. The planner of the Japanese attack on Pearl Harbor, Admiral Isoroku Yamamoto, had warned his superiors in 1941 against attacking America in the first place. Yet he obeyed orders when told to prepare a plan to do just that; and now it was the same blindness to consequences that spurred his masters on. Anyone who had read Roosevelt and Churchill's demands for an unconditional Japanese surrender, issued in July 1945 at the Potsdam Conference, and seen the outcome of the prosecution of the war in Europe, could have told the Japanese leaders that such a surrender was the only acceptable outcome for Japan's enemies. Tojo and his war cabinet were not about to listen to defeatism – and Okinawa was made to pay.

There was to be no such surrender for the people of the island; any who had tried to do so, the Japanese would have shot. There was no surrender either for those same troops. Letters home from these men to their families show that they knew – just as the kamikaze pilots did – that this posting was a one-way mission. US firepower from the invading battle fleet was stupendous: the countryside was pounded daily, whole mountains were reduced to rubble, and a hell on earth beyond Dante's imaginings convulsed Okinawa. The marines who landed at first encountered no resistance, unlike the withering firepower that had mown down so many of them on Tarawa and the other smaller Pacific islands.

Their opponents were dug in further inland, underground in tunnels where many would die later of thirst on the waterless island that could not even supply its own rice (which came from Ishigaki, to the south). Doomed, starving, crazed with thirst, soldiers and civilians alike were either shot in combat or caught in the devastating bombardment. Virtually all the homes on the island were destroyed, and in some of the bloodiest fighting of the war, the Okinawan civilians were crucified on the cross of Japanese imperialism and American revenge.

Since visiting the museum, Neil now had a story to tell me about a small girl sent out to surrender by her grandparents from the tunnel where they

Marine Corporal Earl Brunitt (left) and Private Genare Nuzzi share a foxhole with a war orphan on Okinawa, April 1945. PHOTO: SGT W. A. MCBRIDE OR SGT H. S. ENGLAND. NARA FILE #: 1127-N-118933 WAR & CONFLICT BOOK #: 881.

had all been hiding. Giving her a white flag, the old people reasoned that if she went out, the Americans would not harm a child. The Okinawans had been subjected to a sustained propaganda campaign by the Japanese authorities on what to expect from the brutal foreign soldiers should their invasion of the island succeed. As Neil spoke of this, weaving in and out of highway traffic, his voice choked and I thought he would cry. He was so emotional by now that I asked him if he was okay to drive: 'You're really identified with that girl, aren't you?'

He insisted he was fine as we jousted with the evening traffic. Yes, he did have a hook into that little kid, from the fatherless child in himself, to a figure in a photograph, in a story. It was one he never finished; the subject somehow changed from the girl to the effect of the war on us. I was waiting to hear him say that the Americans had shot her. He'd already given me a long list of their atrocities against civilians on the island. Part of me wanted to interject, to mention the Japanese victim mentality – and what about the Rape of Nanking? I shut up instead and listened to him. It was one of those moments when the truth bubbles up from wherever it's been hiding, saying, 'this is why'. An abandoned child on the crucifix of history: the white flag, the evaporation of all meaning, of any semblance of morality.

The next day as I write this – having woken early at 4 a.m. – a strange parable that ran through my mind as I lay in bed half dozing comes back to me. A man goes to the village sage and asks him, 'Why is my life like it is? What is wrong with me? Why am I so unhappy?' The old man looks at him and says, 'Your problem is that you are refusing to answer your question.' The inquirer is frustrated: 'What question?' The old man replies, 'The question only you can ask, the question you were sent into this life to discover, the question nobody else can ask and answer for you: Why am I here?' Well, it seemed profound at the time: somehow it joined me up to that moment when I responded to Neil's empathetic bond with that terrified little girl in Okinawa, a child forced to face impossible circumstances in a way no child should ever be.

It's about growing up too fast and the manifestations of parental abandonment, a type of what has driven me and what drives him: how to lose something as big as a father. The wind is howling outside right now in Kurume – at that moment in his car, something blew right through me. 'Neil,' I said, 'what you're talking about is what we've got in common – it's what brought me here. That family I visited in Kashima-machi, they'd lost their brother, the parents lost a son in that war – and I lost a father. I know he came back, but half of him wasn't there. It was back on that carrier, and all those other times and places where his life seemed about to stop. They were all like that – they'd seen terrible things and they could never be the same as before.'

They were deeply disturbed individuals, those returned servicemen; many were unable ever again to function as civilians. The war went on in their deepest recesses and spilled out nightly in bad dreams, drunkenness – and violence. What I have in common with these families of kamikaze pilots, I told him, was exactly that: the shadow of the war. I had come to Japan just to be with them for a moment and show my respect for their unspoken losses.

I didn't expect anybody else to understand – it was just something I had to do. I didn't even expect the families here to work me out, to divine what had brought me to their doors – just as long as I found some understanding for myself. I am beginning to right now. There are the answers we are sent to find in this life, and the one nobody gets this side of death. One, you have to live for; the other, you have to die for. Death, what is it? That answer, the six kamikaze and my father now know. Facing a death in life, kamikaze died before they died: knowing I will die, acting as if I will live forever, their courage attracts me in a way I cannot explain.

I think Neil knew what I was talking about: powering his Prius through the evening traffic of Japan and its ghosts, its deep-down suppressed memories, into the weirdness awaiting us in a Japanese-style Costco where there are bargains piled up everywhere, yet no outward and visible sign of the price paid to create the Japan of today.

### Denshinya rice haiku

*egret waits*
*a white spear*
*by green rice blades*

*happy frog*
*by rice blades*
*hears the oxen come*

*foolish oxen-hearing*
*frog forgets*
*the egret's knife*

*egret swallows*
*kicking legs*
*and night has come*

*under the moon*
*the paddy shivers*
*one frog less*

*thousands taken*
*at Tōhoku: no one*
*to eat rice*

*29-4-2011*

# 8

# Ōsaka Soul Food: Okonomiyaki

> Okonomiyaki: a Japanese savoury pancake containing a variety of ingredients. *Okonomi*: 'what you like' or 'what you want', and *yaki*: 'grilled' or 'cooked'. Kansai style is the most common variety of the 'Japanese pancake' or 'Ōsaka soul food'.
>
> *Wikipedia*

**Days Nineteen and Twenty: 30.4.2011 – 1.5.2011. Tachiarai.**
**Interpreters for Ōsaka.**
Today is a preparation day for the Ōsaka trip on Monday: Hideaki Nishida is making some conditions about who is allowed to translate for us. I'm taking an Imperial War Museum DVD of the *Illustrious* for him: film taken of the gunners who shot Dad's kamikaze down. They look extremely happy as they hold up the rubber life raft blown out of the Suisei as it exploded in the sea: seven seconds from looming death, it's not surprising. Neil is away all day and Ritsu is at work; I'm home alone with Aidan who is plainly a bit lost on his own and watches a lot of TV. I am exhausted, almost in pain and woozy, but I just can't sleep. I'm starting to feel very frayed at the edges.

I email Kota back and forth about Nishida-san and his insistence on the translators Neil has kindly arranged not being wanted – and his daughter's ability to handle the job. Having to go through intermediaries (one here and one in New Zealand) makes life difficult, but I have no choice. Kota says they will him ring later today to talk about the meeting. I would agree for the sake of peace that we go with what the family seems to want, but there is another problem for us. Akiko's husband (along with her, one of the two Ōsaka translators) has taken time off his work at Bridgestone, so we just can't tell them 'don't come, we don't need you now'.

When Nishida-san rings later that evening, Neil talks to him and he finally agrees to the translators coming along. Neil is very persuasive and comes back with the news that our man in Ōsaka is finally agreeable. I get on the phone and talk to his daughter, but she can't understand me – not a good sign. She'll have difficulty making sense of my New Zealand accent: talking to me over the phone in her second language, with no visual cues, is tough going. I don't feel very confident about how our attempts at communication will go face to face. Well, at least it looks like we've got a compromise. I collapse into bed for six hours' sleep.

Sunday dawns – May Day 2011. Emails roll in as I set up the little netbook on the Halls' kitchen table while they slumber on. The deal with Nishida-san has proved too good to last: overnight he has emailed Kota. He felt that Neil would not listen to him, so he now wants to meet in a hotel at 2 p.m. for '10–30 minutes'. This is turning to custard. I reply to Kota and say this is not good, but to hold fire until I've spoken to Neil. Part of me just wants to call it off – the game seems not worth the candle – but that's just exhaustion speaking. I'm emotionally burned down after all the changes, and the trip to Ishigaki. The message I send reflects this:

> *Thanks for this. I am disappointed this has happened – I was hoping your part in all this was over. I really want Hideaki to deal directly with us from now on. I will have another talk to Neil about how to proceed. Please don't call Hideaki until I get back to you, okay? Time is short anyway. I have to know what is happening today, one way or the other. I don't really want to go all the way to Ōsaka for what may turn out to be a very short interview. Does he mean we chat in the hotel lobby and then I go to his place without the translators? I spoke to his daughter on the phone and she could not really understand me.*
>
> *I don't think her dad realises how difficult it would be for her if she were asked to translate for us. If I were to go all the way there and this proved to be the case, it would be a major disappointment to him as well. He has his reasons I am sure for not*

*wanting our translators in the mix, but without them, the interview will be difficult. What a saga! I am sooooo sorry you have been caught in the middle of all this, Kota. Anyway, just hang fire, don't do anything, and wait until I get back to you soon.*

Neil Hall and friend James examine the Zero fighter at Tachiarai Peace Memorial Museum.

When Neil gets up, I update him on negotiations, so he just says, 'Okay, let's give him what he wants.' I email Kota to that effect. Neil's English friend James arrives to join us for a trip to Tachiarai Peace Memorial Museum (he's another expatriate and teacher of English, married to a Japanese woman). On the way in the car, Neil's phone rings and it's Akiko, the translator from Nara: her husband has bad stomach pains and has been admitted to hospital. She will have to cancel the offer of helping me. Amazing: so the latest twist goes Nishida-san's way. He no longer has a translator problem – just one of translation. I text Kota and ask him to let them know of this development, and we head to the museum.

When we get there, Neil takes us to the old railway station: during the war, 10,000 people used to arrive daily to work at the place where Japan's aviation industry, civil and military, was founded. Tachiarai was famous for its gliding conditions and, later, as a training base for the army air force's kamikaze. It was severely bombed by the Americans in 1945, the B-29s destroying the base and the surrounding facilities. In the museum, I find Neil has brought with him a document that he gives to Kitahara-san, the director and our guide from the previous visit with Ritsu. This is the Japanese foreword she has written for my book, so that Japanese who read it will see that this is an attempt by a foreigner to understand the kamikaze culture and history from the inside. She wants the museum director to read it and offer any corrections and suggestions.

We tour Tachiarai, Neil having secured free entry for me, and permission to take photographs. I end up again at the video of Hanamichi-san of Wakayama, the crewman who survived a kamikaze mission. I film the video of him talking; at least if I can't get to see him in the flesh, I will have a record of his amazing survival story. We talk to Kitahara-san in a memorial hall for those killed on the base by the US bombing; he says he is happy with the foreword Ritsu has written. Saying goodbye, Neil explains that I will send them a copy of the book, telling them that the real reason for my coming was to show respect. He also says that I went to Ishigaki and scattered the sakura petals on the sea, and floated the ema board with its prayers. You can see it is affecting Kitahara-san. He thumps his heart and says he is very moved; I thump mine too, enacting our feelings. With many bows and a full heart, I leave this man who Neil says will be feeling just that little bit better after my mihi. It's a good reminder of why I need a translator.

Home again, I start packing for Ōsaka. Neil takes me shopping at Kurume for the needful gift to take there: a box of Fukuoka mentaiko (cod roe), a very desirable local delicacy. Later, I write out a list of questions for the daughter to translate, and we're pretty much set. All I need now is to hear back from Kota so I know where to meet them tomorrow. It's all about keeping calm and asking, 'What is all this teaching me?' For one thing, the disparity of rank between Kota and Nishida-san is an insight into how Japanese culture works: the older man has power over the younger. It may be drawing a long bow, but does this relate to how the culture of the day operated on kamikaze: honour and duty, respect for the senior rank? 'Death is light as a feather', I recall the proverb, 'but duty is as heavy as a mountain'.

An email finally arrives from Kota: 'I called Hideaki twice, but he was not at home. So, I sent an email saying that you are visiting his place alone. I also included your arrival time in Shin-Ōsaka and the hotel name. Hopefully, everything is set by now.' I can go to bed and await tomorrow.

**Day Twenty-one: 2.5.2011. Ōsaka. Meeting the Nishida family.**
The dawn of my next major mission: Ōsaka. I get up early and there in my inbox is the message I needed before leaving. Kota writes: 'Jeff, I received an email from Nishida-san. He said that he and his daughter will wait for you at the exit of Hyotan Yama Station.' The message includes the daughter's cell-phone number, but the best part of all is the last line: 'Finally, he said that all his family members are really looking forward to seeing you today. Good luck. Sleepy Kota.' That man deserves a mention in dispatches.

Neil talks flat out; I'm tired before we even hit the road. He gets me to the station in plenty of time for the 9.49 a.m. Shinkansen to Shin-Ōsaka, and soon I'm travelling at warp speed aboard the Sakura (how apt), heading towards my next meeting with the family of a kamikaze. Neil has kindly given me his phone and a list of instructions about what to do and where to go on arrival. I'm all set for my first real test on the trains: voyaging in the swarming subway of a great city, finding the hotel, and then getting out to suburban Hyotan Yama in eastern Ōsaka to meet them.

The train flies across the crowded landscape like a low-level attack aircraft: it's a bit like being in a Skyhawk on rails. I take a video to post on Facebook to show those at home what it's like. The trolley dolly roams up and down selling drinks and snacks. Three hours flash by and we're in the outskirts of the city, rolling up to Shin-Ōsaka Station right on 12.44 p.m. Japan just does not do 'late' on her rail system – except when earthquakes and tsunami buckle rails and cut off the power supply. With Neil's map and instructions, I'm soon navigating the Midōsuji Line on the subway to Namba and the capsule hotel, my bed for the night. I have to ask for help to work the ticket machines – I'm due to meet Nishida-san and his daughter at 2 p.m. and time is running out.

I exit the bustling subway at Namba and find the hotel easily enough: it's virtually in the station entrance. Leaving my bag and paying upfront chews up more time; the Visa is declined, so we have to do it manually. Sorted, I get directions for the entrance and with my shoulder bag packed with gifts, run for the Kintetsu Line next door. This is a bit more complex: my JR pass won't work here. I have to pay, so there is more delay getting a ticket and finding the line. Downstairs, I find a helpful guard with his little green foreign-legion cap.

He tells me that the Sub Express over there – he points to the board – goes to Hyotan Yama in ten minutes. I have to trust that I heard him right – his English is about as good as my Japanese right now. As I wait, a text arrives from New Zealand letting me know Osama bin Laden is dead. Obama has just announced it, DNA evidence apparently. It's weird indeed to hear this underground in Ōsaka. I try to tell the helpful guard the news, but he can't make head or tail of my garbled English. I give up and accept there is nobody here I can tell, when I'm busting to let them all know. Why bother? They'll find out soon enough and get on with their lives.

Aboard the train, I fret until I see Hyotan Yama on a station board, a few stops down. It is just past 2 p.m., so I ring Nishida-san on Neil's borrowed phone to say I'm at Fuse and on my way. He sounds warm enough, but has to hand the phone to his daughter Yuka. I manage to get across to her that I'm running late, but nearly there. We pull in to Hyotan Yama: I try both exits, stand in the street, but still can't see anybody who looks like they're looking for me, so I ring them again. Just as I'm calling, I see them coming down the exit stairs waving and talking to me on the phone. At last we meet.

He is twinkling and jovial: 'Jeffrey,' he says, in pretty good English, 'it is so good to meet you,' shaking my hand warmly in a very Western welcome – as does Yuka, his daughter. That upstages my attempt to bow and do my 'Hajimemashite!' routine, but I know it is appreciated when I do. He is dynamic and friendly, a Kansai trader: straight away I get the feeling this is going to be a good time, despite the speed bumps in getting this far. Dressed a little like Elvis Costello in rocker mode (there's even a resemblance with his glasses), Hideaki leads us to the car park; there's plenty of chat between him and Yuka as I try to relate to her as chief translator. I decide not to mention the other two translators who fell by the wayside, the ones not wanted here.

I'll wait and see if he brings up those negotiations.

The car is a bit of a surprise: a whacking great Mercedes-Benz saloon, dark blue and left-hand drive, it's a very un-Japanese hot rod. It certainly isn't a conservative businessman's executive express either: this man likes power and speed. I sit in the back with Yuka and try out a few opening gambits – can she handle my New Zealand English with the vowels that seem to stump so many Japanese? I tell her that her name sounds like 'Euchre', a New Zealand card game. 'Cards?' she enquires. I demonstrate: shuffle, shuffle. I think she gets it: there are going to be a few more question marks like this over the course of the next nine hours – before I collapse with a raging headache into my capsule bed at 11 p.m.

We drive into a wealthy suburb of East Ōsaka: it's obvious from the size and age of the properties that these jikka don't belong to bus drivers. The narrow street says 'old Japan, old money'. I have to prepare myself to meet the family, as they are all waiting, I'm told, including the navigator's brother, Hideaki's father. We pull up by the carp pool and there they are. First, I meet the younger daughter, Kayo: she's nineteen, a student with a Freaky Brothers T-shirt and the happy aspect of a thirteen-year-old. She will be tested over the day, poor kid, asked now and then by her proud father to practise her high-school English on me.

We arrive at the porch entrance: the wealth and style speak subtly of how Japan can announce its material substance with both traditional and modern trappings – quietly, without insistence. The jikka is lived-in: I meet Hideaki's wife, Kyouko, and do manage to get in some bows and 'Hajimemashites', as well as a handshake. She is elegant, haute-coutured and impeccably styled: the messages keep coming. These people are living at a different level to Nagata-san with his country roots down in Kashima-machi, yet the elements are similar. I'm shown into the living room and seated on the floor as per the country cousins; there are the pictures high on the wall, with Hisashi the kamikaze and his brother who served in the army and their parents. Over in the far corner is the shrine. I almost feel at home.

I have to give the gift of the mentaiko immediately, as the cod roe has been out of the refrigerator for six hours and needs to be kept cool. I hope the ice pack worked. Hideaki receives this very happily and I know the gift has been effective. There are nods of approval as his wife pours green tea and serves me soba noodles, cold with ice (I told them in the car I'd missed lunch, so he phoned ahead). A smiling Hideaki tells me to relax as I rummage nervously amongst my treasures. He's at home now, at ease, and I'm all his: I see the books lined up behind him, tools of research; there are cameras and video recorders galore (they soon start running hot – I'm on film from that moment, till we say goodbye at Namba in the late evening).

The circle is complete: Ōsaka, 2 May 2011. I meet Yoshiaki Nishida, the younger brother of Hisashi Nishida, who died in the attack on *Illustrious* in 1945.

Yuka begins what will be a long day of translating her father's and my obsession – military history. Then the great moment: the grandparents come in and we're introduced. This is Yoshiaki Nishida, Hisashi's younger brother: a child of wartime as is Teruyuki Nagata of Kumamoto, both growing up in the shadow of revered kamikaze elder brothers. He is a tiny bent old man of eighty-eight, bowed like a mountain tree in a Hokusai print. We bow deeply to one another and he too shakes my hand, as his wife Hirokoi-san bows too – so the circle is now complete.

The afternoon passes in a blur: I eat the soba noodles and once more my long gaijin legs and my failure rate with chopsticks get everyone laughing.

It is very helpful at times to be awkward and incompetent. Hideaki tells me how happy he is to have me here: that Hisashi, the dead kamikaze staring down at me from the wall, is very happy too. These moments occur throughout the day – overcome with feeling, he continually expresses his happiness and his pleasure that I have come all this way to meet them. He can manage some English too, which makes all the difference.

His father makes comments and Yuka translates. Hideaki gets out the pictures that are on his website, the originals of the attack on *Illustrious* he had sourced from the Imperial War Museum. I think it must be a good time to give them my photographs: the copy of the strike on the carrier (the image that has led me here); the picture of Dad on the bridge of *Illustrious* (looking hot in all senses of the word); and the ship's crest. The old man fingers the grainy image of the strike. I can see it is affecting him: this might well be the moment of death for his brother and his pilot (or any of the other two crews – we will never know). The family all gather round in this critical moment. I begin to sense what my coming with this ghostly image of the past might mean to them.

I explain about the picture: how I came to have it, where my Dad was on the ship, what he said about the attack, and what the explosion tells us. For each of us in this room, the whole journey hangs on this moment, just as it did for Teruyuki Nagata and his family two weeks ago. There are no tears this time, none that I can see, but the emotion in the room is palpable. I pass over the picture of Dad, which excites much favourable comment: one by one, they look from him to me, approving a resemblance that I have often struggled to see. This changes the room temperature to a more genial level. I pass over the last photo – the three crossed trumpets of the ship's crest: Vox Non Incerta, 'No Uncertain Sound'. It's a Latin tag from St Paul's First Letter to the Corinthians, a military metaphor about giving your trumpets a strong, clear blast when you stand ready to do battle.

Yuka is earning her money now, trying to make sense of my explanation of 'crest' and 'symbol'; in the end, 'badge' has to do the trick (this was why we wanted experts on hand). Then something I could never have foreseen: Hideaki places on the table a pilot's watch, an aircraft clock, and picking up a cloth-wrapped samurai sword from the floor, unwraps it, and hands it to me. I am kneeling in front of my father's former enemies, the family

Clock from the instrument panel of a D4Y Suisei: Hideaki Nishida was given this memento by an American collector repatriating such items to pilots' relatives.

of the man who was trying to kill him that day, holding Hisashi Nishida's sword. I hardly know what to think or say: in the movies, there is always a glib line and mood music – here, only the weight of the act, the silence and the inner life of each person around that table looking on.

I know we are brothers and these are my people now: I ask Yuka to tell her grandfather that in holding his brother's sword, I am thinking of my father. That takes a bit of getting across and I'm not sure he is grasping what I mean. I ask her to say I am thinking of his brother too, and that seems to translate. Can she please tell Yoshiaki-san that I came here to show him and his brother respect? She does, and I hand the sword back. Hideaki unsheathes it briefly to show me its gleaming steel. Just for a moment, I cannot help thinking of those pilots from *Illustrious* shot down by Japanese anti-aircraft fire in the oil refinery raids in Sumatra in 1944, captured and later beheaded with nine others on a beach near Singapore in August 1945. I have to push that thought away – it is not for now. There is no room here for resentment and recrimination.

Then Hideaki asks me, 'Do you have the DVD?' His English works when he wants it to (Kota must have told him I had the movie). I pass over the copy I bought from the Imperial War Museum, with footage of life on the *Illustrious* at the time of the attack. At the end of this short film, there is a clip of the gunners who shot down the last Suisei dive-bomber, smiling and laughing as they hold up the ripped life raft blown from the plane. I was wondering how the family would handle this, but when I explain what it is ('life raft' takes some teasing out), they are genuinely interested and grateful to have it. There is no way of knowing which plane it was that struck the carrier, and they know that; but these mementoes have gravitas and enduring meaning, for all of us. For now we overlook the fact that these happy men are celebrating not just their own deliverance from death through their accurate shooting, but perhaps the death of Hisashi and his pilot, Hajime Kitagara.

All this has meant much more video footage taken of me as I explain things about the DVD. Now it is time for a group photograph under the images of the ancestors. The grandparents kneel in front: it feels very Māori,

Hisashi Nishida, navigator, IJN kamikaze. COURTESY HIDEAKI NISHIDA.

like something from the nineteenth century. The old people are getting weary – too much emotion, I'm sure – so it's time for them to retreat and have a nap, bowing and uttering their respects all the way as they go. How good is this? How much better can it get? It is time for Hideaki and me to get down to some serious discussion on research and what got us on this road, with the must-be-weary-by-now-but-always-smiling Yuka manning the translation station and the electronic dictionary. I like this kid: called upon to do something really difficult, like all the Japanese I have met, she stoically does her duty while remaining civil and obliging. How much they could teach me.

Old Yoshiaki had passed on some memories before leaving: he recalled his brother visiting his school – having just entered the navy at the age of seventeen – when he was only seven. Hisashi too was a top student, a wise young man, and good at martial arts: another potential leader like Chiharu Nagata lost to Japan. I mention to them that Teruyuki had said similar things about Chiharu, and they agree it was a loss – but still, to be a kamikaze and die that death in defence of your country and the emperor was seen as a higher calling, a better end to life than any post-war civilian career and success. Many of the kamikaze themselves, as I am discovering, didn't quite see it that way.

It is this kind of post-mortem thinking that is so hard for my generation to grasp, filled as we were with cynicism in the knowledge of the Great War's mass slaughter, and the poet's bitter cry, 'dulce et decorum est pro patria mori'. We know and accept the way Horace's line is used ironically by Wilfred Owen, insisting that it is not at all sweet to die for one's country. We too in the West once revered honour and duty – but as we became aware of the horror of trench warfare consuming vast ranks of our grandparents' generation, such sentiments have suffered continual erosion. I don't think

The Nishida family. Back row: Yuka, Kyouko (Hideaki's wife), Kayo; front row: Hirokoi (Yoshiaki's wife), Yoshiaki, Jeffrey and Hideaki.

this family would accept that, even while today they say they want no more wars. The sacrifice of the individual to the needs of the group lives on here: ask the workers at Fukushima, who even as we sit talking are risking their lives to contain the post-tsunami nuclear disaster fallout.

Yoshiaki's father was an official involved in the conscription administration, and there is obvious pride here that he helped his son Hisashi choose that road. Neil's comment to me that kamikaze are revered in this country is true wherever I go – and nowhere more so than in their families. While the elders were still present, Hideaki asked me what my father did when he saw the plane coming, so I demonstrated with a mock dive under the low table – a cause of more great hilarity. That much I know is true: my dad said one of the other officers on watch had fixed onto the diving Suisei with his binoculars, tracking the onrushing plane. 'Bloody hell,' he yelled, 'he's going to hit right here!' and they dived for cover. My father got a sliver of steel in his buttock when the plane exploded in the sea – his one and only war wound.

Hideaki then asked me if we in the West thought the kamikaze were suicidal fanatics. What did I think? – be honest. I said some people may still think that, but there was an awareness now that, during the war, propaganda from both sides created a distorted image, in what was a fight to the death. Neither side wanted to understand the other. I told him my view was that they were professional airmen fighting to defend their country, as was my father, a career navy man. There was more I could have said, but it was too complicated and too difficult for Yuka to grasp. I don't think that my relationship to Dad and his part in the war has anything like the same religious intensity as this memorialising culture. They have Yasukuni Shrine, we have Anzac Day and Gallipoli: related instincts, and yet quite dissimilar. Somehow it seems tangled up in the difference between Shinto and Christian roots, as well as the different traditions of Western Renaissance humanism compared with Confucian and Buddhist influences.

He went on to tell me how he'd become interested in the first place from listening to his grandmother talk about the war (as I had also); it was becoming apparent how alike we were in some respects. They had earlier asked me how old I was and it turned out Hideaki was forty-nine – younger than I had expected; nevertheless, it seemed we were brothers in arms. He recounted how he had obtained the pilot's Seiko watch and the aircraft clock from an American in California who had an online mediation service; this seemed to involve the repatriation of wartime relics to the countries of origin (so these were not Hisashi's). Looking at the clock, I thought of the stories in *Kamikaze Diaries* of the young pilots who smashed the clocks in their barracks as the minutes ticked down to their fateful missions.

Taguchi Masaaki (centre, rear), who survived the war and visited the families of his comrades. It was after his visit to Hisashi Nishida's family that Hideaki became aware his uncle had been a kamikaze and he began to study the history of his squadron.

I tried to explain this to them: I was discovering that the pilots were not gung-ho reincarnated samurai, that many of the student pilots in their private diary entries display a genuine anger and anguish at what awaited them in this futile waste of their lives. Still, the duty culture won the day. Out they went to die in unresolved states of crisis. He told me of Taguchi Masaaki, one of the Chusei pilots in Hisashi's squadron who had survived the war, a man tormented by guilt and deep loneliness. He had set himself to visit all the families of his dead tokkōtai comrades, including Hideaki's father, Hisashi's brother. He had come many years ago to visit the old man, and the son remembered him coming. By now I was completely exhausted; I asked Yuka if she could tell her father I needed a rest. So more food and drink arrived to refresh me and she took some time off too.

Hideaki now gave me permission to photograph the returned relics, laying the sword on the matting floor. He was relaxed and laughing, asking Yuka to take pictures of the two of us in the special happi clothing his firm makes, a Japanese tradition of special festival garments that his family has specialised in manufacturing for centuries. They were absolutely beautiful, finished with such superb craftsmanship: Kansai people are famous entrepreneurs, in this case selling happi to Japanese communities worldwide. As a picture was being taken with us standing arms on shoulders, I said, 'I guess this makes you my brother now?' He laughed and corrected me, 'Little brother, little brother!'

Brothers in arms: Hideaki poses with me in happi jackets. YUKA NISHIDA.

The news came that we were going to Namba for a meal: they were taking me out to dinner. It was time to leave, and the old people came for my farewell from the house. Grandfather Yoshiaki-san bowed low, as low as he could; his wife Hirokoi-san was literally on her hands and knees. I was as reverent and low-bowed as I could possibly bend: to a New Zealand onlooker, even someone who knew me, it might have looked like we were acting a part. We were, and one as deeply sincere as any formal Western farewell – for me, a parting full of feeling, resonant with the unspoken. I was doing things their way, respecting their traditions. I meant every bow. It meant as much to me as the nose-pressing hongi back home in daily greetings, or on marae when ihu meets ihu at the harirū, closing a pōwhiri. For this meeting, we had certainly become one – as close as I'm going to get right now to 'being' Japanese. There remained too the knowledge as we parted that we had met this once, forever – and most likely – would never again.

## Ōsaka Soul Food: Okonomiyaki

The pièce de résistance was driving into Ōsaka and Namba where all of life in Japan is swarming on a Monday night in Golden Week, the national holiday. Sweeping along expressways, toll roads and into tiny backstreets, beneath giant twenty-first-century buildings with their neon signs in sometimes hilarious English, and the old temple lit up in brilliant white, it's a postmodern theorist's dream of simulacra: look, look, nothing is real, it is all just signs pointing elsewhere. Well, only if you make sure you don't hit another car or, worse, a cyclist or pedestrian: then a very solid reality would hit you in the form of the Japanese legal system.

Hideaki gets us into the backstreets in the big bad Merc, tooting to let walkers know he's there: do that in London and they'd kick a door panel in, LA and someone might take a shot at you. Here the walkers just melt away; the car-park attendant gets introduced to the gaijin – more bows, more laughter. We plunge into the seething colour and crush of Namba, swarming with its hundreds of thousands, where nobody seems to bump into anyone else, meandering cyclists thread the walkers without really looking, talking on their cell phones, passing droves of other cell-phone mesmerised pedestrians. More photographs ensue, and Kayo the youngest takes another clip of my endless Ōsaka video, until I want to tell her to put it away. Enough already – but I don't, of course.

Poor girl, she keeps getting asked to speak English to me (a father's pride), at which she does her best; a little more classroom exposure to talking and listening is obviously needful. Meanwhile his wife Kyouko has been dispatched to queue for all of us at Hideaki's favourite restaurant (he's been going there for twenty years). We tour the neon valleys and more pictures get snapped: me, and the girls making peace signs. They never seem to tire of this, laughing and giggling with huge enjoyment. Finally, we stop outside the restaurant and after a short wait we're called inside, past a queue of waiting hopefuls.

Okonomiyaki Mizuno I think is the restaurant's name. It's traditional, with huge hotplates in the middle of the table where the meal will be cooked (I'm heading for maximum heat exposure, already). We move to a larger, more private space, where the heat is even more intense, as the artist of food arrives to serve us: drinks, then the okonomiyaki order (a kind of giant seafood omelette with octopus and shrimps). They all play a little joke: offer me a bowl of the raw ingredients, watch my reaction, then snatch them back and laugh fit to bust. This is a sign of pleasure in your company, not what it might be at home – out to make you look silly.

The heat goes on and Kayo starts complaining she's overheated (I'm with her there): Hideaki turns up the air con, and I say to Yuka, 'It's like you get a free sauna with the meal.' Way too complicated, Jeffrey. 'Sauna?' she repeats, 'sauna?' I get the dictionary out and show her, 'Ah, sowna!' – now she knows. There's the problem in a nutshell: the difference between the sounds 'saw' and 'sow' (as in, female pig). She hasn't had enough exposure to idiomatic English and variations in regional speech, so sometimes during the day, I know opportunities were missed. I just had to give up and move on. Overall, she's done really well, and I tell her so.

The food is almost done, and Camp Mother arrives: slim, grey wisps in her hair, she writes on the okonomiyaki like a Kiwi cake decorator, but

Welcome to Ōsaka: Mama-san decorates my okonomiyaki treat.

with mayonnaise – 'Snoopy', 'Hello Kitty', and 'Welcome to Ōsaka'! Oh my goodness, they are even blessing me in the cooking of the food. I dig in and it's delicious. 'Oishii, oishii!' I tell them. 'It's so delicious!' Yuka asks me – for her dad – 'When will your book come out, and what sort of book is it?' I explain that we hope to get it out within the next year or so, depending on the cost of publishing a book with a large number of pictures. She translates this for Hideaki, who says he will gladly give me money to help – and will there be a Japanese translation?

I say we're fine about the money, but I will certainly let him know if he can help (I don't want to be seen as fishing for support here). Yes, if we could get a Japanese publisher interested and have a good translator available, a Japanese edition is a possibility. He asks if Yuka could do the translation work. On her behalf, I explain that while her spoken English is good, to translate a book requires a whole different set of skills. She seems to be nodding agreement: that would be a bridge way too far. I also try and explain that it is a memoir, but also a history and a travel book – but calling it a history of my father and kamikaze works best.

Then at the very end of the day, Yuka just happens to mention Neil and the phone call about the translators. I know now is the right time to say that my friend Neil – who was really trying to help by arranging the translators – says he is sorry if he appeared a little rude on the phone the other night. He told me to say this if it came up at all. Hideaki says 'sorry, sorry' too – and I say, don't worry, let's just leave it, we're here now and it all worked out in the end. I'm glad they brought it up, and now the air is clear. It was left to the end, but it was never going to be left out.

I'm full, I can't eat any more, and it's almost time to go. Hideaki has asked me how long it is since I stopped drinking alcohol (twenty years) and smoking (thirty). He's stopped drinking too, sipping his Canada Dry ginger ale, and smoking after a fashion, puffing on a substitute cigarette. He had a heart attack last year, and he's only forty-nine. I tell him he has to take it easy, so he can get to see his grandchildren and come to New Zealand to visit. It's all jovial and laid back: he keeps patting my arm and showing many signs of affection. You could not have scripted this day better, except maybe in heaven. We leave, bowing deeply to Camp Mother: 'Oishii, oishii desu!' I don't know much Japanese, but I know what this means and it is true: so delicious! It's been a pretty damn delicious day all round.

They walk me back to my capsule hotel at Namba Station, the two girls guiding me like angels on either side through the heavy night-time foot traffic: maybe I do look as tired as I feel, and it is kind of sweet. To them, I'm almost at grandfather level. Hideaki and Kyouko bring up the rear until we reach the hotel and it's time to say goodbye: you don't hug in this culture, but you can shake hands and bow, and bow some more. Hideaki says something warm in farewell, about how glad he is that I came; I was so tired by then, I can hardly recall his words. I just have to turn now and walk into the building and push the lift button in the glassed lobby, all lit up in blue and plainly visible from the road. I look back and there they all are, waving together as I step into the lift, waving back, and the door closes. I make it to my capsule bed with the beginnings of a mean headache, clean my teeth, and collapse.

**Day Twenty-two: 3.5.2011. Capsule hotels. Bullet trains. Japanese trash TV.**
I wake during the night to experience the intimacies of the capsule hotel: latecomers entering the corridor and talking. My neighbour in the next booth is snoring and the air conditioning hums away – but apart from that, silence. I manage to get back to sleep and wake again around 6 a.m. Some movement begins from early risers so I get up and look for the shower on level three below. It's easy to get lost trying to follow the signs and end up wandering the lookalike curtained corridors. I find the showers and they are great: typical Japanese attention to detail. Wicker baskets in which to place your provided pyjamas, a place for your disposable slippers to await your return – it's all sorted.

In the breakfast bar I find myself watching the first TV news I've seen since arriving that chronicles the Tōhoku tsunami and its aftermath: soldiers cleaning up the jagged mountains of destroyed human endeavours. They are camped out in tents, and the breathless female interviewer follows them around firing a barrage of questions. There are images of the survivors: they tell with anguished eyes of the ongoing suffering, of being homeless in temporary accommodation, not knowing the fate of their loved ones and neighbours, or their friends. At Neil's place, trash TV is the order of the day for the kids – endless game shows that help the Japanese escape from the ordered and hierarchical realities of the everyday – while he mostly watches UK sport, football from a former London life, which serves a similar escapist purpose.

Checking out, I head for the subway, back to Shin-Ōsaka and the fast train home: I'm done here and done for. I head for the JR Shinkansen office and join the Golden Week queue to get my reserved seat: some hope. The first train I can get a seat on leaves near to 3 p.m., and it's only just before nine in the morning. The assistant tells me if I get down to Platform Twenty and start queuing before 9.30 a.m., my chances are good. I can't be fagged waiting five hours more (if I'd been twenty, yes, I'd have headed back into Ōsaka). I grab some food for the train and navigate the holiday crush to the platform, joining the queue at Car One. I figure there will be fewer people coming up to the far end of the station.

The train arrives on time, of course. They keep you waiting until the very last minute to board while the cleaners do their work: 9.57 a.m., two

Japan Rail guard, complete with white gloves, Kurume Station.

minutes to go until the train leaves (and it will, on time, believe it). We get to rush for a seat, but in an orderly, Japanese manner. I get one by the window, a young guy slots in beside me and a MacBook Air geek grabs the aisle; the unlucky get to stand. After a few of the early stations like nearby Shin-Kobe, most of those who joined at Ōsaka get seated and the newbies coming in at Shin-Hiroshima and other stops get to stand. By the time we reach Hakata, there are even a few spare seats.

The time on the train gets put to work: I have to write up yesterday and the visit with Hideaki and his family, before things fade. Tiredness is still haunting me, but it has to be done: netbook unfurled, I write for most of the next three hours, the time it takes to fly-by-rail the 600-plus kilometres to Kurume. I hardly bother to look out the window and rail-gaze, until I've packed the laptop away. As we near journey's end, I look out over urban rice fields and there, moving along a pathway at the far perimeter, is a pink umbrella, a lone walker bobbing along in the midday sun, a haiku in the flesh to see and remember this moment by.

Neil is there to meet me with little Kay and we zip home, and I'm grateful to be in a rest zone. Mission accomplished: now it's waiting for Ritsu to return after a fishing trip to Kagoshima with her brother. In the event, they get no fish and have to spend six hours delayed on the expressway; a woman has killed herself, leaping off an overbridge onto the road. A Japanese suicide at the height of Golden Week: how desperate she must have been. Soon, farmers from the Fukushima nuclear disaster will join her in their despair, distraught that their produce is now rejected for market because of contamination from the devastated power plants nearby.

We have bento box food for tea and I watch some game show TV with Aidan, much of which consists of laughing at security camera footage of an American drunk falling about in a liquor store, and other edifying realities. After the news of the suicide, it seems more than a bit hollow. Time must be passed somehow: next up, Man United and a Champions League game, where the Brits toy with a doggedly defensive Schalke in Germany, before a barrage of shots peppering the excellent goalkeeper finally get past him and they stroll through for a two-nil away win. It's a replay: before he heads for bed, Neil helpfully tells me the final score. Good thing I have no investment in the result.

Ritsu finally makes it back, empty-handed, with stories of the tragedy on the road. She asks me about the Ōsaka trip and how it all went, admiring my pictures of Hideaki's samurai sword with its golden sakura rosettes. Tomorrow, it seems, we are going to a barbecue at her parents' house, the jikka. That will be quite something, seeing the elders on their home ground. It's one more privilege on top of the many bestowed upon me over the past two and a half weeks. I have some time now to reflect on all the action and the meetings, the journeys and the returns. There's a raft of Neil's seasoned expatriate observations to think about and sift through; then Ritsu's feisty pronouncements from within the culture; the jigsaw of all these encounters – but that is for tomorrow.

**Day Twenty-three: 4.5.2011. Bowing low. Barbecue time at Takata-machi.**
A sleep-in (6 a.m.!) and now, some time to think about things before we head off to the barbecue at the in-laws – like the way it seems you can understand others (literally, by standing beneath, taking the lower place), and attempting to empty yourself of your invisible prejudices. Of course it is impossible to stand completely outside of your own culture – madness might ensue if such a destabilisation occurred suddenly: extreme culture shock. It is possible, however, to take a fresh view on our perceptions, on what we have received – then to accept or reject this, consciously, as an adult. So much of the interviewing I hear now is people interviewing themselves, interrogating their own preconceptions and agreeing with them. 'I was right all along' – that's how talkback works, and why it thrives, because it feeds the ego.

I'm thinking about this in relation to bowing and politeness in Japan, how for a foreigner it can seem so overdone and feigned. After my experiences – especially in Ōsaka, when I saw that old woman on her hands and knees and her elderly husband prostrated too – I know I can't grasp from inside my own culture what it really means. I have to do it, to echo it, as I did on Monday, to see it come back to me reinforced by my acceptance: it's all about understanding by doing, rather than standing back critically and judging. In other words, don't interview yourself if you want to understand – go and do what they do, do anything that is not a patent violation of your deeply held beliefs and conscience.

By copying – embodying and internalising the bowing behaviour – I am learning what it means by feeling what it does and seeing what it produces. It enacts reverence and respect: those two elderly Japanese, children of World War Two, embodied for me the kind of respect for authority and rank, the performance of duty, that led the kamikaze to their deaths (many against their rational objections, their emotional resistance to oblivion, a denial of our deep survival instinct as humans). Westerners who see this as irrational behaviour – the group mind denying the individual conscience, or the working of reason – might ponder football fans in riot mode, or the slaughter of the Somme and Passchendaele battles when hundreds of thousands of rational individuals stepped up into a hail of fire, following patently insane orders, to a certain death.

As a Christian, I feel that this reverence for the individual springs from a reverence for the Other, a person made in God's image and likeness: many non-Christian religions say this too, whether or not they use the word God. They were bowing to the god in me, and I was bowing in return to the divine image in them. My coming to the Nishida jikka – and to Nagata-san's home in Kashima-machi – was an act of reconciliation and forgiveness. It was something that was desired both ways; I believe in my heart that my motives were sensed, even if never fully articulated. Handing me the sword to hold was a very high honour, a sign that my coming as the son of a former enemy, whose father had taken part in the killing of their brother and uncle, was an act that honoured them – and him. If my father could have done so, I now feel sure he would have come with me. He was somehow there in me, and standing in his stead, I was somehow my father: as big as a father, as small as a son.

There is so much to absorb: now, it's time to go. We all get in the car and head out for the barbecue at around 2 p.m., but first it's the supermarket, where the kids get hungry, and so, to McDonald's. The trip to Takata-machi on the expressway seems to take some time, but soon we're out in rich old farming country in the cooler hills. The jikka is old Japan, a traditional house in the middle of a village by a canal in the midst of rice fields now under wheat. There's a shrine in the centre of the dwellings and some small shops – everything cheek-by-jowl, every space used, and yet somehow, it's not overcrowded.

## Ōsaka Soul Food: Okonomiyaki

Neil Hall at Takata-machi shrine, pointing out the characters for 'Nishida': 'west' and 'field' – rice paddy.

Ushered in and left to amuse myself, I have a short nap on the tatami mat floor. When Neil comes back, we walk around the village and he shows me all the sights, explaining the intricacies of rice culture. I'm really hungry and would gladly eat a bowl right now. He takes me to see a thousand-year-old tree in the grounds of the shrine, struck many times by lightning, and temple buildings that have been on this ancient site for generations. The name Nishida is inscribed on a plinth: the family name, the uppermost kanji for 'west' and the lower for 'field', tracked with pale green lichen. Western rice paddy: symbolically tying Ritsu, her parents and their ancestors to the soul of Japanese agriculture and sense of being. Rice people – they go back a long, long way around here. Back at the jikka, we get into the car and drive over to Yanagawa, famous all over Japan for its many festivals (it's also the hometown of Yoko Ono's grandmother, I'm told). There is a great celebration going on right now in the midst of Golden Week, so we join the festive throng.

This town is also Ritsu's mother's birthplace; as dark is falling, we leave the stalls and entertainments to go to her jikka and pay respects, to the aunt who keeps the place and the relatives who are living there to ensure the ancestral fires stay warm. There is no son to create a new family here, so a blood relation has to step in – a cousin, who is basically getting a free house. It is the same ritual of welcome, of bowing, proffered green tea – then Ritsu explaining who I am, as the non-verbal noises of wonder and assent flow back in response. It's the same as it was down in Kashima-machi – they look at each other and not me. It's a little like being treated as if you are deaf and blind and need to be described and spoken for. But it isn't patronising: this is the way it has to be. We leave after very short respects are paid, but nobody seems to mind: having a gaijin parachute in unexpectedly is all part of life's rich tapestry, even one who very mysteriously has come all this way to study the kamikaze culture.

Ritsu Hall and Kay: goldfishing at the Yanagawa Festival.

Back at home in Takata-machi, it's time for the barbecue: in this case, with a charcoal-fired device that grills the food on a mesh net over what looks to be a cut-in-half forty-four-gallon drum. It works a treat and the food starts to arrive: famous Saga beef and mushrooms. A veritable mountain of food is waiting to be cooked and eaten, but we are very few: Ritsu's mum is the Japanese incarnation of a Jewish mother, and after a few good helpings, I have to cry 'enough' – Neil does too. He reckons that because foreigners like us are large and tall, Japanese think we must eat twice as much as they do. We have to disappoint Ritsu and stop eating before we burst: she is not impressed! Staunch as ever, she thinks 'white guys' like us are just quitters. By the time we get home I'm almost sick with tiredness, but the barbecue in my honour and the jikka visit have been a great success. Old Japan and new Japan in the space of two days: Ōsaka and the neon nightlife of Namba; Takata-machi with its millennial Shinto shrine. They seem to me two different faces of the same deep-down belief: we are Japanese – we are unique in this world.

**Day Twenty-four: 5.5.2011. Goodbye to Ken. The last supper.**
Today is a shopping trip into Hakata Station at Fukuoka to buy family presents and have lunch with Ken to say goodbye and thank you. Neil drops me off at Kurume and I catch the Shinkansen to Hakata: there is something going on, as the JR man at the ticket barrier not only bows, he doffs his cap. Sometimes in Japan it really feels like you just might be back in Victorian England. On the platform, there is a red podium, a red carpet, neat officials, a TV camera and a glamour girl – as well as a table with four neatly placed JR caps and certificates. I ask a guard what's happening. He tells me as best he can that it is Kids' Day, and one of their Kurume JR Shinkansen people has won a prize for being the best at something in all of Japan. A bigwig is coming, for sure.

Getting off at Hakata and venturing into the station concourse, it is bedlam: aha, Golden Week again! A bad time to come shopping, but I manage to buy some gifts, grab a coffee at Mister Donut and sit outside waiting for Ken to meet me at midday. A beggar approaches: he's an old man, a rare Japanese street dweller. He stands there and rubs his stomach until I get the message and give him some money for food. He bows deeply and walks away: what's his story, how did he fall from the great Japanese safety net of belonging? He's a kind of bad news story to his fellow citizens and they studiously ignore his plight as he shuffles out of my life. There will be more of his tribe out there on the fringes of the stagnant Japanese economy.

I see Ken coming, dressed neat as a pin and looking today even less Japanese than he sometimes does: his walk and his style mark him out as being American (his dad), yet he's the same stature as the other people who surge around us (his mum). On the way to the subway to get us out of the Ninth Circle of Consumer Hell, he starts again to advise me on what I will be putting into the book, so I decide to tell him not to do that. I know his feelings are hurt after I've told him it's not a good idea to give writers unsolicited advice – and I wish I hadn't said anything. It's pride, I know, but I can't face another two or three hours of well-intentioned backseat driving.

We get off in Fukuoka and wander through a street of craft shops and tiny restaurants by the river, then share a meal of rice, sweetened beans and those chewy manju balls I like. It's just a snack, sipping green tea with the old ladies who run the place fussing around us – an ideal location to lay back and talk. I brief him on the Ōsaka experience; he tells me of his own time of coming here from America and meeting his relatives, the long-delayed recognition that he'd always had another family here in Japan. He speaks about the huge emotional challenge of visiting his mother's tomb: the woman he had not seen since he was five years old after she was sent back to Japan from Nashville by his father. She died of cancer aged forty-nine, refusing treatment. No matter how much resolution he has found in

My last day with Ken Westmoreland in Fukuoka: one sweet guy.

his lifelong struggle with this abandonment and its consequent depression, his face when he smiles still seems like the sun is lighting up a great sadness from deep within.

He has this in common with the very different English Neil, a man who had no father, whose mother seems to have been violent and narcissistic. It interests me that the two people who responded first to my post on Fukuoka-now.com and offered me hospitality were displaced persons, those who could live and move in Japanese culture – but are not truly Japanese. They are culturally embedded these days and Ken does have whakapapa, but they will always be outsiders. Was it that image of me holding my dad's wartime photograph I posted on the website that spoke to them first? We three have so much that we share, so perhaps it's not so surprising. We take pictures, then get up to go and shop some more, grab a coffee at the art gallery, and a 3-D Hokusai postcard of Fuji-san seen through the waves of a tsunami. Back at Hakata Station, it's time for goodbye at the Shinkansen gates.

I give him a hug and turn away quickly: back at Kurume, I jump on the wrong train going the right way. It's an express, not a local shuttle and I have to get off at Araki, where the train parks up for a while to let another one through. I ask the driver for help: he gets out of his cab and takes me to the timetable for trains to Mie, the station I need. Like an incarnation of the White Rabbit from *Alice's Adventures in Wonderland*, he pulls out his pocket watch (Victorian England again), consults it carefully, then tells me to get over onto Platform Two, go back to Kurume and start again. Hai, wakarimashita! I understand. I am waiting there when a disturbed-looking young man arrives and begins his ritual of circling and recircling the platform: two outsiders in one day, the tramp and the mental patient. Japan is letting its orderly facemask slip just a little.

My driver crosses the overbridge and comes down the stairs with his coat and hat off – it is very hot – just to find me and make sure I am in the right place. Can I imagine this kind of profound helpfulness anywhere else in the world? I say I am fine, we bow, and I shake his hand, thank him profusely and catch the train back to Kurume, then the Yellow One Man Diesel Car that I should have taken in the first place. Home at last. I spend the evening with Neil and Ritsu, taking them all out to a restaurant as a way of saying 'Thank you'. They've chosen a Westernised venue by the name of St Marcs:

all the bread you can eat, they tell me. My lasagne is a little short of any pasta content and the chicken is pretty average too, but they all have a good time and enjoy it – especially Kay with her Hello Kitty tray (someone just made a million dollars out there). Tomorrow it's packing, getting ready to go.

## Day Twenty-five: 6.5.2011. I meet an anarchist. I become Jeffrey Hunter, forgotten movie star.

This is my last full day here at Kurume. I talk to Ritsu over coffee as she fills up bento boxes for the kids' school lunches; the moment I express my admiration for these miniature works of culinary art, lo, one arrives on the table for me too. Beautiful: so deftly presented and packaged that the fish, egg, and preserved plums on the topmost layer compose a picture that will seem almost a crime to destroy in the eating. Criminal behaviour will ensue, however. Once the whānau have all gone to work and school, I head out for the station and my meeting with Kenichi Egami at Kurume Station. He's a young Anthropology MA who I had briefly met through Ken Westmoreland in Fukuoka; he's teaching Japanese here to other Asians, while he considers his options. We meet and head for the shrine gardens near the river: the contents of my wonderful double-decker bento box are still looking too good to eat – but we eat them.

He's a very intelligent and socially committed young man who describes himself as an anarchist philosophically, involved in all sorts of internationalist, green-lefty-anti-authoritarian movements, including anti-nuclear protest and permaculture. He's atypical of almost any Japanese person I have met so far, and the only one willing to talk at length about the nuclear disaster in Fukushima and its implications for future Japanese energy policies. In Fukuoka tomorrow and in Tōkyō, he tells me, there will be street protests against the government's handling of the post-tsunami situation. They will be making demands for an alternative series of energy programmes that eschew the building of more nuclear power plants.

He makes the point that for most Japanese people, the prevailing social order is so naturalised that what is now, is what has always been – and is therefore normal and right. The habit of submission to authority and the deep need to belong to the larger group (always seeking consensus and avoiding open disagreement) plays into the hands of the powerful. I ask him if many Japanese of today are aware of the changes that took place in their society and culture as the Americans occupied the country after World War Two: that historic moment when Emperor Hirohito stood in his formal civilian regalia beside the tall drill fatigue-clad figure of General Douglas MacArthur, both posing for a photograph that was saying to the nation: 'Meet the new boss'? He doesn't think so.

He has just returned from South Korea, meeting with a group of kindred spirits: this too is unusual. Most Japanese over thirty have no love for Koreans and the favour is returned with interest, given the history of Japan's military activities there and in China before and during World War Two. The Chinese feel the same, and for many Japanese in turn, 'Made in China' is a term of abuse. Plenty of history needs facing up to around here, some rivers of very bad blood to cleanse. Kenichi is looking to move across national boundaries and work cross-culturally: he seems to me to be the alternative future of Japan, a nation that will increasingly have to take notice of people like him. I tell him he needs to come to New Zealand to strengthen his already very good English and meet some like-minded people.

My bento box, courtesy of Ritsu: stylish and tasty.

Saying goodbye, I ride for one last time the One Man Diesel Car (sadly, not the Yellow one) and get off at Mie, only to find myself chased by the driver because I've exited via the wrong doors. I flash him my coveted JR Pass: he's happy now, so he's bowing. Then begins a long trek to get some headphones for a Radio New Zealand interview with Kim Hill tomorrow morning. I walk for miles, needing plenty of help with directions. I'm instructed by a cool dude in a freaky DVD store that if I want earphones, I have to go to Yamada-denki for electronics gear.

Several informants later, ending with a very helpful lady in an ice-cream parlour, I make it to the right place and get what I want. I light once more upon that rare bird: a fluent English-speaker in the middle of the Japanese-speaking tourist black hole of light-industrial Kurume. Ko has spent some years in Australia and he's happy to practise on me. Back home after a long trudge, talking to myself en route to prepare my thoughts for the radio interview prior to leaving Neil's place, I start to wonder why I signed up for the extra stress factor. I just want to tell the people back home this amazing story, unfolding from my father's battered old photograph.

I make a Skype call home to test the earphones and the reception: turns out they make me sound like I'm talking underwater. That evening, all the whānau return: Ritsu's mother Asako-san, father Tetsushi-san, and little Kay with them; then Ritsu home from the hospital and later Neil, sunburned from his school hike. The women set to work and produce a feast of tempura: 'Portuguese food!' I tease Ritsu – but wherever they got the idea from, it's great Japanese kai now. I get lots more o-hashi-waving laughs out of brother Yo-san: my chopstick style is still hilarious, apparently. The conversation warms up: I get quizzed about my family back in New Zealand. There is much interest shown in the fact that my son once worked for the police – but I can't elaborate.

It's time for the grandparents to leave and for our goodbyes. The old man grabs my hand and, with a huge grin, quips, 'Jeffrey Hunter, Jeffrey Hunter!' He's hanging onto me with what for a seventy-year-old is a surprisingly powerful grip. He knows he's cracked a really good joke and he's chuckling away, likening me – through my name – to a forgotten Hollywood screen god from the 1950s. In the 1961 blockbuster *King of Kings*, the photogenic Hunter played a very Aryan and hunky messiah. He's counting on me to know what he means, to get the pun – and I do. It's a special moment that cuts through the limitations of our mutual monolingualism. I'm laughing with him: 'That's very good, ha ha ha, very good!' The elders are both saying something to me, and Ritsu translates: 'They're saying, "Come back, come back!"' Time for a lump to rise in the throat – they really do mean it . . .

**Day Twenty-six: 7.5.2011. Kim Hill interview. Fond farewells to the Hall jikka.**
Last day in Kurume: I wake as usual between four and five and head downstairs to get my head around the upcoming interview – and the goodbyes later. I've sent Kim the only earthquake-related poem I have with me – 'Against condescension' – and suggested she read 'Aircraft Carrier: Deck Plans' in my last book, *Fly Boy*. That will come back to bother me later. Neil comes down, gets some coffee going, feeds the cats and goes back to bed. I'm getting stoked up with the usual performance anxiety. I'm going to have to use the bedroom as a studio to keep noise to a minimum, so I wait as long as I can to avoid disturbing Neil again, the three-hour difference between Japan and New Zealand ticking down.

Time comes to have a shower and wake my long-suffering host, but he gets up obligingly. Once I've ejected the kitten from the bedroom, it's time to set up the netbook and hope it all works: 8.30 a.m. arrives and the producer Mark Cubey comes on line. The feed is fine – he can hear me pretty well so there is no need for the earphones. I listen to Kim interviewing the writer David Mitchell about stammering. Ironically, his latest novel, *The Thousand Autumns of Jacob de Zoet*, is set in Kyūshū, with a Dutch protagonist. That history is very weird here – Huis ten Bosch, for instance, a massive US$1.75 billion 'traditional' Dutch village theme park near Sasebo, which recalls their influence in Kyūshū, is incredibly popular with the Japanese (go figure). Mark comes back on, says we're ready to go. She'll just read a couple of emails and drop the song track.

As it turns out, one email (having a crack at an earlier guest, Tariq Ali, on the death of bin Laden) seems to go on forever: I'm in the birdcage by now, snorting like an old racehorse all hyped up to go. She does go to the song, maybe to give her famous voice a rest after three hours on the mike.

# THE LOST PILOT

The song repeats the same lyric over a pretty average tune: I just want the singer to stop. On the point of leaving my host family, that old separation anxiety is doing its worst and so I have to have a wee talk to myself.

Ten minutes to midday, and Kim comes back and starts the introduction. She's talking to me and asking about the time in Japan. How has it been? The next few minutes fly by: coming here, my father's war, the attack on *Illustrious*, meeting the families, reframing the idea of kamikaze as 'suicide pilots' – then it's almost time to go. She listens for long stretches with only a couple of questions, but it's obvious – especially when I speak about Tsuyako bursting into tears when she saw the picture, and carrying it into the family shrine – that she is genuinely moved. 'Extraordinary!' she responds.

I wish we had more time, I say, and so does she – 'We'll have to have you back on.' Then this: 'Well, you've got one minute to read that poem, "Aircraft Carrier: Deck Plans".' Bugger! I don't have it with me – it's downstairs. No matter, she wishes me well and looks forward to talking some more. That's it. She's gone. Mark comes back on and says it was fine. I did well. Let him know when I'm back in the country and where I'll be, he says: they have studios in Hamilton as well as Christchurch. That's wonderful. We must have done some good out there, even though – proud perfectionist – I'm pissed off about not having the poem on tap.

Time for more important things: Neil is getting into the birdcage too; he's ready to go. I say goodbye to Kay and Aidan and give them each a ¥1,000 note. On the spur of the moment, I give wee shy Kay a kiss on the

Aidan Hall drew me a picture of a kamikaze's aircraft: looks like one of mine, age eleven.

## ŌSAKA SOUL FOOD: OKONOMIYAKI

cheek: 'It's okay,' I tell her, 'I'm a grandfather too,' as she snuggles into her mother. I start to shake Ritsu's hand (hugging is un-Japanese, remember), but then I think, 'Bugger it!' and give her a big hug and she responds. She's un-Japanese too when she wants to be, while deep down, Japanese as. 'Come back,' she says, just like her mum and dad did, 'you have to come back!' We have some unfinished business with Hanamichi-san in Wakayama, Ritsu. We'll see – e hoa: mā te wā: time will tell, my friend.

Into the Prius: off for a breakfast at McDonald's and a forty-five-minute run to the airport with Neil talking, me mostly listening and getting a few thoughts in here and there. I don't really want to talk anyway, fretting about my heavy suitcase going over the 20-kg limit. Neil says the local flights don't worry about it and he's proved right. He knows so much, this big-hearted English expat: a man who can't live in England any more, who loves Japan even though the Japanese can drive him mad, a man without a father, a mother who still gives him grief, using his NLP training every which way he can to hold at bay those obsessive–compulsive demons, the monster I know so well from my own childhood hells, old hydra-headed Hyper Vigilance.

At the drop-off, another big hug and he's gone. I'm on my own: burned

Ki-27 ('Nate') kamikaze aircraft: dredged up from Hakata Harbour in 1997, on display at Tachiarai Peace Memorial Museum.

out, sweating in the rising heat, and soon, on my way to Tōkyō, to the same Hotel Nikko Narita I stayed in on Day One. Funny: I came to Japan and never went into that great city. Who cares? As I said to Neil about not using my JR Pass to visit Kyōto ('real Japanese beauty', according to Kota), I found real Japanese beauty right where I was. 'Kyūshū's got stuff most people who come to Japan don't even know about,' he reckons. 'It's all here and you've seen it.' That's right: I've looked into the heart of Japan, and whatever my eyes could see, I saw. Her people are the true and lasting temples – their care and kindness to the stranger and traveller, offering food and shelter as if they were priests who could see in you the impress of a god. Sayonara Kyūshū, sayonara my friends.

**Day Twenty-seven: 8.5.2011. Sayonara Narita, konnichi-wa Newark, NJ.** Back again at the Nikko Narita, after a shower on arrival and a cheap takeaway meal from the hotel's Lawson's convenience store, I bought some presents for Jim and Kelly, my East Coast US hosts, some sake cups for my daughter's family in California, and some nice o-hashi (chopsticks) for home. I surfed the net until I couldn't stay awake, took some Nurofen to knock me out, and tried to sleep. The 8.30 p.m. shift till just after midnight worked fine; after that it was a struggle to sleep, old anxieties bedevilling the system. I finally fell asleep and woke again just after 4 a.m.

I wandered the hotel's manicured grounds before breakfast: mist and greenery, so very attractive, with the restaurant set right into a garden and the trees. I made the coach just fine and found the Lufthansa check-in without any problem. They had some trouble with issuing me a boarding pass: the poor young Japanese woman was getting quite embarrassed and apologised repeatedly. I fired off a few 'Ie, ie!' responses to reassure her all was well – 'Don't worry, don't mention it' – but I was glad we had plenty of time. She finally got me one printed from another station and yes – the case was right on the 20-kg limit (my carry-on bag, of course, was groaning).

I hit the departure gate just in time to hear my name called. They wanted my ESTA, whatever that was, and they didn't know either: turns out it was my online immigration form and code to enter the United States, which I'd taken good advice on and had printed out. All sorted – then they called

At Tachiarai Peace Memorial Museum in front of the Zero, wearing my – literally – cool Ishigaki tourist shirt.

me up again, wanting the number. The giant A380 Airbus rolled up to the airbridge and it was huge: once on board, you get a feeling for its sheer bulk as it trundles out to the runway, wallowing like some huge leviathan of the deep. Once it does get its massive weight under way, yee haa! The monster seems to take forever to reach lift-off, but when it does, the ride at cruising altitude is absolutely smooth, as if it really was created to live at 37,000 feet and not on the ground.

I had an aisle seat ('Tsurogawa no seki, kudasai!' / 'An aisle seat, if you have one!'), and my companion was at the window so we had space between; there were a lot of spare seats all around. It was fine on board and the quality of the screens was excellent; I love the outlook from camera three, up on the tail. You can get a bird's-eye view of takeoff and landing – geeky! I couldn't sleep on the flight: I just rested, watching a wildlife doco on Russia, an old *Mad Men* episode I'd missed, and other distractions. The beast landed at Frankfurt like a train with wings, Dumbo the elephant come back to earth – and not belonging. A very smooth landing it was too, but I liked the A380 best on the wing.

I found the way to the connecting flight to the States at Terminal 1 after a good twice-over through the X-ray machine, then a police escort over to a bored-looking security detail with rubber gloves, for a pat-down and bag search. I hate the intrusion, but as somebody had just written in the *New York Times*, Osama bin Laden has changed the world in ways he perhaps never envisaged. Even though he is gone, the fear, the paranoia and the suspicion live on, ever intensified. I close my last entry before I reach America: there's a young Pakistani or Indian man sitting alone in the departure lounge, looking ahead with a thousand-yard stare. There's no way he could have got through security with anything on his person – is there? How corrosive is that legacy of bin Laden's – the paranoid within me wants to call security. How mad is that: haven't I learned anything about so-called suicide bombers in the past four weeks?

# 9

# THE OLD *ILLUSTRIANS*: WRITING FROM MEMORY

I think we probably wanted to invent him for ourselves.
I think I wanted to tell a story, *and he was available.*

*Daniel Swift*

The moral backbone of literature is about that whole question of memory . . . Memory, even if you repress it, will come back at you and it will shape your life. Without memories there wouldn't be any writing: the specific weight an image or phrase needs to get across to the reader can only come from things remembered – not from yesterday but from long ago.

*W. G. Sebald, the last interview, 24 September 2001*

For Sebald everything is an uncanny memento mori:
even a photograph is a device through which the dead
scrutinise the living.

*Peter J. Conradi*

How can we enjoy memoirs, believing them to be true, when nothing, as everyone knows, is so unreliable as memory? [. . .] To this extent, memoirs really can claim to be modern novels, all the way down to the presence of an unreliable narrator.

*David Shields*

Landing in Newark at night, met at the airport by my Kiwi and American connections, Jim and Kelly, it was time to ease back and wash away some of the emotional toll my journey to Japan had taken on me. I took some days off from writing during my stay with them in New Jersey, before flying to spend time with my daughter's family in California. Between my long, deep sleeps, Jim and I visited the battlefields of the Revolution around the Delaware, as I adjusted to the colours and sounds of big, bold and loud USA after the public and private silences of Japan. Later, in San Ramon, I got to play with my mokopuna, chilling out around the family table as my two-year-old granddaughter rediscovered me and practised her frequent temper tantrums. There was time alone too, and time to think.

On a Sunday afternoon there in May, checking out Radio New Zealand's online podcasts, I found myself listening to Jay Winter of Yale University talking to Chris Laidlaw on the *Sunday Morning* programme. His subject was silence and its many forms: as I listened, it began to occur to me that when it came to breaking silences, to opening up a troubling subject from a particular angle, my trip to Japan was a breach of some very long-held emotional silences. Silences in fact that we could no longer even recognise, broken into by the light of a torn image that had survived its subject for sixty-six years.

Professor Winter referred to New Zealand's national silence on Anzac Day, 25 April (the day when we remember Gallipoli, along with the Turks who we fought in 1915); and also a different kind of silence, where Turkey chokes off anything to do with the Armenian genocide that began on the same day in that same year. Here was an example of a great communal silence – a nation forbidden to speak of an event the rest of the world acknowledges – a silence that if broken can land those Turks who do so in prison. A silence too that New Zealanders will not trifle with, to avoid offending our Turkish brothers.

I thought afterwards of how I had broken silences by entering those lives in Japan – a foreign voice come to meet the families and the kamikaze pilots, to speak and to listen. It was not simply that here was a gaijin with an interest in kamikaze (there have been many of them before me, doing such research in Japan), but rather that I was actually *family* – that I came in my father's stead. The son of an old enemy appears from nowhere with a picture of what might well be the moment of death for your long-lost brother, your uncle – and he wants to meet you. What does he want? Why has he come? What do you say?

Released: the moment of truth for an 'Ohka' piloted rocket, dropped on its one-way mission from a G4N Betty mother ship. KANOYA AIR BASE MUSEUM.

There were many silences for me in those two encounters: with the Nagata family, when my translator Ritsu was at times so involved in talking to them that I was almost a spectator, yet comfortable being so; and in the Nishida household, where Yuka the translator was a family member with limited English. There were inevitable gaps – and peak moments too, demanding silence, as when Hideaki the nephew handed me his dead uncle's samurai sword. I held it with both hands as I knelt, while Yoshiaki Nishida the kamikaze's younger brother looked mutely on. Anything I might write or say now about that moment of silence is only a shadow of a substance that was there – and has passed. The silences we shared did their work, lost in whatever was said afterwards.

And now of course there is another kind of silence: the present, the issue of all those things having happened, never to recur, existing in the memories of a small number of people each of whom has taken something ineffable into themselves from those intense, emotionally loaded encounters. We may never meet again. How can we know that it happened? That we ever met? Only now by telling stories: 'I went to Japan', 'The gaijin came to see us'. Out of the silence of the past forty years and the deep silence of my dead father, his story has begun to speak, summoned from the blurred image of a moment in war – and yet not my father entirely, but all the voices within the picture. What any other person makes of our lives, however, is surely not us doing the speaking – it is them, their side of the story.

Daniel Swift has written in his memoir *Bomber County: The Lost Airmen of World War Two* of his search in Holland's wartime graveyards for traces of a dead grandfather he never knew, a man who died in June 1943 returning home after a night raid on Munster:

> We went to Holland and we didn't find him exactly. But we were cheating a little, as we already knew where he was buried. I'm not sure that we wanted to find him, in the end; I think we probably wanted to invent him for ourselves. I think I wanted to tell a story, and he was available.

I was never sure quite what I was doing, or what might happen if I went on such a pilgrimage to Japan. I am discovering that memoir is invention, a foggy recall stitched together from the fragments of whatever remains; underneath its ragged clothes burns, however fitfully, a desire to remember. My father was available, so I set out to tell a dead man's story. I knew instinctively that if I did not, he would certainly die, die twice over – die so completely he would vanish. As long as I might live, I would have no peace.

This pervasive human instinct to tell stories and to memorialise the dead, until they attain almost mythic proportions, is what separates us from the animal kingdom. Not only does it mark us as a different order of being, it signifies a spiritual nature that can never be wholly satisfied with, nor fully at home in, the material world: 'He has also set eternity in the human heart; yet no one can fathom what God has done from beginning to end' (Ecclesiastes 3:11). Breaking such silences – clothing this sublimated desire with names and dates and places and faces – is in its own way a need to partake of the resurrection of the beloved dead before any such grand event takes place. In calling up my father and his former enemies from the grave of forgetfulness, I want to give them back some kind of life, one where mercy triumphs over judgment, as the Good Book says.

I began this process long ago – in poetry I wrote just after my father died – and I don't think I've ever quite stopped. A feeling of being cheated through his many absences, that I took not enough notice of him when I had him near, or even a stubborn resistance to the idea that death could mean oblivion – all of this, perhaps. 'Father & Son', a poem written in 1973, begins: 'I do not want another father: old man, now / dead, that cancer faded / and swelled you, speechless / at the door, yellow / feathered fingers'. Twenty years later I was still writing about him, in 'As big as a father': '. . . and death's head torpedoes / blew out of the water / the skiff of my father'. It would be a fair criticism that I've made a lot of mileage from losing him early and if he'd lived longer and well, I wouldn't have so much to say. Possibly: but then, if there hadn't been World War Two, things would be very different for all of us today. The war was in him – its ghosts are in me; and that, I would say is the real subject here, his life somehow choosing me. I'm not saying no.

I turn again to that voyager of memory's deeps: W. G. Sebald, a German writer who refused to deny Germany's and Europe's post-war darkness, in his fiction and elsewhere. Speaking in a final interview before his tragic and wasteful death in a car crash ten years ago, he discusses the pain of memories shared by 'a species in despair', where those oppressed by mental anguish are consuming mountains of painkillers, the most vulnerable of whom are the wandering, revolving populations of a huge archipelago of mental hospitals. Bleak stuff: unsurprising from one who was born in 1944 into a Germany on the brink of collapse, a world where, amidst the rubble heaps of his early childhood, nobody would speak of how those broken buildings came to be there in such a devastated landscape. His soldier father returned from Russian imprisonment in 1947, the year I was born: a stranger who also said nothing of where he had been; a ghost from the vanished Wehrmacht.

A silent father, a silenced recent dictatorship, parents and teachers who had made their accommodations with the Nazi regime and now, suddenly, were expected to become a people without a past, a nation that could only have a future. The result was that, for the majority of Germans, there came to be no true present: a radical breach in human time that brought forth a lobotomised Bundesrepublik, where the forgetting and suppression of the Nazi era became a normal mental illness. In many ways, it was the same in Japan post-1945: death or forgetting, as my friend Ken observed when I arrived in Kashii in April. Sebald would make it his life's work to resist this amnesiac psychosis, first by moving his postdoctoral studies to Manchester in 1966; then, in 1970, taking up a post as a lecturer at the University of East Anglia, remaining in England until his death.

The wreckage of a B-29 bomber shot down over Tachiarai.
TACHIARAI PEACE MEMORIAL MUSEUM.

His reflections on a lifetime of dealing with such memories, writing fictions that grapple with the complexity of our relationship to the past, can provide us with clues as to what to do with our own difficulties. There is no real escape, he believed: at the very least, you could subdue painful memories by distractions. His method was to walk his dog – and yet 'that doesn't really get me off the hook. And I have in fact, not a great desire to be let off the hook. I think we have to stay upright through all that, if it's at all possible.' That hook, the pain of memory – I am saying the same about my father and his war – was his subject, and it became his life. Memory, Sebald believed, was inescapable, and its nature changed with age: the older we get, the more we do forget – but that 'which survives in your mind acquires a very considerable degree of density, a very high degree of specific weight'.

My oldest friend killed himself in July 2007, just before his sixtieth birthday, leaving me holding his ticket to a Bob Dylan concert. He'd been to one other Dylan gig here in 1999, but this was to be a shared event for two lifelong fans. A trained mechanic, he ran a hose linked to the exhaust pipe of another car through the window of his diesel engine vehicle, and in the early hours of the morning, sat and waited to die, his mother's picture clasped to his chest and a Bob Dylan tape playing in the cassette deck. I had known him for almost fifty years and was acutely aware of the psychological scarring in his life as we shared our secrets over the decade leading up to his death.

He was a victim of his father's wartime post-traumatic stress disorder: savagely beaten as a child by a man who looked like he couldn't harm a fly. His dad was subject to uncontrollable rages when the lasting effects of terrible head injuries suffered in the war triggered in him irrational eruptions of anger. A sniper's bullet had hit him in the face on an invasion beach twenty years earlier, exiting behind his ear, leaving him partially deaf and unbalanced in his emotional life. Like my father, he had missed death by inches and returned to civilian life scarred by incommunicable trauma; like my father, he attacked his son, giving him entirely the wrong message about his place in the universe.

It was those early messages, finally obeyed, that killed Frank; they overcame him as he struggled with the depression their weight of grief had laid upon him. It is of this specific weight that Sebald speaks: unsurprisingly, some of his own characters are suicides, Holocaust survivors who, like the writer Primo Levi, finally took Hitler's message to heart, in spite of outliving him and his vile regime. Weighed down with such memories, he concludes, 'it's not unlikely that they will sink you. Memories of that sort do have a tendency to encumber you emotionally.' For whatever reason – so far – I feel I have been fortunate. Writing does at least give us the power to address such encumbrances and even use them as a way forward. I think this is exactly what I was doing when I started on the trail of my father's old shipmates in England, back in 1993.

I'd met a former Royal Navy man at the therapeutic community where I was working in rural Kent: Hugh was a Scot on the staff who had warmed to me and we talked a good deal. He discovered I came from a naval family, and hearing of my dad's war on *Illustrious* and his early death, he suggested I place an advertisement in the 'Old Shipmates Sought' column of the *UK Navy News* – which I gladly did. I had three prompt replies: one from Bill Griffiths in Croydon, who had written a book about service life, *My Darling Children: War from the Lower Deck*; another from Bill Weston in Birmingham, an old salt indeed; and the last from Derek Taylor of Colchester, who had actually been trained by my father when he joined the *Illustrious* as a young signalman.

I contacted each of them and made plans to visit. Bill Griffiths had been on the carrier, but in another mess: unsurprisingly, in a crew of over 1200

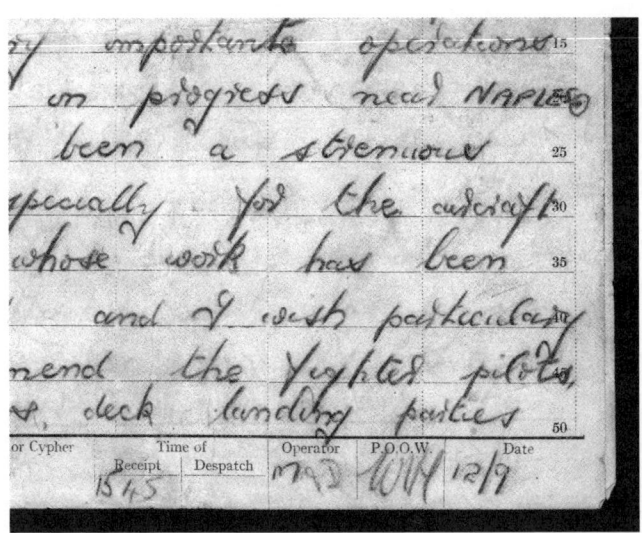

A signal signed off by my father: sent from HMS *Illustrious* in the Mediterranean, September 1943. 'WTH: P.O.O.W.' = William Thomas Holman: Petty Officer of Watch. DEREK TAYLOR.

men he had never met my father. He was pithy and witty on life aboard ship, telling me of his recent book, 'about life below decks, the lot of the ordinary seaman, not the brass hats and admirals'. It is a colourful and authentic account of what it was like to be a sailor during the war, from entry through to discharge; I have used it in the chapter about my father's first experiences in the navy. Derek Taylor too was a fount of knowledge, and better still, he knew Dad.

Derek gave me armloads of memorabilia: the carrier's crest, a painted plywood sailor making the letter 'J' (for Jeffrey) with semaphore flags, and an old signal, sent in the Mediterranean in 1943, signed off with those familiar initials, 'WTH' – William Thomas Holman. When I say he knew my father, it was from the perspective of a lower rank; his primary relationship to him was to receive his instructions and obey orders. Dad was efficient and very professional, Derek recalled, but there was no expectation of any intimacy that might lead to him having any inside knowledge of my father. In a photocopy of a photograph he made for me of the Signals' Mess at Trincomalee, Ceylon, in 1944, there they sit – Bill Weston, my father and Derek – one above the next, almost as if posed for my posterity.

It was with the same impulse of vain desire that I travelled to Birmingham in April of the following year – after the visits to Bill Griffiths and Derek Taylor – to meet Bill Weston. On the phone he'd said, yes indeed, he did remember my father well. He'd be happy to meet me at the Nautical Club and gave me good directions. I boarded a train at Euston Station on one of my weekdays off from Waterstone's bookshop and headed north. The account of meeting him that follows was written on the train back to London, and is reprinted here as set down. I don't want to try and improve on my impressions of what it felt like at the time, nor alter the feeling of the lesson I think it taught me. The dead can be very elusive when they want to be, especially when your spirit guides can only take you as far as the cemetery gate.

*Hard to Remember: after Birmingham and Bill Weston*
 *The train's jerking to a stop at Birmingham International and I've turned off old Bob on my Walkman; with my right ear gummed up, I can't hear him and anyway, I need to write out what's going on inside me. A bellyful of steak-and-kidney*

*pie and chips deadens some of my feelings, but here goes with what's left.*

*Arriving from London, I walked from New Street Station to the Nautical Club in Bishopsgate Street, feeling proud I'd spent money on a map and not on a taxi. At least I've seen a piece of Birmingham close-up, walking under tiled bridges, along streets named Navigation and Holliday. I found the place with the aid of an old salt, steaming in the same direction. I took pictures of the prospect, framed by mines, torpedoes, turreted guns and the obligatory anchor at the door.*

*A silver-headed man emerged, smiling and waving, hailed me over and shook my hand. He posed for me with the doorman and a cardboard sailor cutout: Bill is much more cheery and loquacious than his telephone persona. We chat and then he has to leave me to go into the 'meeting', a large hall full of aged nauticants at tables around the walls. I guess he's got business to attend to, so I wait in the foyer, reading notices bewailing rusty submarines of great antiquity needing TLC and a plea for witnesses (or survivors) of a friendly fire accident in 1939! Contact Seadog X at the address below. I'm still stooging about when another snow-topped sea sage approaches and tells me I'm his man, he can tell by the twang. Bill Weston? The same! So who was . . . ? Who knows, who cares?*

*I mumble, I babble my version of the confusion, but Bill's not fazed. He's dapper in the dark blazer, ship's badge on breast pocket, white shirt, blood-red British Legion tie and grey slacks: a civvy in uniform, still serving. He's outlasted my dad by twenty years and looks good for another double decade. He has a bullet-hole-shaped depression high on the left of his forehead, disguised by rakes of white hair.*

*We sit in the bar and it goes a bit quiet. Is he uncomfortable? I'd better make the running. I thank him for coming to meet me and disgorge my 'wartime' album; Dad's surviving photographs. The Signals' Mess at Trinco, 1944. 'That's me, that's your Dad, that's A, that's B . . .' and the identity parade continues. I show him photos of the great carrier sailing into Sydney, framed by the Coathanger; on patrol in brooding Pacific sunsets and under attack from kamikazes. Krump! Whoomph! Waterspouts, men blown into pieces, half the pilot's skull on the flight deck, one eyeball still attached. He chips in here and there, but not much. I'm doing most of the work and realise that soon, we'll run out of pictures.*

*He buys me a Coke and sips a bitter lemon while all around, ageing Jack Tars, encyclopaedic ironclads, oxidise at anchor, their memories flaking off like rusting boilers, sucking huge pints. He's driving and has a British Legion meeting at three o'clock. He pulls out three photos from his wallet, one with an illegal white silk scarf*

# The Old *Illustrians*: Writing From Memory

Three in line: Bill Weston (top centre), my father (middle left) and Derek Taylor (bottom centre), signals staff, HMS *Illustrious*, Trincomalee, Ceylon, 1944.

*draped around his sailor suit; the other has him posing on a rickshaw in Durban, c. 1939, flanked by a magnificent Zulu warrior in feather headdress and full regalia.*

*'Wouldn't be correct these days, would it?' he reckons, meaning I guess the flavour of Empire and Noble Savage.*

*'It's fifty years, you know,' he reminds me, 'a long time ago.' Birmingham vowels, the Brummie inflections. Well, the photos have all run out and so I have to ask him, 'What was my dad like to work with? How well did you know him?' This is it. 'Oh, we went ashore together a few times.' Silence. Please, give me a tidbit, a glimpse of that man I still don't know. 'Can you remember anything about him?'*

*'Oh well, we were all mates together. You had to be.' Another old salt next door sees the pictures and overhears our chat. He leans over, raises a glass and tells us our reminiscences 'get my lamp swinging!' Aye, aye, sailor! Sup that froth, sir, as the waves break deep within.*

*Bill was on the Russian convoys for a while. 'The banana boats, the escort carriers'*, which makes him a thawed-out statistical miracle. If you took a tinfish, the other ships couldn't stop and you had less than five minutes to live in Arctic waters. We talk a bit about the old Illustrians I've contacted: Derek Taylor at Colchester and Bill Griffiths, the ex-secretary of the association, who answered my ad in the Navy News. 'Bill's dead. He died last year of a heart attack.' Another witness gone, another just-in-time visit.

I tell Bill about Dad joining the New Zealand Navy in 1950, working on the railways, in the state mines, the forestry, and his last role as a cancer patient. I keep wondering why I'm not sat here with my dad, swapping euphoria in some cosy nautical club – but he's dead, isn't he? I begin to want to go now, because Bill won't, can't – why should he? – restore that intimacy I'm craving.

He talks of his garden, living things in the present tense where God is, as well as 'back there' in 1939–40–41–42–43–44–45 in a country never mine. Comes time for Bill to go. Can I get some shots of him now? By the club sign, SNAP, CLICK, over by the anchor, CLACK, CLACK!! I'll send you one if they're any good. Thank you for coming. Take care. God bless. I turn away, sure I'll never see him again.

I walk off down to the lights at Broad Street, heading back another way. I tell myself in words I can't remember now that nothing can change my father's death. It's twenty-two years now, Jeffrey: let go! Poor Bill. He could only give me that much of himself and leave me to get on with it. Bill Weston? Yes, and Bill Holman, too. Shipmates.

'It's fifty years, you know. A long time ago. Hard to remember.'

It was difficult re-reading and re-typing this: the vision of a younger self, greedy for an emotional reassurance that was unobtainable; disappointed in some inexpressible way, and yet grateful for what was given. Bill will be ninety now, if he's still with us, and Derek in his late eighties: wonderful, generous men. As I reflect on the mementoes they passed on to me, and the memories, I see they have given me far more than I realised. They gave me their time. The visit to Birmingham finally taught me that if the dead were invisible yet somehow with us, then in looking for some traces of my father, I had found the living instead – and it was they who mattered. I have long since lost contact, but all three men are with me still.

Reading this twenty-year-old account, I cannot help seeing similarities with my trip to Japan and the things I experienced there. It's almost as

## The Old *Illustrians*: Writing From Memory

if the visits and the meetings are seamless, even though far apart in time and my never having planned to seek out the Japanese side of the story. Storytelling: the dead were beyond recall, yet they cried out to me. Not only are we storytelling creatures, we are makers of myth. Māori once knew this and some still do, and we can rediscover it: that ancestors do become mythical creatures once they depart from this material realm. Only story keeps them alive, as alive as we would have them be, to meet our changing times and needs. In attempting to tell my father's and the pilots' stories as history, inevitably they have begun to merge into myth – if only because word of mouth and text on the page is not them at all, but always something

William Thomas Holman: at the seaside as the war clouds gathered.

other, pointing elsewhere. Where to go now with these storied figures is a mystery to me.

Early in 2010 when the idea for this book was forming more clearly, I read the text of a lecture given by Dr Jennifer Clement, a colleague in the English programme of the University of Canterbury. A Renaissance literature scholar, her subject was humility and the use of personification. In the discussion of the figure of humility, she had this to say: '. . . we turn to the figurative for what can't be understood, or expressed in the literal, even though we use the literal to express the figurative. We turn to the figurative to encounter, at least within our limits, what is unknown in some way.' She was discussing a George Herbert poem, 'Humilitie', where that particular quality, personified, shows the downside of prideful 'Vertues', portrayed figuratively in Aesop's fable fashion as animals.

The lion in the poem is a literal lion indeed, but stands for anger, the turkey for jealousy and the crow for pride, and so forth. She elaborates her points by referring to a well-known memoir by Norman Maclean, *A River Runs Through It* – a fictionalised account of his life with his father (made by Robert Redford into the 1992 film of the same name). The narrator responds to his father's observation that he likes to tell stories. 'Yes, I like to tell stories that are true,' he replies. The father responds, 'After you have finished your true stories sometime, why don't you make up a story and the people to go with it? Only then will you understand what happened and why. *It is those we live with and love and should know who elude us.*' (My emphasis.)

Dr Clement comments: 'The father ties the imaginative, *fictional* effort of restoring the dead to understanding and respecting those dead, and through this tie, the distinction between a true story and a made-up story blurs. Both are, simply, stories. The dead are both too close, and too distant – too close because they haunt us; too distant because they have left us and, perhaps, because we never really knew them.' Personification, she feels, can 'bring the dead into focus . . . [and] make them legible'.

I responded to her at the time: 'Your discussion [from Norman Maclean onwards] on truth and fiction, telling stories and restoring the dead to life lays out, almost perfectly, something I have been trying to articulate to myself, the prospect of writing a memoir.' I go on to talk about making the attempt to write what I am writing now:

# The Old *Illustrians*: Writing From Memory

The story I am calling 'The Lost Pilot', and the prospect of this cross-genre monster scares the shit out of me. But time is short and there is not enough life left for more of the little poems that 'sit up and beg for their cube of sugar, like little pet dogs' (so said Peter Reading, the English poet, reflecting on his epic poem, *Evagatory*). It was what you wrote about the dead that stopped me in my tracks . . . the poetry I have written about my dad is the story – so far – about a stranger. I have this hunch that the only way to approach his truth now is through a fiction, following known facts.

What this amounts to is simple, really: unreliable memory and an unreliable narrator, in the sense that if my father were here now, and read this manuscript, he would have to set about correcting me, as much for my attitudes as the parade of facts. Yet even he – a very well-read man – would have to admit that writing is writing, it is not the life as lived. This is a true story, made up to fill the inevitable gaps, using both fictional and historical techniques. It doesn't do him justice, nor does it do so for those six Japanese airmen who died that day in 1945. Yet for me it is a kind of love letter to those dead; it doesn't matter if I'm only talking to myself. It's payback time, and I want to believe that now, I really have paid something back to someone, in somebody else's mysterious currency.

Ah well, in the end perhaps this is what memoir really is: talking to ourselves as night falls in a vast cemetery at the edge of time. And time that is holy, time paying itself out in strands of unutterable loveliness, weaving us all into a story at the heart of the eternal.

*Ahakoa ka rere atu, ka rere tonu mai ngā tai o ana moana, kāore te heremana ngaro e kitea. The tides of his oceans will continually come and go, but the vanished sailor is nowhere to be seen.*

Epilogue

# TE TAUA MOANA MARAE

On 31 March 2011, I stood at the gate of the sailors' marae in Devonport with my friend, the all-but-blind poet Michele Leggott, as we waited to be called on. She carried a white stick, her poet laureate's tokotoko, while I carried two pictures.

We were a kawe mate: a rōpū bringing our dead onto the marae and into the meeting house, that we might leave them amongst their people so we could finally have rest. Under the guiding hand of my good friend, the marae manager Petty Officer Miru McLean of Ngāi Tūhoe, all had been arranged. The karanga rang out and we came on, with no caller to respond but my tears and my shaking: ka heke ngā roimata, ka heke hoki te hūpē, ka mau te wehi! Taking off our shoes on the porch under the watchful gaze of the tekoteko, Kupe-ki-Uta and his lower companion, Ngahue, we were led to the very back of the house, where the kaumātua, Miru's uncle Bert McLean, recited karakia to bless us and the pictures: the living, the images, and the dead themselves.

Mum and Dad: wedding day, St Luke's Church, Hammersmith, 25 March 1943.

The dead of course were my parents, united again in their 1943 wedding photograph as serving naval personnel, as bride and groom. With them too were six tokkōtai pilots; I had also carried on the image of the explosion beside the ship. Japanese students had died in Christchurch in the 22 February earthquake, along with Te Taki Tairakena, their teacher and my friend; these dead too I was carrying in my heart. On 11 March, a fortnight earlier, thousands of Japanese had lost their lives at Tōhoku, northeastern Honshu, in the magnitude 9.0 earthquake and the following tsunami – they too were with us, even though unknown.

We sat for the whaikōrero: tū atu, tū mai, tau utuutu kawa. As there were only Bert and myself to speak, it was not a long affair before the hongi and the welcome kai that followed. Just to sit and listen to him, to stand and speak in reply, to see the white naval uniforms and to have Michele beside me when we sang 'E toru ngā mea' in response to their waiata – I knew one life was ending and another beginning. After introducing us to the tangata whenua, Miru took us into the room next door where the tūpuna live, the ancestors. Here are all those navy veterans who have died and sailed on: he showed me where Mum and Dad would live now amongst their people. Ahakoa he Māori, he Pākehā rānei, he heremana te katoa. Māori or Pākehā: what did it matter? They were all sailors.

I have carried my father at least since I was thirteen – from the time I became the man of the house – and that's just on fifty years ago now. Today, I have finally put him down. I have left him – and my mother, in his care, not mine – left them where they both belong among their tribe, the sailors. Kua horoia te whakamā, te mamae hoki! The shame and the pain are washed away!

From today, they will rest together inside the belly of the ancestor Kupe on Te Taua Moana, the marae of Tangaroa and his warriors, inside the house Te Whētu Moana, beside the waters of Ngau te ringa ringa at Devonport. Resting with them too I believe are six Japanese navy aircrew: Jaguchi Maasaki (pilot) and Kiyoshi Iida (navigator); Yoshio Minami (pilot) and Chiharu Nagata (navigator); Hajime Kitagara (pilot) and Hisashi Nishida (navigator).

*E ngā mate o te Pakanga Tuarua: o te iwi Māori, o te iwi Pākehā, o te iwi Hapanihi hoki – haere, haere, haere atu rā!*

My parents' grave plaque: Returned Services' Association plot at Karoro Cemetery, Greymouth. She asked to be buried with him, in a final act of reconciliation.

Te Taua Moana Marae

**As big as a father**

*I lost him the first time
before I could grasp
who he was, what he did, where
he fitted with her*

*and it's always seemed so dumb:
how to lose something
as big as a father.*

*I lost him the next time
to the rum-running Navy
who took him and took him
and kept right on taking*

*and it wasn't my mistake
losing a vessel
as big as a father.*

*I lost him a third time
to a ship in a bottle
that rocked him and rocked him
and shook out his pockets*

*and no kind of magic
could slip me inside
with my father.*

*I lost him at home
when floorboards subsided
and he said and she said
went this way and that way*

# The Lost Pilot

*and dead in the water*
*I couldn't hang on*
*to my father.*

*The last time I lost him*
*I lost him for good:*
*the night and the day*
*the breath he was breathing*

*and death's head torpedoes*
*blew out of the water*
*the skiff of my father.*

# Acknowledgements/Mihimihi

RIP

*Yoshiaki Nishida, who I visited in May 2011, died in November of that year: may his soul find rest. Kāore e warewaretia rātou ko tana whānau: I will never forget him and his family. Haere rā e koro: Farewell to you, grandfather.*

There are, as always, a great number of willing helpers to thank for their invaluable support and encouragement. Without them, this book could never have happened: to the dead, haere rā, farewell; to the living, kia ora koutou katoa.

I wish first of all to thank those shipmates of my father who served with him on HMS *Illustrious* at various times during the Second World War, who talked to me so willingly when I contacted them in England in 1993 and 1994. Bill Griffiths of Croydon shared his book with me; Bill Weston of Birmingham hosted me at the Navy Club; and Derek Taylor of Colchester loaded me up with souvenirs, images and stories.

I would like to make special mention of Bill Honan, who wrote the biography of my great-uncle Hector C. Bywater. He was unfailingly helpful when I got in touch with him, to the point of giving me a guided tour of Hector's London haunts when we met in 1990, and blessing any further iteration of the Bywater family story that I might undertake in future.

As for Japan itself, I was overwhelmed by the helpfulness of everyone I approached – and those who approached me – beginning with Philippa Stevenson, a journalist who had interviewed a former kamikaze pilot, Kinase-san, who had visited New Zealand in 2000.

My wife Jeanette King suggested I approach Dr Kota Hattori, a postdoctoral scholar from Kyūshū who was then resident at the New Zealand Institute of Language, Brain and Behaviour at the University of Canterbury. He was instrumental in tracking down the names of the six pilots who attacked *Illustrious* in 1945, enabling me to make contact with two of the surviving brothers. He also acted as an intermediary with the Nishida family in Ōsaka, helping to set up that interview while I was in Japan. This book as it stands would not have been possible without him.

For my time in Japan, I offer heartfelt thanks to my two host families: Ken Westmoreland in Kashii, who gave me shelter the first weekend in Fukuoka; then Neil and Ritsu Hall and family of Kurume, who hosted me for almost a month. They acted as guides, interpreters and became the best of brand-new friends. Words fail me. Ken also edited the sections on Japan, where he appears, as did Neil those sections on him and his family.

The various museums I visited in Kyūshū also deserve mention: the staff at Kanoya, especially our guide, Nakamata-san; at Tachiarai, the director Kitahara-san; and also the staff at Chiran who gave Dr Hattori the details of the crews who died. The Imperial War Museum in London and the Fleet Air Arm Museum in Yeovilton provided a number of file photographs, and were most helpful to me in tracing images from the war.

As well, I have received the warmest encouragement from two other Japanese helpers: Professor Emiko Ohnuki-Tierney, of the University of Wisconsin-Madison, and Risa Morimoto, film-maker. Professor Ohnuki-Tierney has been supportive right from the moment I first contacted her after reading her landmark study of the tokkōtai pilots, *Kamikaze Diaries*. The stories she presented in English, drawn from the private Japanese diaries of those young men – unknown to the West – were matched on film by Risa Morimoto and Linda Hoaglund's epic production *Wings of Defeat* (2007). She, too, has allowed me to use material from this work, the testimonies and the images of the four elderly survivors she interviewed – kamikaze who returned from the jaws of death.

Then there are the brothers: Teruyuki Nagata of Kashima-machi and Yoshiaki Nishida of Ōsaka (since deceased). I have no words to express my gratitude to the Nagata and Nishida families for their willingness to welcome this gaijin, this stranger, into their homes and their hearts.

Thanks are also due to Creative New Zealand and staff at the University of Waikato who awarded me the 2011 writing fellowship and supported me over a fruitful year in their midst: Dr Sarah Shieff (English) and Dr Alistair Swale (Screen and Media Studies), members of the Arts Committee who administer the fellowship; Dr Kirstine Moffat (Programme Co-ordinator, English); Katy Johnson (Secretary, English); Dr Ken McNeil (Convenor, Japanese Programme), who translated material for the book; Dr Akiko Nakayama (Sensei), who allowed me to sit in on some language classes; and Dr Fumiko Nishimura (Tutor) who did some translation for me.

My friends Ray and Ann Harlow were perfect hosts for my first two months in Hamilton, while I waited for a university flat to become vacant; Margaret Maclagan sold me her pristine one-owner 1990 Mazda 323 for transport while away from home; Margaret Samuels offered much appreciated editorial advice and encouragement over a difficult year punctuated by travel abroad and earthquakes at home. Gary and Sally Murdoch of Karori were Wellington hosts, as were Roger Steele and Christine Roberts. My sister Jill Clarke and family of Masterton also had me stay for much-needed weekend breaks. Special thanks also to Julie and Tarina, who have shared so much with me. Julie Noakes, whose husband served on HMS *Illustrious* with my father, has kindly provided some vital photographic material.

For the special occasion that was the pōwhiri at Ngau te ringa ringa in Devonport, I am grateful to my hosts, Michele Leggott and Mark Fryer, especially to Michele for coming onto the marae with me. My mihi goes out to Petty Officer Miru McLean and his uncle Bert, along with all the marae staff of the Royal New Zealand Navy who welcomed us on that day as a kawe mate. Kāore e warewaretia ō koutou aroha.

At the University of Canterbury where I am based, I am grateful to the School of Humanities who host me as an Adjunct Research Fellow; to Professor Patrick Evans who read the book in manuscript and always gives sage advice and encouragement; to Dr Jennifer Clement for permission to quote from her lecture; to departmental administrators Jennifer Middendorf and Douglas Horrell (the latter for his professional help in scanning my old black-and-white photographs); and to all the other staff who have helped me. Thanks are also due to the team at the International Writing Program at the University of Iowa, Iowa City, where my last-minute editing was completed.

Finally, I would like to thank the editorial team: Jeremy Sherlock and Catherine O'Loughlin of Penguin (NZ), my fine copy editor, Mike Wagg and exceptional designers, Keely O'Shannessy and Anna Egan-Reid. Thanks also to Roger Steele of Steele Roberts Publishing (Aotearoa); and to anyone I may have forgotten – my apologies and my gratitude.

Kāti. Nā reira, e hoa mā, tēnei te mihi maioha ki a koutou katoa.

# Sources by Chapter

Cover: *The Great Pacific War 1931–1933.*

## Bibliography and Publishers' Acknowledgements

Every effort has been made to trace and/or contact the owners of copyright material reproduced in this book, but we should be pleased to hear from any copyright holder whom we have been unable to contact.

Those works cited where permissions were sought and gained a response have been acknowledged below; other titles mentioned are background and reference reading.

**Introduction: Saving the Dead**
Theodor Adorno, 'Essay on Mahler' (1936).

## 1. St Valentine's Day
'Father & Son', from *Strange Children* (Fragments Press, 1974).

## 2. Dad's Story
NB: Emphasis in the head quote from Barbusse is authorial.

Allison, David, *Flying Navy: New Zealanders who Flew in the Fleet Air Arm* (Fleet Air Arm Museum of New Zealand, Auckland: 2009).

Barbusse, Henri, *Under Fire: The Story of a Squad* (*Le Feu: Journal d'une Escouade*, 1916), trans. William Wray (1917).

Cameron, Ian, *Wings of the Morning: The Glorious Story of the Fleet Air Arm in the Second World War* (Hodder & Stoughton, London: 1962).

Foster, Simon, *Okinawa 1945: Assault on the Empire* (Cassell & Co., London: 1994).

Griffiths, William, *My Darling Children: War from the Lower Deck* (Leo Cooper, London: 1992).

Hobbs, David, *The British Pacific Fleet: The Royal Navy's Most Powerful Strike Force* (Naval Institute Press, Annapolis, Maryland: 2011).

Masters, A. O. 'Cappy', *Memoirs of a Reluctant Batman: New Zealand Servicemen in the Fleet Air Arm 1940–45* (Janus Publishing Company, London: 1996).

Ministry of Defence (UK) Navy, War with Japan (HMSO, London: 1995), Vol VI, Supplement MAPS. http://www.nationalarchives.gov.uk/doc/open-government-licence.open-government-licence.htm

Pessoa, Fernando, *Selected Poems*, trans. Jonathan Griffin (2nd edition, Penguin, London: 1982), p. 28; used by kind permission of Penguin (UK).

Petty, Bruce M., *New Zealand in the Pacific War: Personal Accounts of World War II* (McFarlane and Company Inc., Jefferson, North Carolina and London: 2008).

Poolman, Kenneth, *Illustrious* (William Kimber, London: 1955); sections on pp. 235–36 (attack on HMS *Illustrious*) and pp. 243–46 (ship's return to UK).

Rawlings, John D. R., *Pictorial History of the Fleet Air Arm* (Ian Allan Ltd, London: 1973).

Smith, P. C., *Task Force 57* (Crecy Publishing, Manchester: 2001).

Tauwhare, Peter, *An Ongoing Journey* (privately published, 2002), pp. 63–65.

Winton, John, *The Forgotten Fleet: The Story of the British Pacific Fleet, 1944–1945* (Michael Joseph, London: 1969).

## 3. Kokutai no Hongi: Japan as the Emperor's Body

Bergamini, David, *Japan's Imperial Conspiracy* (Panther, London: 1972). Material referenced here relates to p. 1009, a quote from military records, and pp. 1027–29, a short paraphrase of the author's account of the first kamikaze missions and Emperor Hirohito's knowledge of this.

Buruma, Ian, *Inventing Japan: 1853–1964* (The Modern Library, New York: 2004), pp. 26–29 and pp. 54–55; © 2003 Ian Buruma, used by permission of Random House, Inc.

Bywater, Hector C., *The Great Pacific War 1931–1933* (Constable, London: 1925).

Gordon, Andrew, *A Modern History of Japan: From Tokugawa Times to the Present* (Oxford University Press, New York/Oxford: 2003).

Honan, William H., *Bywater: The Man Who Invented the Pacific War* (Macdonald, London: 1990); used with kind permission.

Ishimaru, Lt-Comdr Tōta, IJN, *Japan Must Fight Britain* (The Paternoster Library, London: 1936).

Ohnuki-Tierney, Emiko, *Rice as Self: Japanese Identities through Time* (Princeton University Press, Princeton, New Jersey: 1993).

Tasaburō, Itō, *Kokutai kannen no shiteki kenkyū* (Dōbunkan, Tōkyō: 1936); cited in Daikichi Irokawa (trans.), Marius B. Jansen (ed.), *The Culture of the Meiji Period* (Princeton University Press, Princeton, New Jersey: 1969, 1988), p. 247.

Storry, Richard, *A History of Modern Japan* (Penguin Books, London: 1960).

Website: http://www.bbc.co.uk/religion/religions/shinto/

## 4. Fubuki: Falling Blossom, or Human Sacrifices?

1882 Imperial Rescript for Soldiers, cited in Yui, Fujiwara and Yoshida (eds) [1989] (1996), p. 174; cited in Ohnuki-Tierny (2002); references follow: Kasuga Takeo's account, pp. 174–75; Sasaki Hachirō, pp. 197, 207; Hayashi Tadao, p. 216; Nakeo Taketoku, pp. 223, 224–25; Wada Minoru, p. 230; Hayashi Ichizō, pp. 233, 235, 236, 237.

Hanson, Norman, *Carrier Pilot* (Patrick Stephens Ltd, Cambridge: 1979), pp. 235–37; reproduced with kind permission of Haynes Publishing, Sparkford, Somerset BA22 7JJ, UK.

Lamont-Brown, Raymond, *Kamikaze: Japan's Suicide Samurai* (Cassell, London: 1997).

Ohnuki-Tierney, Emiko, *Kamikaze, Cherry Blossoms, and Nationalisms: The Militarization of Aesthetics in Japanese History* (The University of Chicago Press, Chicago and London: 2002); used with permission of the author and publisher.

——, *Kamikaze Diaries: Reflections of Japanese Student Soldiers* (The University of Chicago Press, Chicago and London: 2006); refer to: Hayashi Tadao, p. 96; used with permission of the author and publisher.

Oishi, Corporal Kiyoshi, 'Letter home', see http://geocities.jp/kamikazes_site_e/isyo/isyobun/ooishi.html

Sakai, Saburō (with Martin Caidin and Fred Saito), *Samurai!* (Bantam, Des Moines: 1975, 1978), pp. 288, 290; original authors deceased, republished 2010 by Naval Institution Press (USA), no contacts available, considered 'fair use'.

Tagata, Takeo, see http://www.geocities.jp/kamikazes_site_e/tokkotai-andMe.html

Website: http://wgordon.web.wesleyan.edu/kamikaze/museums/tachiarai/index.htm

This website is one of the most reliable for information on the history of the kamikaze, books, films and other material, plus the main museum sites.

## 5. Japan Calling

Barker, Ralph, *Hurricats* (Sphere, London: 1979).

Clostermann, Pierre, *Flames in the Sky* (Chatto & Windus, London: 1952). This book has an early, post-war discussion of the kamikaze phenomenon in Chapter 9, 'Under the Sign of the Divine Wind', pp. 176–200; reprinted by permission of the Random House Group.

Nagatsuka, R., *I was a Kamikaze* (New English Library, London: 1974). There is a foreword by Clostermann, in which he notes that the section on kamikaze in *Flames in the Sky* was discussed and debated in Japan, and the American authorities in Tōkyō even tried to ban it (see Preface, p. 7). Nagatsuka, who survived his final mission by turning back in bad weather with his entire squad, has written a gripping account of the last days and hours of the tokkōtai pilots (pp. 160–82). The book has never been translated into Japanese.

## 6. On Kyūshū
Dower, John W., *Embracing Defeat: Japan in the Wake of World War II* (W. W. Norton, New York/London: 1999).

## 7. Ishigaki Pilgrim
Smith, P. C., *Task Force 57* (Crecy Publishing, Manchester: 2001).
Winton, John, *The Forgotten Fleet: The Story of the British Pacific Fleet, 1944–1945* (Michael Joseph, London: 1969).

## 8. Ōsaka Soul Food: Okonomiyaki
Hideaki Nishida's website: http://www.awayasu.com/chuseitai.htm
   This Japanese language website contains an account of the attack on the HMS *Illustrious* with images of the pilots and damage to the carrier.

## 9. The Old *Illustrians*: Writing from Memory
NB: Emphasis in the head quote from Swift is authorial.
Clements, Jennifer, Lecture on Prosopopoeia, University of Canterbury, 28.4.2010; used with permission.
Conradi, Peter J., cited in Schwartz, above; used by courtesy of The Permissions Company, PA 18344, USA.
Jaggi, Maya, interview, *The Guardian*, Friday 21 December 2001; http://www.guardian.co.uk/education/2001/dec/21/artsandhumanities.highereducation
Sebald, W. G., *The Natural History of Destruction* (Hamish & Hamilton, London: 2003); used by kind permission of the publishers.
——, *The Rings of Saturn* (Harvill, London: 1998).
——, in conversation with Eleanor Wachtel, 'The Ghost Hunter', in Schwartz, Lynne Sharon (ed.), *The Emergence of Memory: Conversations with W. G. Sebald* (Seven Stories Press, New York: 2007), pp. 54–56.

Shields, David, *Reality Hunger* (Penguin, London: 2010), quote, pp. 25–26; used by kind permission of the publisher.

Swift, Daniel, *Bomber County: The Lost Airmen of World War Two* (Hamish Hamilton, London: 2010), quote, p. xxvii; used by kind permission of the publisher.

**Epilogue: Te Taua Moana Marae**

Holman, Jeffrey Paparoa, *As big as a father* (Steele Roberts, Wellington: 2002).

# Index

*Page numbers in italics refer to photographs and illustrations*

## A

*A River Runs Through It* (Norman McLean) 294
AA guns 82
abandonment 38–9, 65, 66, 73–4, 242, 271
Abbey Kennels, London 66
acts of reconciliation 41, 43, 161, 228, 266, 298
Admiralty Islands 80
Adorno, Theodore 13
'Against condescension' (Jeffrey Paparoa Holman) 275
aircraft carriers 8, 59, 75–6, 95, 104, 109, 115, 144, 161
 *see also* fleet carriers
'Aircraft carrier: deck plans' (Jeffrey Paparoa Holman) 275, 276
Airey, Eunice Winifred 24–6, *25*, 67–8, *67*, 69–74
Airey, Fred 73
Aizu 92
Akiko 245, 246
alcohol dependency 14, 18, 19, 32–40, 43, 65, 109, 110
Allied GHQ, Tōkyō *99*
Allies 16, 75, 94, 96, 110, 113, 117, 122, 135, 149, 236–41
America 61, 94
Americans and Japanese in the Pacific 104–11
Americans in Japan 89, 91–2
ancestors 293–4
anti-aircraft attacks 56, 82, 85, 114, 141, 237–8, 253
anti-Japanese sentiment 151–2, 155
Anzac Day 35, 213, 221, 223, 256, 282

Araki 271
Araki, Corporal Yukio *113*
'As big as a father' (Jeffrey Paparoa Holman) 178, 183, 285, 299–300
*As big as a father* (Jeffrey Paparoa Holman) 183
Asako-san 203–4, 221, 267–9, 274–5
Atomic Bomb Museum and Peace Park, Nagasaki 218–20
atomic warfare 88–9, 113, 121, 131, 135, 142, 195
Avengers 75, 77

## B

B-25 bombers 98
B-29 bombers 89, 114–15, 116, 117, *129*, 147, 199, 218, 247, *286*
Barracudas 75
Bashō, Matsuo 155–6, 158, 211
Battle of the Atlantic 75, 104
Battle of Britain 100, 110
Battle of the Coral Sea 98
Battle of Leyte Gulf 86, 120
Battle of Midway 98, 111, 143
Battle of the Somme 266
Battle of Tsushima 109
Battle of Yalu River 101
battle cruisers
battleships 57, 95, 104, 107, 109, 117
Barrytown 42
Baxter, Sub-Lieutenant 78
Beach Boys 155
Bennett, James Gordon 102
Best, Elsdon 164
*The Big Show* (Pierre Clostermann) 153–4
bin Laden, Osama 249, 280
Birkenhead, Merseyside 63, 69–70
Birmingham 289–92
*Bismarck* 104

311

Bismarck Straits  86
Blackball  14, 22, 24, 26, 28, 31, 39, 41, 50, 233
Blue Impulse Japanese aerobatic team  205
Bluecoat School, Wavertree  70–1
Bofors guns  83, 84
*Bomber County: The Lost Airmen of World War Two* (Daniel Swift)  284
Bowlby, Prof John  70
Bridgestone Tire Company, Kurume  194, 203, 214
Britain  61, 75, 86, 91, 95, 109–110, 148, 159
British Pacific Fleet  62–3, 75–80, 81, 86, 119, 145, 237
British Royal family  223
Brunitt, Marine Corporal Earl  *241*
Buckman, Dick  42
Buddhism  89, 90, 126, 178, 256
bushidō (the way of the warrior)  122, 152
Bywater, Eunice  64
Bywater, Hector  93, 94, 100–11, *110*, 115
Bywater, Lily  24
Bywater, Mary  24
Bywater, Peter Daniel  24, 70
Bywater, Ulysses J.  64, 100
*Bywater, The Man Who Invented the Pacific War* (William Honan)  100–11

**C**
Caidin, Martin  153
California  111, 257, 282
Calman, John  161
Cameron, Ian  21
cancer  13–14, 42–6, 72, 270–1, 285
capsule hotel, Japan  262
Carlton Mill Rd, Christchurch  18, 42
Castlecliff, Wanganui  69
*Catch 22* (Joseph Heller)  153
Catholicism  219, 222
Ceylon  61, 75, 289, 291
Chamberlain government  109
cherry blossoms  98, 120, 122, 124, 128, 176, 180, 181–2, 183, 223, 230, 238
China  91, 94, 95, 98, 106, 115, 117, 273
Chiran Peace Museum  162
Chisun Resort Hotel, Ishigaki  228, 238
'Choir Boy' (Jeffrey Paparoa Holman)  45–6
Christchurch  18, 42, 214
Christchurch earthquakes  161, 165–6, 167, 185–6, 204, 213, 215

Christchurch Public Hospital  42
Christianity  16, 31–2, 90, 127–8, 157, 215–16, 219–20, 222, 256, 266
Churchill, Lieutenant  85
Churchill, Winston  109, 240
Chusei Squadron  80, 119, 162
  *see also* kamikaze pilots
Clement, Dr Jennifer  294
Clostermann, Pierre  153–4
coal mining  24, 45, 99, 233
Cole, Nat King  36
colonisation  91, 94, 95, 97, 98–9, 169
Combat Air Patrol  82
commercial colonisation  99
Confucianism  90, 212, 256
Conradi, Peter J.  281
Conradson, Bernie  35–6
Convention of Kanagawa 1854 (Japan/America)  91
Corsairs  82, 84, 145, 236
Couston, Dr  39
cruisers  56–7, 59, 86–7, 95
CTV building, Christchurch  166
Cubey, Mark  275, 276
Cumming, Sir Manfield  100
The Curve, London  65, 88

**D**
D4Y-3 Suisei  *85*, *103*, *120*, 160
darts  33, 38, 43, 45, 46
Dazaifu shrine  178–80
Delaware  282
'Denshinya rice haiku' (Jeffrey Paparoa Holman)  243
Denshinya Undersea Telegraph Station  228, 236, 237, *237*
'The Departed' (Jeffrey Paparoa Holman)  149
Devonport Naval Base, Auckland  12, 167, 296–8
Dominion Hotel, Blackball  *33*, 38, 49
Doolittle, Lieutenant Colonel Jimmy  98
Durban  60, 61, 62, 76–7, 291
Dutch colonisers  75, 95, 97, 98
Dylan, Bob  32, 287, 287

**E**
earthquakes
  Christchurch  161, 165–6, 167, 185–6, 204, 213, 215
  Japan  166, 167, 170, 171, 182, 204, 232–3, 262, 297

# INDEX

East Asia  97–9, 104–5
East China Sea  85, 180, 231
Edo (Tōkyō)  92
Edo Bay  90
Egami, Kenichi  272–3
Ei-ichiro, Captain Jo  115
804 Squadron  154
'Emily' (flying boat)  189
Eri  184
*Evagatory* (Peter Reading)  295

## F
F-15  182, 183
F-104 Starfighter  182
Falliace, Gaetano  99
'Father & Son' (Jeffrey Paparoa Holman)  285
Faulkner, William  20, 154
Firestone factory, Papanui  214
First Air Corps  119
'First Light' (Ena Takehiko)  134
First World War *see* Great War
*The First World War: An Illustrated History* (A. J. P. Taylor)  153
*Flames in the Sky* (Pierre Clostermann)  153
Fleet Air Arm fighters  24, 28–9, 78, 180, 237–8
fleet carriers  56, 60, 77
*Fly Boy* (Jeffrey Paparoa Holman)  275
Focke-Wulf 200 Condor bombers  154
food  135, 198, *203*, 204, 259– 61, 268–9, 273
football  51, 57, 202–3, 266
forgiveness  42–3, 175, 266
Formosa (Taiwan)  80, 85, 93, 117, 119
Frank  287
Frankland River, Western Australia  155
Franklin St, Greymouth  13, 43
Frankfurt  279
Fraser, Peter  68, *68*
French colonisers  97, 98
French Indo-China  98–9, 110
Friedburg, Max  156
Fuchida, Mitsuo (pilot)  108
Fuji-san  173, *174*
Fukuoka  162, 167, 173–86, 214, 238–9, 270
  *see also* Kurume
Fukuoka-now.com  163, 271
Fukushima  256, 264, 272
Fumiko  178, *179*, 231

## G
G4N Betty  283
gaijin (foreigner)  196, 201, 204, 214, 223, 225, 268, 282–3, 284
Gallipoli  51, 57, 106, 256, 282
gambling  18, 21, 24, 33–4, 55, 56
Germany  60–1, 66–7, 74–5, 95–6 103, 182, 285–6
Gibraltar  86
*Gneisenau*  57
Goering, Hermann  148
Golden Downs, Nelson  18
Golden Week, Japan  259, 263, 267, 269
Goto Islands  194
Gray, Eddie  169
Great Depression  48, 51, 69, 73, 108
Great Meiwa Tsunami  232
*Great Pacific War, The* (Hector Bywater)  94, 100, 105
Great War  48, 51, 55, 57, 94, 106, 108, 126, 153, 255, 256, 266, 282
Grey Hospital  43–5
Greymouth  13, 39, 43, 155, 298
Greymouth Workingmen's Club  43
Griffiths, Bill  288–9, 292
Guam  107, 116

## H
HMNZS *Achilles*  56
HMNZS *Pegasus*  21
HMNZS *Rotoiti*  150
HMS *Drake*  59, 87
HMS *Eaglet*  66
HMS *Formidable*  61, 209
HMS *Furious*  56–7, 59–60, *59*, 86, 110, 154
HMS *Gambia*  86
HMS *Ganges*  53, 56, 58
HMS *Glorious*  57, 110
HMS *Illustrious*  9, 16, 78, *78*, 82, *83*, *84*, 244, 252, 253–4
  attack on Japanese-held oil refineries in Indonesia  77–8
  attacked by Suisei dive-bombers near Okinawa (6 April 1945)  14–16, 81–5, 159–61, 162–3, 180, 190, 207, 224, 244, 252, 253–4, 256, 276
  attacked in the Mediterranean  60
  collision with *Formidable*  61
  emergency repairs in Australia  86
  inspected in the Philippines  86
  repaired in Sydney  78, 80

repaired in Virginia 60–1
HMS *Indefatigable* 77
HMS *Indomitable* 76, 78
HMS *Mercury* 87
RMS *Rangitiki* 170
HMS *Victorious* 76
Haberfield, Sub-Lieutenant 78
Hachirō, Sasaki 124, 126
Hakata 225, 264, 269–70
Hakata Harbour 200, 277
Hall, Aidan 189, 198, 244, 264, 276–7, 276
Hall, Kay 189, 193–4, 200, 264, *268*, 272, 274, 276–7
Hall, Neil 163, 167, 175, 184–5, 186–8, *187*, 188–214, 221, 223–5, 239–48, *246*, 261, 264–9, *267*, 271–2, 274–8
Hall, Ritsu 188–214, 221, 247, *190, 208*, 264–9, *268*, 271–2, 274–7, 283
Halsey, Admiral William F. 117
Hamilton 165
Hammersmith, London 48, 53, 64, 297
Hanamichi-san 200, *201*, 247, 277
Hanson, Lieutenant Commander Norman 84, 85
Haruda 178
Hardy, Thomas 20
Harlow, Ray and Ann 164
Harris Treaty of 'Amity and Commerce' 1858 (America/Japan) 91–2
Haruda 178
Hasenburg, Carl 24
Hattori, Dr Kota 162–3, 165, 192, 202, 224, 244–8
Hawai'i 108, 109, 110–11
Hawker Hurricane fighters 154
Heinkel He-111 bomber 52, *52*
Hellcats 82, 236
Heller, Joseph 152
Herbert, George 294
Hill, Kim 165, 275–6
Hinschu base 80, 81, *148*
Hirohito, Emperor 95–6, *96*, 98, *99*, 114–18, 207, 273
Hiroshima 89, 116, 121, 131, 135, 142, 147, 240
Hiryu ('Flying Dragon') Ki-167 bomber *199*, 200
Hitler, Adolf 52–3, 73, 75, 89, 103–4, 109, 147, 287
Hoaglund, Linda 131
Hokitika 39, 45, 158
Hokkaido 89

Holland 75, 284
Holman, Airey and Woollam families 88
Holman, Beth *42*
Holman, Doreen 53
Holman, Eric 24, 39, 40, 47, 86, *88*
Holman, Geoffrey 53
Holman, Jeffrey Paparoa 19, *37, 50, 164, 212, 232, 251, 255, 258, 279*
Holman, Jill 27, *37*
Holman, Mary Elisabeth (*nee* Woollam) 19, *47, 63, 67, 68, 72, 74, 88, 297*
described 66
eclampsia 87
early years 69–74
in WRNS 63, 66, *74*, 77
Holman, Pat 53
Holman, William George 51
Holman, William Thomas 14, 15, 19, 23, *42, 47, 49, 54, 293, 297*
early years in London 48–55, *88*
illness and death 13–15, 41–6, 157, 292, 299–300
intellectual abilities 19, 53–4
marriage to Mary 63–5, 297
in New Zealand Royal Navy 56, 62, 150, 217, 292
discharged ashore by purchase 87
prison and release 21–4, 26–30
in Royal Navy *9, 57, 59, 62, 76, 78, 151, 291*
Acting Yeoman of Signals 62, 68
Boy 1st Class 58
Boy 2nd Class 53, 56
Leading Signalman 62
Ordinary Signalman 59
Petty Officer of Watch 288
Signal Boy 58
training 55–9
Yeoman of Signals *9*, 75, 86
Holman family *54*, 88
Holocaust 31, 287
Honan, William H. 100, *101*, 103, 301
Hong Kong 98
Honshu 166
Hopkins, Henry Ivor 22
Hopkins, Jim 22, 23, 26, 30
'Humility' (George Herbert) 294
Hunt, Sid *9*
Hunter, Jeffrey 274
Hunters Lane, Wavertree 71
Hurricats 154
Hyakuri 135, 141

# INDEX

Hyotan Yama, Ōsaka 248–50
hyper vigilance 277

## I

Ichizō, Hayashi 127–8
Iida, Kiyoshi (navigator) 81–4, 298
*Illustrious* (Kenneth Poolman) 21, 29–30
Imperial Japanese Navy 80, 94–5, 107–8, 117
Imperial Navy Torpedo School 108
Imperial Rescript for Soldiers 1882 93, 121–2
Imperial War Museum 244, 253–4
India 99
Indian Ocean 62
Indonesia 75, 77–8
Ishibashi, Shojio 214
Ishigaki 82, 85, 180, 227–8, 234–8
Isle of Dogs, London 52
Issa, Kobayashi 158, 178, 211
Iwo Jima base 118

## J

J Force 156
James *246*
Japan 89–98
   being Japanese 171–3, 258, 265–6, 269
   bushidō (the way of the warrior) 122
   cultural complexities 184–5, 247–8
   kokutai no hongi (sacred national body) 96–9
   Meiji Restoration 90–3, 95–7, 121, 158
   religion 89–90, 122, 128, 156, 222
   Yamato spirit 96, 98, 124–4, 147
'Japan style' 186, 202
Japanese and Americans in the Pacific 104–11
Japanese cars 155, 158–9, 178–9, 235
Japanese writing system (kanji, katakana, hiragana) 157, 158, 211
John Paul II 221–2
Judys 84, 114

## K

Ki-27 ('Nate') 200, *277*
Ki-167 ('Flying Dragon') *199*
Ki-67-I Kai ('Peggy') 200
Kagoshima 113, 185, 192, 264
*Kamikaze, Cherry Blossoms, and Nationalisms* (Ohnuki-Tierney, Emiko) 120
*Kamikaze Diaries: Reflections of Japanese Student Soldiers* (Ohnuki-Tierney, Emiko) 120, 257
kamikaze pilots 8, 11–12, 14–15, 56, 80, 81–5, 88, 97, 107, 111, 112–31
   Kazuo, Nakajima 140–2
   Shigeyoshi, Hamazono 143–5
   survivors 131
   Takehiko, Ena 132–6
   Takeo, Ueshima 137–9
   wills 119, 122, 123, 124
Kanoya Air Base Museum 190–2
Karoro Cemetery, Greymouth 298
Kashii 174–82, *177*, 226
Kashii-gū 176–7, 181
Kashima-machi 190, 205
Kawanishi Type-2 flying boat ('Emily') 189
Kazuo, Nakajima (gunner) *140*, 140–2, 145
Kei 184
Kent 51, 100, 288
Kibblewhite, Dr 13, 20, 43
Kinasi, Prof Nobuya 161
King, Corinne 41
King, Ernest J. 75
King, Jeanette 166, 167, 168, 170, 185–6, 197
Kinoshita-san 156–8
Kita-Kyūshū 218
Kitagara, Hajime (pilot) 81–4, 298
Kitahara, Isao 199–200, 247
*The Knights of Bushido* (Lord Russell) 152
Kohama 228–33
Kokubu 141
Konoye, Prime Minister 111
Korea 89–90, 93, 95
Korean War 150, 175, 217, 273
Koseki, Yūji 112
Kuinaki, General Koiso 116
Kumamoto 195, 226
Kuroshima 135
Kurume 163, 188, 189, 192, 193, 195, 212–14, 221, 264–5, 272–7
Kushira 134
Kwajalein 94
Kyōko 183
Kyōto 278
Kyūshū 114, 115, 162, 173, 200, 203, 275, 278

## L

Laidlaw, Chris 282
Lambe, Captain 83
Leggot, Michele 167, 296–8

Leicester  69, 72
LeMay, Major General Curtis  89
Leyte Gulf, Philippines  86, 120
Lime Street Station, Liverpool  64
Limehouse, East London  34
Line, Joe  51
Liverpool  25, 34, 63–4, 67–8, 70–1
London  13, 34, *34*, 48, 51–5, *52*, 64, 65–6, 74–5, *88*, 100, 110, 297
'The Lost Pilot' (Jeffrey Paparoa Holman)  160–1, 295
Love Hotels  212
Loveridge, Rev Barry  31–2
Luftwaffe  34, 52, 66–8

**M**
Maasaki, Jaguchi (pilot)  81–5, *298*
MacArthur, General Douglas  *99*, 273
McGuire, Bebe  49
McGuire, Ivy  49
McKenzie, Dave  169
McLean, Bert  296–8
McLean, Miru  167, 296–8
McLean, Norman  294
Mai  184
Malta  60, 65
Manchuria  93, 220
Manila  117
Manyoshu Tanka Poem memorial stone  181–2
Marianas  133
Marx, Karl  121, 124, 125
Masaaki, Taguchi (pilot)  257, *257*
Masamichi, Shinta  112, 122
Maseru  232, 234
Masuda (former pilot)  182–3, 230
Maxims  92
Mediterranean  60, 65, 80, 86, 288, 289
Meiji Restoration  90–3, 95–7, 121, 158
Mekkonen (taxi driver)  168–70
memoir  11, 12, 153, 160, 261, 281, 284, 294–5
memorialising  256, 284–5
memory  13–14, 74, 158, 281, 287, 295
Michizane, Sugawara no  179
Mie  271, 274
Minami, Yoshio (pilot)  81–4, 191, *192*, 207, 298
Mindanao  117
Minoru, Wada  112, 126–7
missiles  34, 75, 116
*Mister Roberts* (film)  151, 152

Mitchell, Brigadier General Billy  95
Mitchell, David  275
Mitchell, Jimmy  107
Mitchell, Lillian  25, 69, 72, 73
Mitsumasa, Admiral Yonai  116
Miyako  85, 238
model-making  22, 36, 107
Mombasa  61–2
Mori-san  198
Morimoto, Risa  131
Morse code  58
motorcycles  155
Mt Fuji  173, *174*
Mt Kaimon  142, 144, 145
Mt Ufudaki  233
Muirhead, Percy  24
Munroe, Marilyn  223
Munster  284
Murray St, Greymouth  39
*Musashi*  109
*My Darling Children: War from the Lower Deck* (Bill Griffiths)  288

**N**
Nagasaki  216–20, 224
Nagasaki bombing  89, 116, 121, 131, 142, 147, 195, 203, 218
Nagasaki Peace Park  218–20
Nagata, Chiharu (navigator)  81–5, 125, *189*, 190, 191, 206–12, 255, 298
Nagata, Hideharu  206–12, *206*, *208*
Nagata, Shizuko  208–9, *208*
Nagata, Teruyuki  208–11, *208*, *210*, 252, 255
Nagata, Tsuyako  206–12, *208*, 276
Nagata family  201, *208*, *212*, 266, 283
Nagoya  173
Nakada, Bishop  220
Nakamata-san  *190*, 191
Namba  258–9, 262
Nansei Shoto  238
Narita airport  173
*Narrow Road to the Deep North* (Matsuo Bashō)  155–6
Nautical Club, Birmingham  289–92
Naval Limitation Conference  109
naval strategy  94, 104–11
Nazi regime  152, 285–6
Neilson, Ron  45
Nelson  18, 41
Neptunes  189
New Guinea  80, 98

# INDEX

New Jersey 282
New Zealand
  as tourist destination 159, 233
  trade with Japan 159
Newark 282
Niitaka Squadron 119
Nikko Narita Hotel 171, 278
Nimitz, Admiral Chester W. 114
9/11 146
Nishida, Hideaki 162, 192, 210, 244, 245, 249–62, *255, 258*
Nishida, Hirokoi 251, *255*
Nishida, Hisashi (navigator) 81–4, 146, 162, 250, 251–8, *254*, 298
Nishida, Kayo 250, *255*, 259, 260, 262
Nishida, Kyouko 250–1, *255*, 259, 262
Nishida, Yoshiaki 251–8, *251, 255*
Nishida, Yuka 249–62, *255*, 283
Nishida family *255*, 266
Norway 57, 65, 154
Nuzzi, Private Genare *241*

## O

Oedipal moments 28, 38, 40
Ohka piloted rocket 116, *283*
Ohnuki-Tierney, Prof Emiko 120, 124, 163
oil refineries 75, 76, 77–8, 253
oil shortages 95, 98, 104, 117, 145, 214
Oishi, Corporal Kiyoshi 129–30
Okinawa 78, 81, 85–6, 114, 117, 126, 133, 138, 144, 147, 200, 226–7, 239–42, *241*
102nd Tokkōtai 80, 119, *148*
Operation Iceberg 79, 80
Operation Meridian 77
origami 233, *234*
Ōsaka 195, 248–50
Oscars 114
*Ostfriedland* 95
Owen, Wilfred 255

## P

Pacific islands 232, 240
Pacific region 94–5, 97, 98, 159
Pacific War 93, 94, 100–11, *110, 118*, 232, 239
Pakistan 99
Palembang oil refinery attacks 77
Pangakalan Brandan oil refinery attack 77
Paparoa Ranges 99
Paparua Prison 21

Parewanui 69
Passchendaele 266
Paul 186, 187
Pearl Harbor 61, 92, 94, 95, 100, 106, 107–9
Perry, Commodore Matthew 89 90–1, *91*, 92, 95
Philippines 86, 94, 106, 107, 111, 115–20, *134*
Philippine Sea 115, 133, 224
Pike River Mine explosion 162
pilgrimages 135, 167, 178, 180, 224, 284
Poolman, Kenneth 21
Port Arthur, Manchuria 93, 159
post-traumatic stress disorder 18, 34–5, 55–6, 285, 287
Potsdam Conference July 1945 240
*Pylon* (William Faulkner) 154

## Q

Queen Anne's Mansions, London 65, 74

## R

Rabaul Air Base 111, 144
racism 103, 108, 151, 175
Rape of Nanking 220, 241
Ratana, T. W. 220
Reading, Peter 295
Recreation Hotel, Greymouth 43
Returned Services' Association (RSA) 19, 35, 45, 198, 298
Reynolds, George 49–50
rice 202, 216, 240, 243, 267
Richards, Craig 42
*The Rise and Fall of the Third Reich* (William Shirer) 152–3
Roa 32, 45
Roosevelt, Franklin D. 106, 240
Rosyth 86
Royal Navy 55–9, 76, 81, 85, 103–4
Royal New Zealand Navy 56, 62, 150, 217, 292
Russell, Lord 152
Russia 93, 97, 101, 102–3
Ryoma, Sakamoto 92
Ryukyu Islands 82, 117, *227*, 236, 239–40
  *see also* Okinawa

## S

Sailors' Hymn 30
St Luke's Church, Hammersmith 64, 297
Saipan 94, 114, 116

Saito, Fred  153
Sakai, Saburō  118, *119*, 130, 153
Sakishima Gunto  81, 86, 180
Sakishima Islands  15, 46, 85, 180
sakura (falling cherry blossoms)  98, 120, 122, *123*, 124, 230–1
Sakurajima  192
samurai  89, 92, 116, 117, 191, 257
*Samurai!* (Saburō Sakai)  118, 153
samurai swords  16, 114, *146*, 252–3, 265, 283
San Ramon, California  282
Sands, Florence Annie  51–2, 53
Sasebo  150, 217, 230
Sawako  213, 214
*Scharnhorst*  57
*The Sourge of the Swastika* (Lord Russell)  152
*Sea Power in the Pacific* (Hector Bywater)  102, 104
Seafire  85
Seaview Hospital, Hokitika  39, 45
Sebald, W. G.  281, 285–7
semaphore  58, 65
Sendai  167, 196
sepukku (ritual disembowelment)  92
72nd Shinbu Squadron  *113*
701st Air Corps  119, 162
Shakespeare  44, 45, 121
Sheilds, David  281
Sheppard, David  30
Shiga Prefecture  152
Shigeyoshi, Hamazono (pilot)  133, 141–2, 143–9
Shikoku  125
Shin Tosu  197, 216
Shinei Peace Park  234
Shinichi-san  198
Shinji  178
Shinkansen (trains)  197–8, 216, 225, 248, 263–4, 269
Shintoism  89–90, 154, 175, 178, 181, 222, 256, 269
Shirer, William L.  152–3
shoguns  89, 90, 92
Shotley, Ipswich  53, 57–8
silence  282, 283–4
Singapore  78, 253
Sino–Japanese War 1894–5  93
Smith, Tony  168
Soengai Gerong oil refinery attack  78
Solomon Islands  232
South Africa  60, 61, 62, 76–7, 291
Spitzer, Dr  87

Steele, Roger  164
Stevenson, Philippa  161, 302
Stevenson, Robert Louis  20
storytelling  293–5
Street, Fred  64
Strongman Mine disaster  162
submarine battle  75, 104
submarine torpedo kamikaze  112, 126–7
suicide  12, 39, 111, 116, 145–9, 264
suicide bomber terrorists  8
Suisei dive-bombers *see* Yokosuka Suisei (Comet) dive-bombers
Sumatra  76, 77, 253
Swears, Rev Peter  44
Swift, Daniel  281, 284
Sydney  61, 78, 86, 209, 290

**T**
Tabard St, London  51, 52
Tachiarai  247
Tachiarai Peace Memorial Museum  199, *246*, 247, *279*
Tadao, Hayashi  125–6, 130
Taffy One  118
Tagata, Warrant Officer Takeo  112
Tainan Air Base  80, 119
Tairakena, Te Taki  166, 297
Taiwan  117, 119, 147, 162, 236, 238
  *see also* Formosa
Takata-machi  187, 266–9, *267*
Takehiko, Ena (pilot)  *132*, 132–6
Takeo, Kasuga  122, 127
Takeo, Ueshima  *137*, 137–9, *139*
Takeshi  228, 229, 234, 236
Taketoku, Nakao  126
Takijiro, Admiral Onishi  115, 117
Talgarth Rd, West Kensington  77
Tangaroa  298
Tarawa  240
Tasaburō, Itō  81
Task Force 57  56, 76, 78, 79, 82–6, 236
Tauwhare Marae  166–7
Tauwhare, Pita  56
Taylor, A. J. P.  153
Taylor, Derek  65, 288–9, *291*, 292
Te Taua Moana sailors' marae, Devonport  12, 167, 296–8
Te Whetu Moana meeting house, Devonport  167, 298
terrorists  8, 122
Tetsushi-san  193–4, 203–4, 221, 274–5
Theresa  41–2, 44, 45

# INDEX

*The Thousand Autumns of Jacob de Zoet* (David Mitchell) 275
Tinian 116
*Tirpitz* 104
Togo, Admiral 103, 105
Tōhoku earthquake 166, 171, 182, 232–3, 262, 297
Tojo, General Hideki 96, 98, 116, 240
tokkōtai (special attack) units *see* kamikaze pilots
Tōkyō 93, 98, 104, 138
Tondern naval base 59
torpedos 183, 285
torpedo bombers 107
Towton, Roma 40–1
Trincomalee Naval Base, Ceylon 61, 75, 289, 291
Truk 94, 232
Tsuchiura Naval Air Base 122–3
tsunami 166, 167, 182, 232–3, 262–3, 297
Tsushima Strait 93, 95, 105, 109
Turkey 213, 282
Twines Hotel, Durban 77

## U

U-boat fleets 75, 103
*UK Navy News* 288
US Army Air Service 95
US Navy 60, 75, 145
US Pacific Fleet 111
US Strategic Bombing Survey 120–1
USAF B-29s *129*
USAF F-15s 226
USS *Essex* 120, *134*, 160
USS *Kitkun Bay* 85
USS *St Lo* 118
USS *Santee* 118
USS *Saratoga* 75
USS *Suwanee* 118
University of Waikato 12, 161, 165
Urakami Catholic Cathedral, Nagasaki 219–20, *219, 221*, 222

## V

V-weapons 25, 34, 52, 74–5
Vickers-Armstrongs shipbuilding works 30
Vietnam 99
Vietnam War 55

## W

Waikato 164, 166–7
Waituna 40
Wakeman, Jane 161
Wakeman, Keith 161
Wallaby Language School, Haruda 178
Wanganui 69
Wapping, London *52*
war films 151–2
Wehrmacht 285
West Coast Hospital Board 158–9
Western Australia 40, 41, 155
Westmoreland, Ken 163, 167, 174–86, *176*, 221, 270–1, *270*
Weston, Bill 288–92, *291*
Westport 158
White City dog tracks, London 54–5
Whitehall, London 100
Wilson, Jim 278, 282
Wilson, Kelly 278, 282
*Wings of Defeat* (Risa Morimoto and Linda Hoaglund) 131
*Wings of the Morning* (Ian Cameron) 21, 28
Winter, Prof Jay 282
Woollam, Samuel Thomas 69–70
Woollam family *88*
Women's Royal Naval Service (WRNS) 63, 66, *74*, 77

## Y

Yaeyama 224, 231,
Yakuza 187
Yamaguchi 195
Yamaguchi, Lieutenant Yashinori 120, 160, 198
Yamamoto, Isoroku 106, 108, *108*, 109, 110–11, 240
*Yamato* 109
Yamato spirit 96, 98, 124–4, 147
Yanagawa 267
Yanno-san 194, 224–5
Yap 107
Yasukuni Shrine 122, 126, 256
Yellow One Man Diesel cars 196, 224, 271, 274
Yo-san 201, 202, 209
Yokosuka Suisei (Comet) dive-bombers 80, 81–5, *83, 85, 103*, 112–32, *120*
*see also* kamikaze pilots
Yoshida, Ichitaro 108
Yuji 213

## Z

Zero fighters 114, 117, *130*, 143, 191, 192, 199, *246, 279*

Kawasaki Hien Ki-61 (飛燕, Swallow), a fighter used as a kamikaze aircraft.
DETAIL FROM A PAINTING BY RAINE HOLMAN, AGED 13.